THE BIBLE STUDY HANDBOOK

A Comprehensive Guide
to an Essential Practice

LINDSAY OLESBERG

Foreword by AJITH FERNANDO

IVP Connect

An imprint of InterVarsity Press
Downers Grove, Illinois

InterVarsity Press
P.O. Box 1400, Downers Grove, IL 60515-1426
World Wide Web: www.ivpress.com
E-mail: email@ivpress.com

*InterVarsity Press® is the book-publishing division of InterVarsity Christian Fellowship/USA®, a movement of
students and faculty active on campus at hundreds of universities, colleges and schools of nursing in the United States
of America, and a member movement of the International Fellowship of Evangelical Students. For information
about local and regional activities, write Public Relations Dept., InterVarsity Christian Fellowship/USA, 6400
Schroeder Rd., P.O. Box 7895, Madison, WI 53707-7895, or visit the IVCF website at <www.intervarsity.org>.*

Scripture quotations, unless otherwise noted, are from the New Revised Standard Version of the Bible, *copyright
1989 by the Division of Christian Education of the National Council of the Churches of Christ in the USA. Used by
permission. All rights reserved.*

*While all stories in this book are true, some names and identifying information in this book have been changed to
protect the privacy of the individuals involved.*

Cover design: Cindy Kiple
Interior design: Beth Hagenberg
Images: Badge icons: shopping: © Cagri Oner/iStockphoto
     Badge icons: education: © Cagri Oner/iStockphoto

ISBN 978-0-8308-1049-9

Printed in the United States of America ∞

Library of Congress Cataloging-in-Publication Data

Olesberg, Lindsay, 1960-
  The Bible study handbook : a comprehensive guide to an essential
practice / Lindsay Olesberg.
     p. cm.
  Includes bibliographical references.
  ISBN 978-0-8308-1049-9 (pbk. : alk. paper)
  1. Bible—Hermeneutics. I. Title.
  BS476.O53 2012
  220.071—dc23

                                                            2012027648

P	20	19	18	17	16	15	14	13	12	11	10	9	8	7	6	5	4	3	2	1
Y	29	28	27	26	25	24	23	22	21	20	19	18	17	16	15	14	13	12

To my beloved Jon,
who supported me every step of the way.

And to our dear children,
Michael and Mary—may you come to enjoy the
riches of God's Word as your parents do.

Contents

Foreword

Each era in Christian history has faced unique challenges to the task of getting the message of the Bible to its people. Great Christian reform movements, like the sixteenth-century Reformation, were characterized by their success in getting the Bible to the ordinary Christian. Today too we face some unique challenges.

First, people in our digitalized generation find it difficult to stop long enough to let the Word of God penetrate into their inner being. They are so busy spending their spare time with mobile phones and the computer, with gaming, chatting and social networking, that they don't have the time to linger with the Bible and learn from the God who inspired it. Speed-reading techniques taught to students during the past few decades may have contributed to the phenomenon of a generation of people too lazy to dig conscientiously into what is written in a book.

Second, the welcome return to emphasizing the importance of the spiritual nature of life in this postmodern world has brought with it an unfortunate byproduct: some Christians are asking "How does this text make me feel?" without finding out what that text really says. Some are imposing spiritual interpretations on texts said to be given to them directly by God, seemingly bypassing the hard work of finding what the author, inspired by the Holy Spirit, really intended to say in the text. The spiritual interpretation is somehow considered more authentic than God's written Word, as it claims to be a direct, personal revelation from God to the interpreter.

Third, I am discovering that people reading the Bible today are finding it increasingly difficult to answer the question, "What is the author trying to say in this passage?" I have not done extensive research into the reason for this, but I think it has something to do with people getting out of the habit of reading. Reading written words in books does not seem to be a primary way many people get information today.

Yet our surest source of God's truth is in the written Word. Despite these cultural challenges, studying what the Bible says is a key expression of devotion to its ultimate author, God. If this is God's Word, and if we are devoted to God, then we should study it carefully, seeking to know what the God-inspired author intended to communicate to his readers.

One of the most effective tools God has used in the past century in helping people get the message of the Bible has been what is now known as "inductive Bible study." This method aims to help the reader discover what is communicated in the Scriptures. This can be a joyous and exciting exercise in discovery and could help capture the attention of our preoccupied generation, resulting in a new crop of careful Bible readers in this digital age.

I had the thrill of studying inductive Bible study under one of its great proponents, Dr. Robert A. Traina, while I was a student at Asbury Theological Seminary. Graduate studies in New Testament took me to Fuller Theological Seminary, where I was, at first, disappointed that I could not have the famous Dr. George Eldon Ladd as my primary mentor. Instead I was given another proponent of inductive Bible study, Dr. Daniel P. Fuller, and an amazingly happy relationship between mentor and student continues to this day.

I use what I learned from Drs. Traina and Fuller every day when I read the Bible. And even though my calling has included some public preaching to large audiences, my first love continues to be helping young Christians dig into the Scriptures in a small group setting.

What a thrill it was for me to discover a kindred spirit in Lindsay Olesberg. I worked closely with her as she coordinated the Bible expositions at the 2006 Urbana Student Missions Conference and the Lausanne III Congress in Cape Town, South Africa, in 2010. I learned many lessons from Lindsay about how to study the Bible and help others get its message. Naturally, I welcome her *Bible Study Handbook* with great enthusiasm.

I, and I'm sure Lindsay also, have benefited greatly from seminary-level hermeneutics books written, for the most part, by people skilled in teaching theological students. The wonderful insights in these books, however, are somewhat inaccessible to the theologically uninitiated. For a general audience we need works by practitioners who are skilled at helping the uninitiated dig into the Scriptures. Lindsay has the experience and the qualifications to write such a book. I am so grateful that she has done such a superb job in giving us a comprehensive and easily accessible guide to Bible study.

Ajith Fernando
Teaching Director, Youth for Christ, Sri Lanka

Introduction
SOLID

King David? Who's that?" The other teens in the room looked at me like I was from Mars. I flinched ever so slightly as I saw incredulity followed quickly by criticalness pass across some of their faces. I was new to youth group and already felt self-conscious. Not knowing about King David, it turns out, was like not knowing about George Washington or Abraham Lincoln.

Wishing I had kept my questions to myself or asked the leader later, I listened carefully to the answer given: "The greatest king of Israel and forefather of Jesus." The answer didn't help much. I only had a vague idea of where Israel is and absolutely no sense of what it or its kings had to do with me as a new follower of Jesus.

I had been overjoyed at age twelve to hear for the first time that there is a God who created me and loves me. I found it remarkable that this God would want a relationship with me and had sent his Son to the cross to make that relationship possible. Becoming a Christian was the most wonderful thing that ever happened to me, better than a Disney vacation or winning the lottery. But it also plunged me into a very foreign world.

I grew up in a completely secular home. No one read stories to me from a children's Bible with a picture of shepherd Jesus on the cover. I had never attended Sunday School or acted out the story of David and Goliath. It seemed to me that the kids in my youth group were natives of a culture that, until recently, I hadn't known existed.

As an only child being raised by a single mom, I was eager to fit in and to be liked. As a young girl yearning to grow in a newly discovered relationship with her Heavenly Father, I was eager to learn as much as I could. This meant learning the lingo, discerning the unspoken rules of how to behave in church settings and figuring out the right questions to ask.

After enough experiences of feeling stupid, confused or unsatisfied in youth group because I didn't understand most of what was being said, I made one of the most important decisions of my young life. I decided to study the Bible on my own.

Now, I had absolutely no idea how to go about studying the Bible by myself. But nonetheless, during the summer between ninth and tenth grade I studied the Bible for over an hour a day. I wrote down thoughts and questions in a notebook. I made lists. I looked up cross-references. Slowly I began to feel like I could make out the basic story.

DISCOVERING MANUSCRIPT STUDY

It was great to not feel stupid in youth group and to understand the lessons. But soon a subtle shift took place in my heart. As I continued to read and study the Bible, pride crept in.

In addition to my hunger for connecting with God, I also became motivated by a different desire: to be a "top student." Rather than deepening my relationship with Jesus, I grew increasingly focused on accumulating facts and knowledge. In fact, when I arrived at the Claremont Colleges and was invited to join a small group Bible study for freshmen, I declined. By that point I was so self-assured that I assumed a Bible study for freshmen would be too basic for me. That's embarrassing to admit, but it's the ugly truth.

And then something remarkable happened to me.

I was invited to what my InterVarsity group called a "Dig-In." Yes, the name is corny, but it captures the spirit of the event well. A dig-in is a ten- to fifteen-hour intensive study of a single book of the Bible, using something called the "manuscript method." It's not a retreat weekend in a beautiful setting with a dynamic speaker, moving worship and funny skits or games. A dig-in is simply an extended time of hard work, digging deeply into God's Word, with a few meals and prayer tucked around the edges.

I liked the campus minister who invited me to the dig-in, and I was looking for deeper relationships with the Christian community on campus, so I said yes to the invitation. I felt confident about my Bible knowledge and figured that it was a setting in which I would shine. (The ego is an amazing motivator.) But when I walked into the classroom where my group met, my heart sank a little. I didn't recognize any of the students seated around the table. I became a little anxious and thought, *What have I gotten myself into?*

You wouldn't expect lots of students to give up their weekends to participate in such an intense study. But fifteen students did, and I soon discovered why. The leader, Tom, briefly explained the inductive method, and then he passed out the book of James. It was printed on standard paper. I was intrigued, but flipping through the James manuscript and realizing that I could read it all in less than fifteen minutes made me wonder, *How in the world can we spend twelve hours on this?*

That first night, Tom encouraged us to look closely at the first page and a half of the manuscript. He encouraged us to look closely and mark what we observed. As I read through the first page I noticed words like *trial* and *testing* and decided to circle them with a pink pen. I highlighted all the commands in green (like "ask God") and wrote a question mark next to the sentence about being joyful in trials. After a few minutes of quiet reading and studying, Tom invited us to share with each other what we had seen in the text.

For the next twenty minutes the comments came fast and furious. Paul, a sophomore, had seen variations of the word *give* six times. A girl with big glasses and long braids said, "There is a contrast between line six, where it says 'God gives generously' to all who ask for wisdom, and line nine, where it says the double-minded 'must not expect to receive anything from the Lord.'" Each time someone shared an observation I hadn't seen, I added it to my manuscript. Before too long my sheet was littered with observations about the text.

The next few hours were glorious. We talked, discussed, laughed, even argued as we worked to understand the meaning of the text. Tom taught us to challenge each other gently with questions such as "Where do you see that in the text?" When we would ask Tom for "the answer," he would refuse to give it to us and direct us back into the text to dig deeper. Our work paid off as God gave us more and more clarity. We felt as if we were in a lively conversation with God

James

James, a servant of God and of the Lord Jesus Christ, To the twelve tribes in the Dispersion: Greetings. My brothers and sisters, whenever you face trials of any kind, consider it nothing but joy, because you know that the testing of your faith produces endurance; and let endurance have its full effect, so that you may
5 be mature and complete, lacking in nothing. If any of you is lacking in wisdom, ask God, who gives to all generously and ungrudgingly, and it will be given you. But ask in faith, never doubting, for the one who doubts is like a wave of the sea, driven and tossed by the wind; for the doubter, being double-minded and unstable in every way, must not expect to receive anything from the Lord.
10 Let the believer who is lowly boast in being raised up, and the rich in being brought low, because the rich will disappear like a flower in the field. For the sun rises with its scorching heat and withers the field; its flower falls, and its beauty perishes. It is the same way with the rich; in the midst of a busy life, they will wither away. Blessed is anyone who endures temptation. Such a one
15 has stood the test and will receive the crown of life that the Lord has promised to those who love him. No one, when tempted, should say, "I am being tempted by God"; for God cannot be tempted by evil and he himself tempts no one. But one is tempted by one's own desire, being lured and enticed by it; then, when that desire has conceived, it gives birth to sin, and that sin, when it
20 is fully grown, gives birth to death. Do not be deceived, my beloved. Every generous act of giving, with every perfect gift, is from above, coming down

Figure I.1.

himself and that he was actively speaking to us. The book of James had come alive.

By the end of that dig-in, I was hooked on manuscript Bible study. For the first time I understood how faith and works are connected, and I had some very specific ways that I wanted to act on the Word in the coming week. I felt energized, stimulated and met by Jesus. I even had the beginnings of some real relationships with other Christian stu-

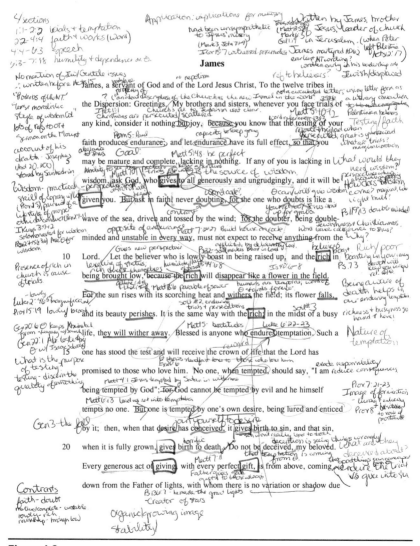

Figure I.2.

dents. My earlier motivations for Bible study melted away. My drive to know a lot and be thought well of was replaced by fascination with the Bible and a hunger to experience Jesus through his Word and with his people. God had given me far more than I had given him. I couldn't wait for the next dig-in.

SHIFTING MOTIVATIONS

Our campus fellowship spent a week every summer at Campus-By-The-Sea, a camp on Catalina Island off the coast of California. We immersed ourselves in manuscript study of Mark's Gospel. As we studied, Jesus seemed to jump off the page. Studying Mark that week caused me to fall in love with Jesus and to know him deeply with my both my head and my heart. Not only my group but many InterVarsity chapters across the Los Angeles area were gripped with zeal to make Jesus known on campus and to take huge risks of faith together because of those Mark studies.

Throughout my twenties, I threw myself into practicing and teaching manuscript study. In my spare time, I created manuscripts of new books of the Bible to share with InterVarsity students and staff. In my early thirties I brought a new motivation to Bible study: the need for stability. Though my fascination and hunger had not waned, I hit a point in life where I felt pressed beyond my limits. My husband and I had two young children; my husband was finishing graduate school, and I had shifted from full-time to part-time work as an area director for InterVarsity Christian Fellowship. I was trying to do in twenty hours a week what I had previously done in fifty. Our church had lost its pastor and was slowly falling apart. I was disoriented by the shift from full-time ministry training dynamic young leaders to endless hours of changing diapers, stacking wooden blocks and folding laundry. To top it off, I was deeply shaken by the recent divorce of an important mentor.

During that time, I read a line from my favorite psalm: "I keep my eyes always on the Lord. / With him at my right hand, I will not be shaken" (Psalm 16:8 NIV). But I did feel shaken—and shaky. My life was like a tiny rowboat on a stormy ocean. I felt disoriented, vulnerable and scared. I needed an anchor, something to tie my boat down so that it didn't drift off to sea or get caught on the rocks.

As I prayed, God showed me that he had already given me an anchor. Through meditating on the Bible every day I could experience the Lord at my right hand. Like Joshua as he faced the formidable challenge of attacking the Canaanites without Moses' strong presence, I needed to keep God's law ever before me and not turn from it to the right or the left (Joshua 1:7-8). I didn't pick up my Bible because of commitment to spiritual disciplines. Meeting God through the Bible was an utter necessity. During those challenging years, Scripture itself would be that solid, fixed place for me.

One of the ways God provided mooring for me was through a manuscript Bible study of the life of Abraham. Because I came from a secular home, I hadn't grown up in the church knowing older believers and seeing models of people whose faith stayed vibrant through the challenges of life. As I studied Abraham, I felt like I was getting to know a long lost grandparent. Watching Abraham closely, with all his faults as well as his faith, had a stabilizing effect on me. I saw the faithfulness of God even when Abraham (then called Abram) did really dumb things like telling the Pharoah that Sarai was his sister (Genesis 12:10-20). I witnessed the transformation of Abraham into a man of deep trust in God, even to the point of being willing to sacrifice his son Isaac. The stories of Abraham's life assured me that others have made it through the challenges of life and that God would be faithful to me.

It wasn't enough for a friend to tell me, "All new parents feel like this." I needed the stories of God's people to get inside of me, to expose my unspoken fears and to speak to my heart. God's Word gave me what I needed.

BECOMING WISE

I might be particularly prone to shakiness or instability, but my guess is I'm not alone. In fact, Jesus' parable of the wise and foolish builders shows that all of us will be shaken at some time or another. The question is, will we fall down or remaining standing?

> "Everyone then who hears these words
> of mine and acts on them will be like a
> wise man who built his house on rock.
> The rain fell, the floods came, and the
> winds blew and beat on that house,
> but it did not fall, because it had
> been founded on rock."
>
> MATTHEW 7:24-25

In Matthew 7:21-28 Jesus describes two men who each decide to build a house. Building a home is a universal human activity. We all need a place to live, a place to keep our possessions, a place where we belong. Homes provide security and stability for families physically, emotionally and financially. Like all of Jesus' parables, this is a picture of ordinary life.

In the parable, the problem comes when the two men discover that they have built in a flood plain. One was ready for the flood by putting extra work into the building process; one was not.

I live in Iowa, where flooding occurs almost annually. Our farms do not need irrigation because it rains regularly in the summer. The state is crisscrossed by small and not-so-small rivers. The extensive network of creeks and rivers provides great drainage and a constant supply of fresh water for the many ponds and lakes. Most summers, however, some part of the state experiences severe flooding, when heavy rain exceeds the capacity of the rivers and lakes. All Iowans are familiar with photos of submerged cars and of homes that look like small islands surrounded by water on every side.

In the verses preceding this parable, Jesus makes the bold claim that he is the one who will determine who enters the kingdom of heaven and who doesn't (Matthew 7:21-23). He is the Judge before whom all will stand "on that day." Like a good school teacher who tells the class clearly what will be asked on the final exam, he makes the criteria on which he will base his judgment quite clear: doing the will of the Father.

And how do we know the Father's will? By paying attention to Jesus' words. "Everyone then who hears these words of mine and acts on them . . ." Because Jesus is the Judge we will all stand before, his perspective is the only one that matters. He alone accurately describes reality. He can see it all, and he knows where it is going. It is utter foolishness to ignore his words. Not making Jesus' teaching the center of our lives and choices is as stupid as building our dream home ten feet from the Iowa River.

Wisdom involves seeing reality clearly and making good choices in light of reality. The Word of God describes reality and shines light into our lives so that we can be aligned with what is true. It takes work and effort to study the Bible so that we are really hearing Jesus' words. It takes more work to examine our lives, soften our hearts, and change our attitudes and actions in response to what we hear. Yet the effort is worth it. The more we study God's Word and let it shape our lives, the more stability and security we have. We become more solid and substantial people.

JOURNEY TO MATURITY

I was first introduced to the idea of solidity of character in C. S. Lewis's wonderful book *The Great Divorce*. Through an imaginative narrative, Lewis describes the kind of people who inhabit heaven and hell. He depicts hell as a shadowy, flimsy place where people are self-centered and caught up in petty arguments or complaints. In contrast, heaven and the people who live there are large, robust, vibrant and substantial.

The narrator comes to the edge of heaven and discovers that he is a mere wisp; he can see through his own body like smoke from a campfire. The grass of heaven is so real and solid that it hurts his feet to walk on. All are welcome in heaven, but many turn back because of the pain of confronting their own flaws and being transformed into solid beings.

I've come to understand that this solidity that I found so attractive in others is what the Bible calls "faithfulness" or "maturity." I have found the path of faithfulness to be challenging. As much as I like the idea of being a mature person, I often cringe at the process required to develop that maturity. I wish we lived in a world where one could just be born an Olympic-level athlete rather than getting there through hard work and practice. Likewise, I wish I could just ask God to make me mature and have it happen automatically. Instead, he invites us on a journey with him, guided by his Word and marked by hundreds of choices of obedience.

The earliest memory I have of deciding to obey the Bible involves gossip. It seems that most people are susceptible to the temptation to talk about other people, but gossip seems to be a particularly strong temptation for teenage girls. It is as if juicy morsels of information about other teens are a form of currency. The more you know, the wealthier you are.

One night at youth group, we read Ephesians 4:29: "Let no evil talk come out of your mouths, but only what is useful for building up, as there is need, so that your words may give grace to those who hear." As I began to understand that God wants us to control what we talk about and that we are to only say things that build others up, I thought, *Uh oh. I'm in big trouble.* I was an avid gossiper, regularly talking about my friends behind their backs in order to feel "in" with other girls. But there it was, in the Scriptures, and I had to deal with it. My progress in turning from gossip was slow and difficult; it felt awkward to interrupt a conversation with friends and ask that we change the subject. But that discomfort was nothing in comparison to the shame I felt when a friend in college came to me and said, "I hear you said these things about me." Thankfully that friend was willing to extend forgiveness to me, but the pain of being confronted with my sin provided the motivation I needed to more diligently resist the temptation to gossip.

Though I still stumble in this area, a life relatively gossip-free has provided me a lot of relational stability and security. I know many friendships, families and churches that have been damaged by gossip, but I have been spared that pain. By and large, my relationships are solid, built with respect, trust and love. People feel safe to share vulnerably with me because they know I won't expose their weaknesses to others to somehow make myself look better.

It would never have occurred to me to pursue a gossip-free life. God's Word led me to that, and I am so grateful for the benefits. I desperately want a secure, stable and fruitful life. By letting the light of the Bible shine on my life and attempting to respond with faithfulness, I am slowly becoming a more solid and mature person.

The process of becoming that kind of person is like a journey on a long and winding road. The road sometimes is narrow and unpaved; at other times it is obscured by fog. But God has not left us to find our way on our own. As the psalmist so aptly puts it, "Your word is a lamp to my feet and a light to my path" (Psalm 119:105). Through the Scriptures the Holy Spirit provides illumination. Actively studying and obeying the Bible provides stable footing and a sense of direction, no matter how challenging the journey.

MOTIVES MATTER

Before diving deeper into this Bible study handbook, it will be beneficial to identify your motivation. I have described the various motivations I have had for Bible study over my thirty-plus years as a Christian: desire to fit in with Christians, desire to accumulate facts and knowledge, hunger to connect with Jesus, need for stability and security. What are yours?

> "It isn't easy to let a text 'read' you. Your thirst for knowledge and information often makes you desire to own the word, instead of letting the word own you. Even so, you will learn the most by listening carefully to the Word that seeks admission to your heart."
>
> **HENRI NOUWEN,** *Letters to Marc About Jesus*

Our motivations for studying often reveal (or shape) our view of what the Bible is.

Those of us who approach the Bible primarily for knowledge tend to view it like an encyclopedia. Bible study is boring unless we see something new or have an opportunity to show how much we know.

Those seeking guidance or help in making decisions are often tempted to view it as a Magic 8 ball. You know what I mean: we pray and then point to a random verse, expecting God to speak to us as if he were a fortune teller or a horoscope column.

Others of us want to know what is expected of us to be approved of by God. We view the Bible like a manual from the Department of Motor Vehicles. We look for the rules and figure out what will be on the test. Intimacy with God isn't our goal, because no one wants to be close to a powerful guy whose job is to evaluate and critique.

These motivations distance us from God rather than draw us closer. But there is another motive that leads to the opposite problem.

We have been told that God's Word is like a love letter to us, and so we read it looking for inspiration or comfort. The problem with that view of the Bible is that we make it all about us, rather than God and his purposes in history taking center stage. When we view the Bible as a love letter, we hone in on favorite verses such as "I know the plans I have for you" (Jeremiah 29:11) and "He . . . will rejoice over you with singing" (Zephaniah 3:17 NIV), while jumping over the parts we don't immediately connect with, like Leviticus, Deuteronomy or genealogies. I believe deeply in the love of God, and I am convinced that giving us the Bible is one of the major ways God expresses his love. But to take the love-letter approach is to narrowly define love and to cheapen God's Word.

If we believe Jesus when he says that his words are key to living within reality and experiencing the solidity and fullness of life God has for us, then we will set aside inadequate views of the Bible and seek to understand it on its own terms. We will welcome it into our hearts and allow the Holy Spirit to use the Bible to renovate our lives. In doing so, we will discover—as I did in my first dig-in—that God gives himself generously to those who seek him through his Word.

USING THIS HANDBOOK

The Bible Study Handbook is designed to help you do that. It is arranged in three sections: foundations, building blocks and, finally, a tool box. The five chapters in the "Foundations" section address the presuppositions behind inductive Bible study, including the nature of the Scriptures, the importance of keeping the text itself central and the benefits of becoming people of the Word. These chapters each stand on their own, so you can read them in any order, though I suggest you read chapter one before turning to the material in the "Building Blocks" section. Each of the chapters in the "Foundations" section ends with a reflection exercise, designed to assess your heart's posture toward the Bible. Like going to the chiropractor, the "Foundations" chapters should help to realign your heart and mind so that your relationship with God through his Word can deepen.

There are six chapters in the "Building Blocks" section. These chapters build on each other and should be read in order. Here I explain in detail how to study the Bible inductively and illustrate the various elements by working with the same Gospel passage throughout. The practicum exercises at the end provide an opportunity for you to put the training material into practice. When you finish the series of practicum in section two, you will have completed an inductive study of a passage in Mark.[1]

The final section of this handbook is a series of short chapters about a variety of topics that affect and enhance inductive Bible study. Like a hammer, screwdrivers and wrenches in a tool box, you can use these chapters at any time and in any order according to your needs. This section is meant to be a reference for you as you grow in inductive Bible study. Each chapter includes a practicum to practice the skill presented. When first using the handbook, you will be focusing on the basics. But as you get more experience and begin to study a broader range of books of the Bible, various questions might emerge that you didn't have at the beginning. I have attempted to provide answers to the kinds of questions that come up along the way.

You can also use section three to challenge and stretch yourself as a student of God's Word. Dipping into a chapter or two of the "Tool Box" section periodically will stimulate your thinking and enable you to access more of the richness of the Bible. A list of additional resources is available in appendix E.

My prayer for you is that using this handbook will increase your love and enjoyment of God's Word, develop your skills in studying it, and provide many opportunities to encounter Jesus. May you find yourself more fully rooted and established in God as you learn to delve into his Word.

REFLECTION EXERCISE
Identifying Obstacles to Bible Study

For most of us, studying the Bible is harder than it needs to be because of internal obstacles. These obstacles are often unnamed, but they influence us nonetheless. Read the statements below and mark the ones you resonate with.

_____ I don't have enough time.

_____ I have heard most of the Bible stories before.

_____ I get easily distracted when reading the Bible.

_____ I feel guilty that I don't read the Bible more often.

_____ I read the words, but most of it goes over my head.

_____ I had some bad experiences in Sunday school or small group Bible study.

_____ The Bible seems irrelevant to my life.

_____ I don't like reading.

_____ It seems like too much work.

_____ I don't feel adequate to interpret the Bible and would rather learn what experts think.

_____ If I studied the Bible, I'd be challenged to change parts of my life.

_____ Growing as a Christian isn't that important to me.

_____ I don't know how to study it.

_____ I don't have anyone to talk about it with.

Which of the items you marked is the strongest? In your own words, describe that obstacle.

In the coming week, tell a trusted friend or leader about this obstacle and ask them to pray for God to overcome it.

Part One

FOUNDATIONS

1

Centrality of the Word

Let's be honest with ourselves: the Bible is a strange book. It talks about ancient societies with customs we find odd, mentions people with names like Salathiel and Eliud, and uses words that are far from contemporary vocabulary, such as "uncircumcised" and "covetousness." Yet it is God's Word and central to the Christian faith, so we know we can't completely abandon it to the realm of university Religious Studies departments. We sense our need for this book, but reading it can be challenging.

One way to deal with this tension is to focus on individual verses such as "For God so loved the world that he gave his only Son" (John 3:16) or "We know all things work together for good for those who love God" (Romans 8:28) but leave the rest of the Bible for pastors and scholars. Those verses are wonderful and true, but they are really just terse summary statements. Do you want to know what it means that "all things work together for good"? Then you need to know the rest of the story, even though that may mean plunging into foreign waters.

Another way we deal with the strangeness of the Bible is to make "Bible study" synonymous with "Learn what an expert has to say about the Bible." We feel inadequate and unqualified to understand the Bible ourselves, so we turn to scholars and seminary graduates. We sign up for adult Sunday school classes where a pastor or elder will teach through a book of the Bible (perhaps asking a few questions along the way to encourage group participation). We read commentaries and listen to famous preachers expound on the Word. We purchase study Bibles with copious notes to explain what we are reading.

I thank God for pastors, teachers, authors and scholars who have invested their lives in studying the Scriptures and in communicating what they've learned. Their gifts are invaluable. But most of us tend to pay more attention to the words of experts than to the words of the Bible itself. We desire to learn from the Bible and believe it alone is authoritative for Christian faith and practice, but *in practice* we turn to the experts and let the Scripture be sidelined.

The purpose of this handbook is to train God's people to study the Bible for themselves rather than relying on "professional Christians" to explain it. The method I use is called *manuscript Bible study* and uses an *inductive* approach. Studying the Bible directly is like watching a one-person show, where the text of the Bible is the primary actor and all focus is kept on it. Input from other sources is like minor characters coming on stage briefly to play bit parts. If our attention becomes diverted by these other actors, we must refocus our selves on the star of the show. Inductive Bible study is an effective method of keeping the text of the Bible in the spotlight.

Keeping the words of the Bible front and center is easier said than done. As a young Christian, I was eager to read the Bible. When my youth pastor suggested a study Bible that was popular in our denomination, I read along, reading first a verse of the Bible and then the explanatory notes below. On some pages there was more space given to the study notes than the biblical text itself. I could tell by the formatting which sections were explanatory notes and which were the Bible itself, but in practice I ascribed the same weight to both.

It wasn't until a few years later, when I began to interact with Christians from different churches, that I realized that my study Bible promoted a particular theology—some of which I would later come to view as incorrect. But at the time I had no way of knowing. If I read it in my study Bible, I assumed it was true.

That very night the believers sent Paul and Silas off to Beroea; and when they arrived, they went to the Jewish synagogue. These Jews were more receptive than those in Thessalonica, for they welcomed the message very eagerly and examined the scriptures every day to see whether these things were so. (Acts 17:10-11)

The book of Acts provides a valuable model of people who worked hard to keep the Bible front and center, and to not get sidelined by the opinions of experts. The Jews of Beroea are described by Luke in Acts as unique in their response to Paul's preaching. The Beroeans didn't just listen to the preaching of Paul and Silas; they compared Paul's words to the Word of God.

No doubt Paul's message of Jesus crucified and resurrected was different from how they had become used to thinking about the Messiah. But rather than focusing on the teaching of their rabbis or being persuaded simply by Paul's charisma, the Beroeans examined the Scriptures directly to discern what was true. They did this not just once, but for several days. The Beroeans did the hard work of examining the Scriptures themselves, attributing authority to the text, not to authoritative teachers. They kept the text front and center.

ABDICATION

Too often, we leave the work of understanding complex things to others. We do this in many areas of our lives. Voters make decisions on who to vote for based on endorsements from people they respect rather than by learning for themselves a candidate's position on key issues. Likewise, many students would rather read the CliffsNotes summarizing an assigned novel than the novel itself. By taking this shortcut, they rely on someone else's interpretation and undercut the process of developing critical thinking skills.

At one level, taking advice or input from experts is a good use of our time. We can't all be specialists in medicine, nutrition and auto repair. A specialized society enables us to benefit from the investment of those with different interests and abilities than our own. However, Christian faith and spiritual formation are too important to leave the work of understanding the Bible to experts. Sermons and books by skilled teachers and thinkers are valuable, but they can't replace the life-giving words of the Bible itself. To become mature and vibrant followers of Jesus, we must engage with the Bible directly. We must learn to keep the Scripture itself in the center of our study. Then, once we've studied a passage inductively, reading a commentary by a reliable author can highlight elements we may have missed, provide additional insights and raise new questions that cause us to engage further with the biblical text.[1]

I have three convictions that I believe affect our ability to rightly understand the Bible, use biblical scholarship appropriately and keep us in a posture of humility and submission to God's Word.

1. Facts before theories.
2. Author determines meaning.
3. Understanding requires application.

CONVICTION #1: *Facts Before Theories*

The sixteenth-century scientist Galileo Galilei found himself in a predicament. He loved and worshiped God, but his telescope and his inquiring mind landed him in a heap of trouble with the Catholic Church. By paying careful attention to the movement of the stars, Galileo came to believe that the earth moves around the sun, rather than the other way around. From his perspective, the evidence was undeniable, yet it contradicted the longstanding assumption of geocentrism that the church at the time thought was inherent to a biblical worldview.[2] Galileo was tried for heresy, forced to recant and placed under house arrest for the rest of his life.

On one level, I am sympathetic toward those church leaders. They took their responsibility to protect the church from false teaching seriously. Until Galileo expressed an alternate theory, the preconception of geocentrism was widely assumed to be truth.

We can gain a valuable lesson from the church's experience on the eve of the Scientific Revolution: assumptions and theories aren't the same as truth. Theories, whether they are the laws of nature or theological statements, are attempts to summarize truth, but they are not the truth themselves. Truth lies in reality itself, not in the theories used to describe that reality. Theories and beliefs must be the servants of truth, not the other way around.

There are two complementary processes we use to learn and explore. One is to move from the general to the particular: to use what we know to be true to help us further investigate and better understand specific situations. The other approach moves from the particular to the general—to notice details and then develop a generalization that makes sense of that information. The scientific world calls the first approach *deduction* and the second *induction*. These approaches are used every day by children, farmers, friends, artists, business people, scholars and doctors. Deduction and induction are what humans do, whether we are conscious of it or not.

Photography as an art was developed (no pun intended!) using deduction. Once it was discovered that light-sensitive chemicals could capture images onto metal or glass plates by focusing light through a lens, inventors were able to experiment using general principles of photography (focus, exposure, etc.). Armed with a general knowledge of capturing images using light and chemicals, they varied the chemicals, camera designs and techniques for developing film. Eastman Kodak began to sell flexible photographic film to replace the standard thin glass plates. Eventually photographers learned how to capture the image in color, and to adjust settings, aperture and film speed to achieve different effects. By applying the general principles of "drawing with light" (the literal meaning of the word *photography*) to the process of exploration, hundreds of new insights—both scientific and artistic—were made. Soon photography joined painting and sculpting as a recognized art form.

Induction, by contrast, starts with details and builds out to a general theory or synthesis. The inductive process analyzes a set of facts in relationship to one another and develops an understanding that holds the particulars together in a coherent whole. Inductive study can be seen in toddlers as they explore their world. Early on, for example, a toddler notices that if she drops her spoon off the highchair, it falls to the ground, and an adult leans over to retrieve it. The same thing happens not just to spoons but crackers, cups, balls and toys: regardless of which item is dropped, an adult responds by moving to pick it up. Long before she can even pronounce the word *gravity*, she has developed awareness

of a general truth, a law of nature: objects fall. But she has also identified another "law of nature": adults compulsively pick up dropped
things. Her experiences with particular utensils, toys and pieces of food
have been effectively synthesized into a general conclusion. In combination, these two laws of nature provide no end of entertainment for
the toddler.

Deduction enables us to anticipate what will happen in a new situation or interpret a new experience, based on what is already known.
Induction enables us to test our current understandings and to learn
more. Scientists use the two in tandem to extend our knowledge of the
universe. Both deductive and inductive thinking can be used when
studying the Bible as well. I find, however, that most Christians don't
approach the Bible inductively unless they are intentional about doing
so. Our default seems to be a deductive approach.

> "Induction is the influence of the new on the old;
> deduction is the influence of the old on the new."
>
> HERMAN H. HORNE,
> *The Psychological Principles of Education*

I consider it a spiritual discipline to intentionally put facts before
theories. There are many places in our lives were what we already
"know" can lead us to miss what is really happening. This causes no
end of trouble in arenas such as crosscultural relations, scientific ex-
perimentation and criminal investigation. But it is particularly important to put facts before theories when it comes to studying the
Bible, since inductive study helps us to read the Bible with an openness
to be changed. It trains us to resist our tendency to make a general
conclusion before all the facts have been accounted for. Without such
openness, the Bible becomes the servant of our preconceived ideas.
The famous detective Sherlock Holmes would describe this as twisting
facts to suit theories.[3]

Humility and teachability require that we let the Scripture speak for itself, even if that means laying aside our current views.

> When used in connection with Bible study, the term "inductive" simply means that procedure of Bible study which approaches a book of the Bible with no general conclusions, but rather, begins by observing the particulars of a book, and, after observing these adequately, comes to some general conclusions of their meaning.[4]

As one Ethiopian Christian leader testified after studying the Gospel of Mark inductively using the manuscript method, "I can no longer make Scripture say what I want it to say but must let it speak what it is meant to speak to us. This style of study forces us to listen to the Word itself. It's been life challenging and life changing. I will never be the same after studying the Gospel in this way!"[5]

Inductive Bible study follows three primary phases: *observation, interpretation* and *application*. This means that the question "What?" comes before the questions "So what?" and "Now what?" (I will address these phases in significant detail in part two of this handbook.) Such a commitment to putting facts before theories through studying the Scripture inductively is invaluable in keeping our focus on the text and submitting ourselves to its authority. The second conviction—that the author determines the meaning—goes hand-in-hand with the first.

CONVICTION #2: Author Determines Meaning

Most Christians are eager to hear from God through the Bible, but they are highly subjective when interacting with it. How many times have you been in a Bible study when someone said, "What this means to me . . ."? Living in a relativistic and pluralistic society, we have become used to the idea of "personal meaning." Existentialist philosophy and postmodern literary theory have asserted that truth is an arbitrary construct and that meaning is created by individuals or communities.

Many of us who follow Jesus carry this perspective into our faith in subtle (or not so subtle) ways. Our personal experience reigns supreme, and our interaction with the Bible is deeply subjective. Perhaps without realizing it, we function as if *we* determine the meaning of the Scriptures.

We don't. The author of each of the books of the Bible determines the meaning. In chapter six I explain the reason and implications of this conviction—including the relationship between God as the ultimate author of the Bible and the human authors he worked through. Though the Bible contains transcendent truth, it was not dropped from the sky. Behind every book of the Bible is a human author inspired by God, writing from within a specific situation to a specific audience. Biblical authors used language, historical examples and literary conventions of their culture to influence their audience toward faith and obedience. They had a purpose and objective when they sat down to write.

In the world of literary studies, this is referred to as "authorial intent." A commitment to authorial intent means we seek to understand what the author was trying to communicate to his original audience rather than what it sounds like to us. By continually asking, "How would this have sounded to the original audience?" we are forced to think outside of ourselves and our own experience; without this posture, we would be blind to the parts of Scripture which challenge our cultural assumptions.

Authorial intent involves taking the crosscultural and literary nature of the Bible seriously. Through looking closely at content, structure, form (genre) and cultural/historical context, we seek to discern what the author wanted to communicate. Pursuit of understanding the author's intent takes the Bible on its own terms rather than ours.

One implication of the conviction that the author determines meaning is that each book of the Bible must be understood as a unique composition. In inductive Bible study, cross-referencing books that a particular book's first audience wouldn't have had access to doesn't make sense. (The parts of the Scripture that the original audience had available to them is an important part of their perspective.) Everything that is needed to understand a particular book is in the book itself when heard from the perspective of the original audience. Too often, we don't do the work of understanding a particular author because we use other parts of the Bible to interpret his work. It is a mistake to turn to a parallel passage in Luke or Matthew to answer a question about Mark rather than looking for the evidence Mark has provided to effectively communicate to his audience. Believing that the author determines meaning involves staying within the text at hand and discerning the author's purposes and intentions before comparing what has been written to other parts of the Bible. Together, the sixty-six books of the Bible—when each is understood on its own terms—tell a richly woven story of God's commitment to redeem all of creation.

CONVICTION #3: *Understanding Requires Application*

The first two convictions I am proposing aren't exclusively related to studying the Bible. In studying *any piece* of writing or work of art, one can approach the text with a commitment to facts before theories and to authorial intent. These presuppositions bear fruit whether reading *Hamlet* or watching *Titanic*. Likewise any person, regardless of their religious beliefs, can study the Bible inductively and consider its original context. Students in "Bible as Literature" classes will benefit from these approaches whether or not they believe in the God of the Bible. Atheistic New Testament scholars can (and do) have insight about the letters of Paul or the unique vision of the Gospel of John.

But for followers of Jesus, this is not sufficient. For those of us who have put our faith in Jesus as Savior and Lord, understanding God's Word requires application to our lives. When we come to the Bible we must come to it as holy Scripture—God's address to God's people. As his people our posture must fit that of subjects before a beloved king: open, expectant, eager to do his bidding. New Testament scholar Joel B. Green writes that "such dispositions and postures and gestures as acceptance, devotion, attention, and trust [are] more necessary than familiarity with ancient peoples and their cultures, more basic than learning the biblical languages, and more essential than good technique in interpretation."[6]

The Bible is not merely a text to be studied, analyzed and explained. The author of Hebrews describes it as a double-edged sword that is "able to judge the thoughts and intentions of the heart. And before him no creature is hidden, but all are naked and laid bare to the eyes of the one to whom we must render an account" (Hebrews 4:12-13). The Bible reads us even as we read it. Whether or not we allow ourselves to come under its scrutiny has everything to do with our heart posture. Thus commitment number three is essential: understanding requires application.

We do not truly understand something until we have lived it. It is one thing for a medical student to memorize the steps in a surgical procedure but quite another to be a surgeon. Until she has performed the surgery, knowing the steps does not equal understanding. Likewise, it is impossible to actually understand the Bible without living it out. For example, when I was a student at a small liberal arts college, slanderous things were said about our Christian community because of our bold witness. We had been seeing God's hand at work on our campus, including a number of public conversions and some dramatic changes in students' lives as they turned from materialism and a drive to worldly success. Our highly secular environment viewed Jesus' resurrection as fairy tale and tolerated faith only as long as it was kept private. It wasn't until I had to meet with a college dean to discuss concerns about our ministry that I understood Jesus' words about not being ashamed of him (Mark 8:38) or the promise of the help of the Holy Spirit when standing before governors (Mark 13:9). Living out parts of the Bible gave me understanding of those texts that I hadn't gained from merely studying them.

Have you ever noticed that people who have played a sport in high school tend to be faithful followers of that sport later in life? That is because understanding that comes from *doing* creates a sense of connection. Their experience as athletes enables them to see more than others who haven't played the sport before; even as spectators they have an insider's perspective. I am a runner. In high school I ran on the cross country team in the fall and middle distance during the track season. (I even tried hurdles but soon learned I'd better keep my feet on the ground.) To this day, I love watching world-class athletes run. I could never match their speed and endurance, but I feel a connection to them because I know what it is like to compete as a runner. I can easily imagine what they are feeling at the two-thirds point in the race. I know the joy of crossing the finish line having run with everything I had.

My enjoyment of watching others run is greater because of my own experience with running. When we put biblical understanding into action, it deepens our passion to know more of the story of God's interactions with his people and enables us to see things that we could not have seen without those experiences.

It is in applying the text to our lives, obeying it in concrete ways and submitting ourselves to the process of being transformed at its direction, that we come to understand the Scriptures. A true Christian understanding is an integrated understanding, not primarily a conceptual one. A passionate commitment to listening to God's Word and living it out is essential if we truly understand what the Bible is and its purpose in our world. As Dietrich Bonhoeffer wrote,

> In our meditation we ponder the chosen text on the strength of the promise that it has something utterly personal to say to us for this day and for our Christian life, that it is not only God's word for the Church, but also God's word for us individually. We expose ourselves to the specific word until it addresses us personally. And when we do this, we are doing no more than the simplest, untutored Christian does every day; we read God's word as God's word for us.[7]

The application of Scripture to our lives isn't optional. We can't claim to have studied the Bible inductively if we haven't wrestled with its implications for our world and our lives in particular. Our understanding is at best incomplete and at worst distorted if we haven't responded to the text and been shaped by it. Chapter eleven explains how to discern God's invitation to apply the Word to our lives.

DISCOVERY

These three convictions (facts before theories, author determines meaning and understanding requires application), along with the determination to not abdicate our understanding of the Bible to experts, put us in position for one of the great joys of life: the joy of discovery.

I recently stayed in an urban residential neighborhood during a business trip. While I was out walking, an unusual building caught my eye. Tucked away on a side alleyway, its clean, modern design stood in contrast to the bungalows and Victorian-style homes on the street. As I ventured down the alley to get a better look, something else caught my eye: a bright blue arrow pointing further down the alley. Propelled by my curiosity, I followed the arrow and found myself at a cultural center called the Meso American Institute. Just when I was about to turn around and head back to the main street, I noticed something else that I hadn't expected to find in the city: a pathway lined by trees, which seemed to be an opening to a small park accessible only by foot. By this point, I was having such a good time exploring that I couldn't resist going further to discover what I might find.

At the bottom of the park, hidden to those who stayed on the paved alley, was a beautiful wooden bridge over a babbling creek. I was delighted! The park was cool, quiet and secluded. It's the kind of place I would enjoy escaping to with a picnic blanket and a good book.

What had begun for me as a walk through an urban neighborhood—with all its pavement, tiny yards, garbage cans and street lights—had become a joyful discovery of a beautiful natural retreat hidden away from sight. I could have been told by my hosts that there was a lovely park nearby, but it was so much more fun to discover it myself. In fact, the process of discovering this tranquil park on my own was as much a part of the joy as the beauty of the wooden bridge and the sound of the creek.

> "The Bible is in fact more than a fixed library; it is a world we have to enter for ourselves, an adventure to which we are summoned: that of a people seized with a passion for God."
>
> FR. ÉTIENNE CHARPENTIER,
> *How to Read the Old Testament*

Studies show that we retain more when we figure something out for ourselves. Learning that involves proactivity, genuine curiosity and hard work engages us at a deeper level. Rather than an "in one ear and out the other" experience, participatory and learner-driven study (as opposed to teacher-driven study) stays with us long after the study session is over. Discovering the riches of the Scripture for ourselves deepens our motivation to learn and increases our level of comprehension.

Inductive Bible study is a process of discovery, an adventure. This adventure can be experienced whenever an individual sits down with the text and makes space in their heart and mind to engage it deeply. But it is also an adventure that communities of believers can (and should) embark on together. The group as a whole looks closely at the text, asking questions of it and working together to determine its meaning. When there is disagreement, the text—not the teacher—is the arbitrator. Inductive Bible study teachers function as facilitators in the discovery process, not as lecturers, and they are not given the final word. All comments and conclusions must be supported by the data in the text, without reference to explanations in study Bibles or by pastors. The group keeps the Scripture front and center and enjoys the adventure of discovery together. Chapter five will more fully address the communal nature of inductive Bible study.

The following description of a student's experience of a manuscript study of Mark's Gospel highlights the power and the joy of an inductive approach toward the Scripture:

> I would read through the passage on my own and I would find the passage mildly interesting. But as we entered group discussion, my peers around the table would verbalize their questions and the text, and I would find myself more intrigued and engaged. I would be forced to look again at the passage, more carefully this time. Suddenly I would see something new for myself. I found great joy in the process of discovery and also in being able to ask questions of the group. . . . The word became a mirror and I saw a new picture of myself. I was wrapped in thorns and choking. No one else had judged me or told me how I needed to change. Rather, I saw myself in those bad soils, and the images were haunting. Prior to this, I was accustomed to other people telling me that I needed to change, and I had become adept at pushing aside such comments from others. This time I saw it for myself and I could not push it out of my head. I had arrived at my own conclusions about Jesus for the first time in my life . . . and surrendered my life to Jesus.[8]

I write this handbook in the hope that many of God's people will have their own story to tell by studying the Bible inductively. The Bible might be a strange book, but once we have learned how to explore it there is no end to the joy we can have discovering its riches.

REFLECTION EXERCISE
Convictions

On a scale of 1-5 (1 being lowest and 5 highest), rate your level of conviction about each of the three premises of inductive study described in this chapter. If you desire to see any of those levels of conviction increase, how will you pursue that?

Conviction #1: Facts Before Theories

Conviction #2: Author Determines Meaning

Conviction #3: Understanding Requires Application

2

Power of the Word

Good things happen when soft-hearted people come in contact with the Bible. When I am training Bible study teachers, I stress that the most important thing they can do as a teacher is to create space and time for people to get in front of the Bible and let it have its effect on them.

Teachers tend to focus on skills and methods, but the reason people are transformed through Bible Study is the inherent power of God's Word. I have experienced this power and witnessed its impact on people and communities of faith for over twenty-five years. One of those people is Tim, a young man utterly convinced about the dynamic power of God's Word.

A missions pastor at a church in Los Angeles had created an urban ministry internship, hoping to build a team of interns with strong social skills, initiative and the ability relate crossculturally. Motivated by his love for God and desire to grow as a Christian, Tim applied for the internship. During his interview, Tim's social awkwardness was readily apparent. The missions pastor seriously doubted Tim's ability to become effective in ministry, especially in a crosscultural setting. Nonetheless, Tim was admitted to the summer internship and assigned to an immigrant neighborhood.

Tim did not speak Spanish, but somehow he made a connection with a Spanish-speaking family who had recently moved from Mexico to Los Angeles. Tim wasn't able to share the gospel directly because of the language barrier, but he knew God's Word could speak to them, so he arranged to meet weekly for a Bible study. Tim began each study by reading aloud a passage from the Gospels out of a Spanish Bible. Then he read six simple inductive questions, translated into Spanish, that he had been taught in his internship. The questions were straightforward and applicable to any Bible story:

1. What did you like best about this story?
2. What did you like the least?
3. What don't you understand?
4. What did you learn about God?
5. What do you personally need to do about it?
6. Which phrase or verse do you want to take away with you?

Since Tim didn't understand what the family said as they discussed the passage, he merely waited while they talked with each other about the question he asked. When the talking died down, he asked the next one.

Tim and the family continued on like this all summer long. At the end of the summer, a Spanish-speaking Christian came with Tim to the study. The family eagerly turned to the visitor and asked, "How do we become Christians?" In the following months, they returned to Mexico and began the same type of Bible study in their village. Through that Bible study, most of the village entered into Jesus' kingdom.

God loves to use the Bible to draw people to himself. He uses it to reach the hearts of those who haven't known him, and he uses it to bring his people into deeper relationship with him. What is it about the Bible that makes it God's chosen tool? To understand the uniqueness and importance of the Bible, we must first consider the value of words.

WORDS

Like the air we breathe, we take words for granted. We use words all day long whether we are talking on the phone, reading a magazine, making a grocery list or watching a movie. Yet it isn't until we meet someone who speaks a different language or encounter someone who isn't able to use words effectively, such as a child with autism, that we become aware of how central words are to life and relationships.

Words stand as representatives of things, ideas, people and emotions. Yet words aren't the thing itself. You can't eat the word *banana*.

But I bet that as soon as you read the word *banana* an image came to your mind of a long, slender object with yellow skin covering whitish fruit. Using the word *banana*, I am able to communicate effectively to you whether or not an actual banana is on hand.

Just as a sewing machine enables a seamstress to sew more than she can with only a needle and thread, words enable us to do much more than we could without them. Try this experiment: for fifteen minutes use no words in your interactions with people. When you're done, write down what you noticed about the experience.

My guess is that you will feel severely limited in communicating. Pointing and drawing can only get you so far. We experience some of the same frustrations and confusion when traveling to a country where our language isn't spoken.

Tim must have felt similarly. Without any command of Spanish, he was left with only nonverbal communication to make a connection with the immigrant family. Their interactions weren't able to move to a deeper level until Tim began using words—the words of the Bible and the Spanish script he had been given.

Tools can be wielded to create and build, but they can also be used to destroy and harm. The same hammer used to build a backyard play-house can also be used to smash a window, depending on whether it is being wielded by a parent or a thief. As tools, words can function in the same way. As a child, I was confused by the chant "Sticks and stones can break my bones, but names can never hurt me." That saying seemed completely backward. Hearing "You're ugly" from a classmate during recess hurt much longer than a punch in the arm. Careless or cruel words can lodge in our hearts and minds, damaging our confidence or fueling our resentments. We all know that words have the power to shape us for a lifetime. Since words have latent power for good or for ill, we would do well to handle them thoughtfully and with love.

Recorded words are an even more powerful tool. Writing enables communication to move beyond the bounds of location and time. Records can be kept, ideas can spread, discovery and knowledge can be shared and built upon. The ancient civilizations of Egypt and China became great after the development of written language. Likewise, the philosophical, political and mathematical accomplishments of ancient Greece have influenced and shaped Western civilization for more than two millennia because their ideas were written down, translated and read broadly.

The same holds true for a digital age. Recorded words—whether dialogue or narration in videos, songs, blogs or ebooks—are central to communication and influence. Advances in recording and dissemination are opening up the way for more of us to be heard and read by a broader audience. If you want to reach large numbers of people, you must use the tool of recorded words in one format or another.

Imagine if every book, magazine, instruction manual, label and email could only be produced using images and graphics. Likewise, what would happen to our relationships if we couldn't use words? If I were limited to communicating with my family only through gestures, facial expressions, body language and drawing, we might laugh a lot (as we do when playing a game of charades), but we would also experience a lot of frustration, misunderstanding and isolation. We wouldn't be able to tell stories about our days, discuss politics, or share why we are feeling joyful, angry or sad. Without words, our relationships would be severely limited. We need the tool of words to live together in a meaningful way.

BEYOND CHARADES

In the Bible, God has availed himself of the powerful tool of recorded words. He has not left us to play charades with him, trying to interpret what he is saying through the night sky, natural disasters or the changing of the seasons. He communicates more directly and clearly than that. He is eager to be in relationship with us, and relationships need words.

Of course, God's creation does communicate something to us about who God is. King David wrote, "The heavens are telling the glory of God; and the firmament proclaims his handiwork" (Psalm 19:1). Paul reminds us, "Ever since the creation of the world his eternal power and divine nature, invisible though they are, have been understood and seen through the things he has made" (Romans 1:20). When we take the time to gaze out over the ocean or walk through a forest, we become freshly aware that God is real, he is powerful, and he is good.

But we can't know merely by observing nature that God desires relationship with us. We need the words of the Bible to show us that the creator of the universe is a relational God. We learn about God's relationality through the stories we read about God in the Bible, through the conversations we see God having with biblical characters. We learn that God has a mission for his people, and that his mission is irrespective of their character flaws or personal limitations—and we learn it through the words laid out in the Bible. We learn that God suffers with us and demands justice from us and offers mercy to us, and we learn these things through the particular communication of the Old and New Testaments. We are able to learn about God because God communicates about himself to us through the Bible.

To connect with Jesus deeply we need to "see" for ourselves how he treated sinners, healed with compassion, spoke with authority, submitted himself to crucifixion and rose from the dead. Hearsay is not enough. Early church leaders understood this; they were painstakingly careful to write down and pass along eyewitness accounts of Jesus. Luke, for example, "decided, after investigating everything carefully from the very first, to write an orderly account for you . . . so that you may know the truth concerning the things about which you have been instructed" (Luke 1:3-4).

God has not left us to grope around in the dark with a vague sense of who he is and what he is up to. Jesus came to earth in a physical body precisely because God wants us to know him. As the apostle John explains, "No one has ever seen God. It is God the only Son, who is close to the Father's heart, who has made him known" (John 1:18). The whole point of Jesus' incarnation was to set the record straight about who God is: a loving, compassionate God who will pay any cost to deliver creation from its corruption and make all things new. If you want to know what God is like, look no further. Jesus makes him known.

But the vast majority of people in world history could not experience God-in-the-flesh if it weren't for the Bible. The very nature of being in the flesh is to be limited by time and space. How often I have envied the people I read about in the Gospels who were able to hear Jesus' voice, look into his eyes, feel his hand on their shoulder. God's gift of Jesus would be an exclusive gift, accessible to only a relatively small number of people, if it weren't for the Bible. The Bible makes God's self-revelation available to all, regardless of when or where they live. Through the Bible we come to know Jesus and the bigger story of God's work in the world.

MORE THAN A GOOD BOOK

For many, the Bible is an old, dusty book that we know we should think highly of but that we don't actually enjoy. If I asked you to play a word association game with me and I said "Bible," I'm guessing that "powerful" wouldn't be the first word to pop into your mind. It is all right to admit that sometimes when we read the Bible, we feel bored. (In chapters six and seven, I'll explain some of why we might feel that way and how to remove that obstacle.) Nevertheless, the Bible is not just good for us; the Bible is also a *powerful* book.

God's words are powerful. It might seem blatantly obvious that the words of the Creator of the universe are powerful, but many of us don't see it that way. Power is the ability to effect change. A stick of dynamite (the term is rooted in the Greek word *dynamis,* which means "power") has explosive, destructive force. A beautiful piece of music has the power to change our mood. Antibiotics have the power to cure infection. Words have power to move a nation to war or to seal a marriage covenant.

Not all words are equally powerful, of course. Many of the words we hear, read and say are like chaff—they blow around but have no substance or lasting value to them, like headlines about the latest arrest or divorce of a Hollywood star. (As hard as I try, I'm not able to keep myself from reading those magazine headlines when I'm waiting at the grocery store checkout.) Other words are said with emphasis or conviction, but they don't make any difference (consider, for example, the promises of a politician). So many words lack the weight of wisdom or true authority, like a stick of dynamite without any explosive compound. A statement of conviction that doesn't compel the hearer is like a piece of music played on the air guitar.

One of the most valuable things I learned in college was how to study the Bible. The more I grew in my ability to study inductively, the more I got out of the Bible—and the more I got out of my school books. When it came time to write my senior thesis on a piece of Chinese literature in Asian Studies, I decided I wanted to use the inductive method I had been using to study the Bible. I chose the novel *The Travels of Lao Ts'an* by Liu Tieh-yun, one of the most treasured of all Chinese novels around the turn of the twentieth century. Through it the author artfully delivered social critique, challenge and hope during a time of tremendous instability in China.

I thoroughly enjoyed all those afternoons in the library marking up a Xeroxed copy of the book. (I don't think the library would have taken kindly to me writing all over their only copy.) I used colored pens to follow repeated words in *The Travels of Lao Ts'an*. I researched historical and cultural context. I asked probing questions and sought to answer them with the evidence in the text.

Some days I would do manuscript study of *The Travels of Lao Ts'an* during the day, and then participate in a manuscript study of the Bible in the evening. I noticed something: Liu's book, while excellent, didn't transform me. When studying the Bible, I became aware of my fears and God's invitation to trust him. I was able to believe the tremendous promises of Jesus instead of the paltry claims of advertising. I grew in my capacity to love, reconcile and serve. When studying *The Travels of Lao Ts'an*, I felt as if I was standing in a small pool of fresh water. When studying the Bible, I felt as if I was standing under a mighty waterfall that flowed out into a vast ocean.

> "When you or I open the Bible, we are beholding the very words of God—words that have supernatural power to redeem, renew, refresh, and restore our lives to what he created them to be."
>
> **DAVID PLATT,** *Radical*

The Bible is unlike any other book because its author is everlasting. In fact, the Bible is a portal of sorts, a setting for our encounter with the living God, whose words are living and active. We read a good book and are perhaps transported to another time and place; we read the Bible and are encountered by God incarnate, entering into our time and place.

The Bible is powerful because it is spiritually alive. The Holy Spirit is actively present in it, thus an encounter with the Bible is an opportunity for an encounter with God himself. The power of the Bible is not primarily in its ability to inform, instruct or inspire (though it certainly does that). Its power is seen in its ability to bring light, to reveal what's really happening in my heart. As Jeremiah says,

> The heart is devious above all else;
> > it is perverse—
> > who can understand it? (Jeremiah 17:9)

The Holy Spirit uses God's Word to cut through self-deception, to reveal our true motives, and to show us a path that leads to life.

MIRACLE SEED

One of my favorite New Testament stories is the parable of the sower (Mark 4:1-20). I have a painting above my desk, from the *St. James Bible*, of Jesus in blue jeans carrying a woven basket, his right hand outstretched as he scatters seed.[1] Some of the seeds are in mid-air, falling down the side of the painting. Beneath his feet are four mounds of earth, with cutaway views revealing that each mound is made of a different type of soil. A bird pecks at the ground on top of the first mound. A very small plant with shallow roots comes out of the mound whose soil is full of rocks. The third mound has a larger plant that is entwined by a thorny briar. Standing in stark contrast to the others is the fourth mound, a tall wheat plant with stalks of golden grain. The plant from the good soil stretches halfway up the painting, pointing to calligraphy of Jesus' closing line of the parable: "Let anyone with ears to hear listen."

If you and I had been standing near the lake on the day Jesus taught this parable, it is likely that we would have turned to each other and said, "We walked all that way for *this*?" In his story about the farmer who scattered seed, Jesus draws attention to the obvious: seeds only grow in good soil. It is common sense that birds will eat seed that falls on hard packed ground, like paths, and never gets below the surface.

Seeds sown in rocky places obviously won't survive long. And if you don't keep on top of the weeds, your crop is lost. (Unfortunately, knowing this basic agricultural fact hasn't helped me to be diligent in weeding my vegetable garden.) The only thing that is surprising about this story, in fact, is that Jesus describes the crop that comes from the good soil as having a yield of 30, 60, even 100 percent. The typical yield for grain would have been three or four times, maybe six times in a really good year. (Even genetically engineered grain from Monsanto, which claims to offer "Better Seed for a Better Future," can't come close to this kind of yield.) Jesus is announcing a miracle seed; any hard-working farmer who was paying attention should have asked, "Where do I get some of that seed?!"

Figure 2.1.

By ending with "Let anyone with ears to hear listen," Jesus calls the audience to realize that there is more to this story than meets the eye (or, in this case, the ear). Some of them follow Jesus back to his campfire and ask him about the parable, where he explains that the seed is the Word of God and that the four soils are different heart conditions. The seed bears no fruit in the people represented by the first three types of soil: those with hard hearts toward God can't even take the Word in; those who aren't willing to persevere through the suffering that inevitably comes with following Jesus soon fall away; those whose lives are full of distractions, including a thirst for comfort and wealth, are unable to bear fruit.

But those who "hear the word and accept it . . . bear fruit, thirty and sixty and a hundredfold" (Mark 4:20). Jesus knows that not everyone who hears God's Word will really *hear* it. He knows that many who read the Bible won't be changed by it. But there will be those who take his Word in, truly listen and wrestle with it until they understand. These kind of people let themselves be transformed by the Word and bear so much fruit that all who witness it recognize that God is at work. The seed of God's Word planted in these people reveals its miraculous power.

Our role in bearing fruit is to get ourselves into God's Word and allow God's Word to get into us. This involves seeking God for soft hearts, perseverance in obedience, and weeding out aspects of life that crowd out the work of the Spirit. We don't have to manufacture spiritual growth. God's power is present in the Word and bears good fruit in those who "hold it fast in an honest and good heart" (Luke 8:15).

The seed of God's Word was sown into the hearts of Tim's Spanish-speaking friends. It found soft-hearted people who received the good news, bore fruit and became sowers of the Word themselves. In a village in Mexico, many families are bearing fruit and sowing the seed of God's Word in others because a seemingly powerless young man believed in the power of the Bible. What might God do in and through us if we approached the Bible with the same confidence in its power?

REFLECTION EXERCISE
Soil Testing

1. In the box marked "Seed Received," list the various passages of the Bible you have read or heard in the last week. Include things like personal reading, small group Bible study and sermons.
2. Read Jesus' description of the different types of soil in Mark 4:15-20.
3. Reflect on your response to each passage you have listed. Which soil were you in response to each Scripture? Write the reference next to the appropriate drawing of the different types of soil.
4. What do you notice about the condition of your heart toward God's Word? What will it look like to become good soil more consistently?

Seed Received

_____

_____

_____

_____

Soil #1: The Path

Soil #2: The Rocky Soil

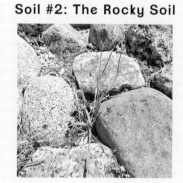

Soil #3: Seeds with Weeds

Soil #4: Good Soil

3

Authority of the Word

I love stories about missionaries. It's exciting to learn how God works to bring people of all cultures and languages to himself. A good missionary story inspires me to trust God more fully and to take risks in making Jesus known. Additionally, missionary stories highlight elements of God's character in dramatic ways.

Don Richardson, in his book *Eternity in Their Hearts*, tells a series of stories that demonstrate how God has prepared people throughout the world to welcome the good news of the gospel. His account of the Karen people of Burma is one of my favorites. In his village in the hill country, Ko Thah-byu was known as a rough man with a violent temper; he had earned a reputation as a thief and a murderer. He left his village to seek employment in the capital city of Rangoon, allowing him to escape his reputation and earn some money to pay a debt. At the house where he wound up working, Ko Thah-byu met Adoniram Judson, an American Baptist missionary who was staying there. Judson had arrived in Rangoon in 1817 to preach the gospel to Buddhists and spent long hours translating the Bible into Burmese.

The Karen people believed in one true God, Creator of the universe, who gave their ancestors a book so that they might know him. The ancestors were careless, however, and lost the book, thereby losing their connection to *Y'wa*. Village teachers called Bukhos kept alive an ancient prophecy that someday a "white brother" would come with a copy of the lost book. Since his youth, Ko Thah-byu had heard stories about

Y'wa's lost book, and he became increasingly interested in Judson's project. He asked countless questions about the book—where it had come from, what it contained. But Ko Thah-byu was illiterate and so couldn't read the book himself.

Later on a missionary named George Bordman arrived to join the Burmese mission. He opened a school for illiterate peasants, and Ko Thah-byu was one of the first to enroll, motivated by his eagerness to read the lost book from *Y'wa*. Ko Thah-byu learned the good news that *Y'wa* had come to earth in Jesus and given his life to restore relationship with all who are estranged from him. Filled with incredible joy, Ko Thah-byu returned to the hill country of the Karen to preach the gospel. In village after village, the Karen people received the message with joy, turning from their idols and asking to be baptized in the name of Jesus. "Almost as quickly as Karen were converted and baptized, they became missionaries to spread the good news still further among their own people."[1] The white missionaries who followed the Karen missionaries found thousands of converts eager to be taught from the book. Over the next century, over 250,000 tribal people in that area became Christians.

Why were the Karen so eager to receive the Bible? Because they wanted to know God. They knew that God created them, that he is powerful and good, and that they had lost their connection to him. They even recognized that he is the only source of salvation: "If *Y'wa* does not have mercy on us, there is no other one who can. He who saves us is the only one—*Y'wa*."[2] But they had no idea how to bridge the chasm between themselves and *Y'wa*. And so they waited eagerly for arrival of the "white brother" and the book he carried. Long before any contact with Christianity, the Karen people understood that God reveals himself through a book.

> "Scripture is not in and of itself divine, but we should respect, even reverence, Scripture as the divinely appointed medium by which God chooses to reveal himself to us."
>
> **DONALD BLOESCH,** *Holy Scripture*

BEYOND RUMOR

People seem to have in insatiable interest in the lives of the rich and famous. An enormous number of books are written about beautiful, powerful or controversial public figures. Amazon.com offers 468 biographies about the iconic actress Marilyn Monroe; if it is Al Capone you are interested in, there are 146 options. When you consider all the magazines, tabloids and made-for-TV movies that explore the private lives of public figures, it becomes clear that gossip is a lucrative business. The gossip industry thrives throughout the world because rumors can be addictive.

As any teenager knows, rumors are not only tantalizing but dangerous. Rumors can lead to distrust, resentment and broken relationships. Victims of rumors and gossip may object that their motives have been misconstrued or that their political enemies are twisting facts to discredit them. In order to set the story straight, more well-known victims of gossip and rumors sometimes sanction the writing of an "authorized biography." Books that include the phrase "In Her Own Words" are presumed to be more reliable than those that claim to be "The Untold Story."

In Genesis 3, the serpent is depicted as the world's first rumormonger. Prior to the serpent's entrance on the scene, God and the humans relate directly, face to face. Adam and Eve know what God is like through his kind actions and his clear commands. In Genesis 3:1-5, the serpent introduces doubt about God's motives, and does so while talking behind God's back (sounds like junior high!). Adam and Eve allow the rumors to distort their view of God and carry more weight than their direct experience of him. The results are disastrous: humanity loses true knowledge of their Creator and is left with only rumors and speculation.

The Lord of the universe wants to be known. Hearsay is not sufficient. To overcome the lies and defeat the claims of false gods and empty philosophies, God created a people for himself and, ultimately, chose to come to earth in the flesh. "No one has ever seen God. It is God the only Son, who is close to the Father's heart, who has made him known" (John 1:18). As theologian Donald Bloesch puts it, "Because God has acted decisively in the particular history of biblical Israel culminating in Jesus Christ, the Bible becomes normative as the primary witness and record of God's mighty acts."[3] The epic story depicted in the Bible traces God's relentless commitment to cut through the rumors and reveal himself to the world. The Holy Bible is God's authorized biography.

> **"First of all you must understand this, that no prophecy of scripture is a matter of one's own interpretation, because no prophecy ever came by human will, but men and women moved by the Holy Spirit spoke from God."**
>
> 2 PETER 1:20-21

TRUTH

We don't have to search any further to know what is true about God, the way he works in the world and what he expects from us. We have the authorized version, God's own telling of the story. It is his story and created by his inspiration. As biblical scholar Ben Witherington puts it:

> The Holy Spirit guided and directed and motivated human authors so that what they said was not their own creation or imaginings, but the very word of God himself: the truth. Thus the Spirit is the motivator or originator, the guide or guard of the words of the human author so that what he says can be declared to be spoken from God.[4]

We live in a world that tells us truth is personally and culturally constructed. We are told that truth is relative and that the highest virtue is tolerance rather than goodness. Against this assertion, the Bible is known to be true because God is true and the source of all truth. Jesus declared, "I am the way, and the truth, and the life" (John 14:6). Paul echoed, "Truth is in Jesus" (Ephesians 4:21). In one of John's heavenly visions, the faithful sing, "Just and true are your ways, / King of the nations!" (Revelation 15:3). Truth is not an abstraction or an ephemeral concept but a personal being: the embodiment of truth took on flesh, walked among us and lives forever in a glorious resurrected body.

The Merriam-Webster Dictionary defines *truth* in various ways, including as "being in accord with fact or reality" and "a transcendent fundamental or spiritual reality." Despite the plethora of opinions about it (including those who would say that all reality is subjective), there is a fundamental, objective reality in our universe. The true God has been revealed by Jesus and is attested to in the Scriptures. In describing the nature of the Scripture's authority, biblical scholar Chris Wright writes, "His, therefore, is the authority that those Scriptures mediate, because we have no other access to YHWH's reality than through these Scriptures."[5]

Because the Bible is God's authorized communication, we can trust it to reveal the truth. When we interact with the Bible, we are interacting with something that embodies reality and shines light on our lives and world, exposing what is actual. We are adept at putting a favorable spin on things so that we look better than we really are (and others look worse). Half-truths and self-deception are a prison and keep our lives, marriages and cultures in shambles. Without the truth there is no freedom. As Jesus said to the Jews who had believed in him, "If you continue in my word, . . . you will know the truth, and the truth will make you free" (John 8:31-32). By his grace, God who is the truth has given us the Bible to lead us into truth and his Spirit to enable us to live out the truth.

A SURE GUIDE

If the Bible is true, then to live in light of reality will involve giving Scripture primary place in our thinking. This means that all of my beliefs, values and practices are to be lined up in relationship to the Scripture. As a Christian, I am not free to do whatever I want with my money; I must seek to regard and use my money as the Bible instructs. Growing as a disciple of Jesus involves the shaping of my life by the truth of the Scripture. I learn from others (both Christian and non-Christian) in a myriad of formal and informal ways, but in the end any ideas or teachings that contradict Scripture are to be rejected.

The Bible is a sure guide for matters of faith and practice. It provides the community of faith in all ages and all places a means of evaluating itself. As the Westminster Confession puts it:

> The supreme judge by which all controversies of religion are to be determined, and all decrees of councils, opinions of ancient writers, doctrines of men, and private spirits, are to be examined, and in whose sentence we are to rest, can be no other but the Holy Spirit speaking in the Scripture.

Just as the Protestant Reformation called the medieval church to account for doctrines and practices that were beyond the bounds of biblical truth, so God's people must continually evaluate all that we do and teach by the standard of faithfulness to the Bible.

Human history is filled with charismatic leaders who gather a following around persuasive ideas and assertions. Some of those leaders and teachers have done great good in the world and mobilized people into just living and trust of God. But countless people (and even whole societies) have been led astray and manipulated by leaders who are self-serving or just plain wrong. Problems abound when people are dependent on a human leader who claims to speak for God. Thus, the Bible is an incredible gift not just to individuals but to the church, because it provides an external standard of evaluation and relativizes the authority of all earthly leaders and systems. God, through the Bible, sets the standard for truth.

SUBMISSION

As the Creator and righteous judge of all, God has supreme authority. The "authority of the Bible" is Christian shorthand for "God's authority revealed through the Bible." The distinction may seem subtle, but it is important to clarify that God himself is the authority; we submit to the teaching of the Bible as an act of submission to him. When calling ourselves by the name of Jesus, the rightful king over the universe, we are claiming that he is our king. King Jesus uses the Bible to communicate his character, his values and his commands.

The notion of submission to a king sounds archaic in contemporary society. Twenty-first-century culture applauds self-determination above all else and is skeptical about most forms of power. Individual autonomy and democratic government are our ideals. Many do not want to be told what to do or think by our teachers, our religious leaders or our government. Others are ambivalent about authority and comply with leaders (parents, pastors or professors) because it is the path of least resistance, but they have little conviction about the value and goodness of authority.

Often our view of authority has been created by the world rather than by God. The Bible presupposes that authority and power are a fact of life and calls those with authority to use their power rightly. Parents are commanded to train their children in righteousness while not provoking them to anger (Ephesians 6:4). Pastors are called to "not lord it over those in your charge, but be examples to the flock" (1 Peter 5:3). Governing authorities are "God's servant for your good" (Romans 13:4). All earthly authorities will be held accountable for their use of power—whether or not they used their position for the good of those under them. Godly authority matters to God, in part, because all authority is meant to be a reflection of him. As damaging as wicked, oppressive authorities can be, however, no abuse of authority can ultimately discredit the value of authority itself, and certainly not the authority of God.

Christians submit themselves to the authority of the Bible even on topics that they struggle with, out of faith in the goodness of God and trust in his benevolence. Jesus said, "I came that they may have life, and have it abundantly" (John 10:10). Like a good shepherd, he uses his authority in our lives for our benefit. He guides us to good food, clear water and a safe place to rest (Psalm 23). He protects us from harm and binds up our injuries when we are hurt. He is a good king, utterly committed to truth and justice, full of grace and mercy.

In the United States, *freedom* is often understood as freedom *from* constraints. To be free from work, taxes or familial obligations sounds ideal: a secular utopia without government, where anything goes between consenting adults and no questions are raised about morality or ethics. The reality, however, is that those who pursue this kind of "freedom" often find themselves lonely and untethered, bewildered that the joy they envisioned from being a free-spirit has eluded them.

God cares about freedom as well, but the path to freedom is found not in independence from all authority or responsibility but in submission to our Creator, living under his benevolent rule. Time and time again, I have found that what the Bible teaches about how to handle my sexuality, my money or my relationships has proven to protect me from harm and led me into life. The freedom Jesus offers delivers us from bondage to sin and the cravings of the flesh; it sets us free to be people of love, marked by the fruit of the Spirit (Galatians 5).

As I have wrestled with the teaching of the Bible around various topics, the underlying questions I am continually faced with are, "Will I trust God? Do I believe that he knows reality far better than I do? Am I convinced that the truth will make me free (John 8:32) or am I succumbing to the serpent's rumors and doubting God's goodness?"

God wants to be known, and he wants us to experience life as he intended it: under his reign, living abundantly. He has provided us the Bible to reveal himself and to mediate his authority. Through the Bible we have access to truth, a sure guide for faith and for life. Actively submitting ourselves to the authority of God's Word is our demonstration of trust in God and his goodness.

REFLECTION EXERCISE
Wrestling with the Truth

Which of the following biblical topics of belief or practice do you struggle with?

- Salvation in Christ alone

- Final judgment and hell

- Sexual morals

- Other _____

How does trust in God's goodness and authority affect how you wrestle with that issue?

4

Water for the Soul

A few months ago my friend Helen went to the doctor for a routine physical. She doesn't particularly like going to the doctor and was several years overdue for a check-up. She had recently moved to a new city and hadn't yet selected a physician, but the end of the fiscal year was coming, and Helen's husband still had some health savings money to use up, so he scheduled an appointment for her.

During the exam, a small lump was detected in one of Helen's breasts. Tests showed that it was cancerous. The diagnosis shocked her family and friends. She looked and felt fine, but something deadly was growing inside of her, hidden from view.

Helen and her family envisioned months of chemotherapy and the loss of Helen's beautiful thick hair. Thankfully, however, she was able to see a top specialist quickly and had a lumpectomy just a few weeks after the initial exam. The surgery was successful; the cancer cells had not spread, and chemotherapy was not required.

Thank God for health care. Helen's story could have ended differently had the cancer not been detected so early. In countries where health care isn't readily available (or is very expensive), people suffer needlessly. In the United States, health care is a major political topic and will continue to be so because physical health is so important to a happy life. We all know experientially that our quality of life is greatly affected by the state of our bodies.

Humans are more than physical bodies, however. We are spiritual beings. There is an inner, intangible aspect to humans. The soul is just as significant as our bodies and just as central to our existence. We are able to relate to God because we have a soul, which scholar N. T. Wright suggests is "really a way of speaking about 'who I am in the presence of God.'"[1] Our quality of life is just as affected by the health of our souls as it is by the health of our bodies.

In chapter one I asserted that true inductive Bible study requires a desire to meet God and be changed by him. The place that happens is first and foremost in our soul. Inductive Bible study is one way we welcome the Holy Spirit's work in our soul. In his book *Eat This Book: A Conversation in the Art of Spiritual Reading,* Eugene Peterson calls Scripture and the soul "the primary fields of operation of the Holy Spirit."[2] If Peterson is right, and I believe he is, then we can expect to encounter the Holy Spirit whenever we actively bring the Scripture and the soul together.

It might be unexpected to find a chapter about the soul in a Bible study handbook. I have included this reflection on the nature of the soul and the significance of regular Bible study for its health to make it loud and clear that inductive Bible study is not merely an intellectual exercise. Rigorous thinking and spiritual formation need not be viewed as separate pursuits. It makes all the difference when we sit down to study that we consciously bring our whole selves to the text—heart, mind, soul and strength. Developing awareness of our soul can help us to be integrated people as we approach the Scripture and more attentive to the work of the Spirit in our lives.

A MAN IN A MAN

Most cultures around the world, both contemporary and historically, believe in the soul. Traditional African thought affirms the existence of a "little me within the big me."[3] In the words of an ex-slave who had been treated as a beast of burden by his owners, "There is a man in a man. The soul is the medium between God and man. God speaks to us through our conscience, and the reasoning is so loud, we seem to hear a voice."[4]

In the modern era, however, Westerners have downplayed (or even completely disregarded) the soul. Since the Enlightenment, understanding of the nature of humanity has shifted from the biblical view to a materialist one. Because the soul can't be seen or measured, many intellectuals have come to deny its existence. And once the concept of the soul is rejected, the logical conclusion is that life is fundamentally meaningless: human existence is nothing more than a series of electrical and chemical reactions. The materialist viewpoint asserts that when your physical body dies, who you are (the soul in N. T. Wright's definition) ceases to exist. There is no transcendent self, no soul.

The biblical view is that the soul is what distinguishes humans from all other animals. The life that is in us is markedly different than the life in dogs, cats, monkeys or dolphins. We are more than organic organisms with rationality and highly developed verbal communication skills. We have a soul. As attested to in the biblical creation accounts, humans are unique above all of creation. Only humans have been made in God's image (Genesis 1:26-27) and animated by his breath (Genesis 2:7).

The Hebrews saw humans as an integrated whole of inner and outer being. The body and the soul are interdependent. The inner being, referred to in the Bible as "spirit" or "soul," is the core and serves the whole person by guiding and directing the outer aspects. The outer being, the body, enacts the will of spirit or soul. The relationship between them is dynamic; neither inner nor outer being is complete without the other.

The Greeks introduced the idea of a dichotomy between body and soul: the body temporal and the soul eternal. They concluded that the soul was more important than the body and that experiences in the body have little effect on the soul. This dualism laid the foundation for many harmful cultural assumptions in the Western world, among them that sex is merely a bodily function, and that religion is a private affair to be kept in the home and kept out of the academy, the marketplace or the political realm.

The early church leaders vehemently opposed the Greeks' denigration of the body. The apostle Paul, for example, clearly sides with the Hebrews over the Greeks in passages such as 1 Corinthians 6:15: "Do you not know that your bodies are members of Christ?" Jesus' incarnation validated our bodily experience. He got sore feet and became exhausted at the end of a long day, just as we do. Likewise, Jesus' resurrection wasn't just spiritual; his followers were able to touch his hands and feet. They saw him eat and felt his embrace. His resurrected body was indeed flesh and blood.

At the final resurrection, those who are in Christ will be renewed in both body *and* soul. We hope in a resurrection in which we will stand fully before God as whole beings, not disembodied spirits. Additionally, the soul is not inherently eternal, as the Greeks claim. The soul does not autonomously give or maintain its own life. Only God is self-existing; he has being and life in himself and receives it from no other.[5] Life is a gift of God, sustained by God continually. If God withdraws, life ceases. God upholds our being day by day, moment by moment. Eternal life is a gift from the one who subjected himself to death on the cross, not an inevitability. The gospel is good news for both our bodies and our souls. Our whole person—body and soul— will share in Jesus' resurrection.

If our soul is a fundamental part of our being and a gracious gift from God, then we would do well to tend to it. Our world and the church is full of people who are sick in their souls and aren't getting the health care they need. It is imperative that believers come to understand the nature of the soul and learn to care for it. Bible study has a significant role to play in nurturing healthy souls and healing sick ones, because in studying the Scripture we open ourselves to the very presence of God.

> **"Every word in the book is intended to do something in us, give health and wholeness, vitality and holiness to our souls and body."**
>
> **EUGENE PETERSON,** *Eat This Book*

SOUL CARE

"Eat more vegetables." "Visit the dentist every six months." "Drink eight glasses of water a day." "Exercise at least four days a week." Instructions and encouragement to take care of our bodies abound. And that's a good thing. It's easy to neglect some of the habits which would actually help us be physically healthier. More and more the wider culture attempts to reinforce proper care of our bodies.

When it comes to the soul, however, we are left high and dry. Since spiritual topics are considered outside the bounds of the public arena, you will never see a billboard that says, "Who do you need to forgive?" or "Regular silence for a happy soul."

Just as parents are responsible for feeding, comforting and obtaining medical care for their children, so each of us is responsible for the health and welfare of our own soul, the "little me." Fulfilling this responsibility requires that we become intentional about checking in with our souls. Can you recognize the signs of soul sickness or malnutrition in yourself? During a time of prayer and reflection it can be helpful to visualize your inner self, not because the soul is a separate entity, but in order to develop greater awareness of your soul's state. Is it frail, bloated, lethargic or distracted? How much energy and joy does your soul have? What temptations have you been facing? Compulsion toward alcohol, food, sex or spending, for example, is often a mask for the soul's thirst, hunger or need for attention.

Soul care involves learning what the soul needs to thrive and being diligent in meeting those needs.[6] Do you know when your soul needs solitude and silence? Confession? Celebration? Can you recognize when your soul is longing for a long drink of God's Word?

The soul's greatest need is time in God's presence. Our souls get discouraged, agitated, worn out and tattered. God's presence nurtures and restores our souls. Consider this selection of Scripture describing the soul's need for God:

> As a deer longs for flowing streams,
> so my soul longs for you, O God.
> My soul thirsts for God,
> for the living God.
> When shall I come and behold
> the face of God? (Psalm 42:1-2)

Why are you cast down, O my soul,
    and why are you disquieted within me?
Hope in God; for I shall again praise him,
    my help and my God. (Psalm 43:5)

For God alone my soul waits in silence,
    for my hope is from him. (Psalm 62:5)

My soul clings to you;
    your right hand upholds me. (Psalm 63:8)

Come to me, all you that are weary and are carrying heavy burdens, and I will give you rest. Take my yoke upon you, and learn from me, for I am gentle and humble in heart, and you will find rest for your souls. (Matthew 11:28-29)

Worship, prayer, solitude and meditation are all means of putting our souls in the presence of God. Unfortunately, Bible study doesn't usually make that list. Our perception of Bible study has suffered from the dichotomist worldview we inherited from the Greeks. Too often, Bible study is viewed as something we do with our minds; contemplative reading or *lectio divina* are seen as the way to engage the Word with our souls. However, since body, soul, mind and heart are an integrated whole, the whole person is to be engaged whether we are praising the Lord in musical worship, participating in a manuscript study or sitting silently in a sacred space.

We should expect (and welcome) a soul encounter with God whenever we interact with the Scripture. As Sri Lankan leader and teacher Ajith Fernando reminds, "Studying the text carefully is an expression of devotion to God. . . . When we give time to be close to the Word we become receptive to hearing from God."[7] Inductive Bible study requires effort and intellectual engagement, but it is as much a way of bringing our soul into God's presence as taking a silent retreat at a monastery.[8]

LIVING WATER

Jesus, when quoting Deuteronomy said, "One does not live by bread alone, but by every word that proceeds from the mouth of God"

(Matthew 4:4). The Bible is our soul's food and drink. The Word of God is as basic to spiritual life as bread and water are to physical life: "Over and over again, we find that when we strip away the stained glass, incense, prayer beads, or gilded domes of religious expression and peel it down to its basic core, we will find an open book."[9]

Psalm 1 uses the imagery of a thriving tree to describe those who are nurtured by God's Word:

> Happy are those who do not follow the advice of the wicked,
>> or take the path that sinners tread, or sit in the seat of scoffers;
> but their delight is in the law of the LORD,
>> and on his law they meditate day and night.
> They are like trees planted by streams of water,
>> which yield their fruit in its season, and their leaves do not wither.
> In all that they do, they prosper.

Water is an apt metaphor for God's Word. Without water, fruit trees wither. Without God's Word, souls become anemic.

When I left for college, my mother gave me two house plants to decorate my dorm room. Unfortunately, I neither inherited her green thumb nor learned from her modeling about how to care for plants. I watered them when I thought of it (which wasn't very often). Within a few months the plants were all but dead.

At winter break I brought both plants back to her. She watered them, gave them plant food and trimmed away their dead leaves. By the end of winter break they were healthy and growing again. Resolved to keep them alive, I took them back and put them closer to the window so that they received better light. However, the new spot I picked for the plants was inches from the radiator. I hadn't thought about the amount of heat the plants were exposed to via the direct sun through the window and the building's heating system that ran full steam in the winter months. Though I was more diligent about watering the plants, the amount I gave them wasn't enough for the conditions they endured. Within a few weeks they were completely dead. Not even my mother could revive them.

In Iowa, flowers and grass erupt everywhere when the spring sun provides enough warmth to melt the snow and warm the soil. For a while, these plants do fine whether or not it rains because there is so much moisture in the ground from the winter's snow. By midsummer, however, if there isn't enough rain the grass at the side of the road becomes dry and brown and the flowers fade. The water in the soil is gone, and the plants are dependent on rain (or irrigation) for their survival. The trees that line the creek running through my neighborhood have a different experience. Their leaves don't wither with the heat of summer like the grass and flowers. They continue to thrive whether it rains or not. They always have enough of what they need because the creek is a permanent source of water.

A tree planted by a stream has access to as much water as it needs, regardless of how the conditions fluctuate. The Bible is that permanent source of living water.[10] The Bible mediates the presence of God by the power of the Holy Spirit. We can be assured that, like the tree in Psalm 1, our soul will thrive despite the conditions we endure if we are drinking in God's Word daily.

DAY BY DAY

A few years ago, I felt invited by God to train for a sprint triathlon. Several months of intensified athletic activity accentuated my need for hydration, food and rest. I became more aware of my eating habits. It wasn't enough to eat healthy meals a few times a week. It mattered what I ate every day and that I drank enough water every day. On days where I ate fast food or too much sugar, my body dragged. I found that if I hadn't had enough water the day before, my distance run was more difficult. Sufficient hydration is needed throughout training, not just on race day.

Our souls are asked to endure challenges far beyond a few hours of swimming, biking and running. Strained relationships, anxiety over money, work and school deadlines all tax the soul. In just the last few months, various friends of mine have experienced cancer treatment for a child, the exposure of marital unfaithfulness, deep disappointment in career, the pain of addressing childhood hurts and the death of a parent. Coming through these experiences of suffering well requires a healthy soul. From the reservoir of a soul nurtured by God comes hope, resilience, capacity to forgive, peace and the ability to endure pain without being crushed by it. Dry and undernourished souls don't have the resources to finish the race well.

Many people draw near to God in times of difficulty, feeling their need for spiritual resources. God welcomes us in our need, but our souls need to receive from him more than in times of crisis. You can pour water on a plant that is starting to wither and perhaps keep it from dying, but there is only so much water a plant can take in any one watering. Likewise, going to church or praying with a friend when under stress is good, but it is not enough to provide our souls with what they really need. There is no substitute for caring for our souls day by day.

The habit of daily Bible reading seems to be falling by the wayside as our lives get busier. External distractions abound, and when we come before the Word we soon discover that the internal distractions are just as rampant. "The key to spiritual depth is lingering in the presence of God in prayer and in meditation of his Word. But meditation requires that we slow our mind down so that we can concentrate on the object of our meditation. That is where our problem lies. We are unaccustomed to slowing down."[11]

Inductive Bible study is a way of slowing down and concentrating on the Word. Manuscript study can't be accomplished in a quick ten minutes before running out the door. It requires an investment of time, a lingering in the presence of God. Whether we are aware of it or not, our souls are being watered and nourished as we do the work of observing, interpreting and applying the text.

Daily Scripture reading and periodic in-depth Bible study are a great combination. Most people who are committed to interacting with the Bible daily (including me) don't do inductive study every time they sit down with the Scripture. My daily reading and mediation is more like weeknight meals in my home—nutritious but requiring less than forty-five minutes to make. On the weekend, however, the menu might become a little more elaborate, including food that takes more preparation and more mess in the kitchen. It's a meal that often warrants inviting friends to join us. As we will see in the next chapter, like a great weekend meal, inductive study is fun to share with a group.

Each person's soul is a both a gift and a responsibility. Sick or neglected souls do not honor their Maker, but healthy souls bear witness to the Life Giver. We must learn to pay attention to our souls, seek healing when they are sick and provide nourishment so they can thrive regardless of circumstances. Rigorous mind-engaging, soul-nourishing Bible study is essential to the soul's flourishing. As Psalm 1 promises, those who take in God's Word regularly "are like trees planted by streams of water, which yield their fruit in its season, and their leaves do not wither."

REFLECTION EXERCISE
Soul Check

During each of the next seven days, take time to check in with your soul. What is taxing it? What does it need? Reflect on what you have done to feed or care for your soul that day (e.g., prayer, silence, worship, Bible reading or study, etc.).

At the end of the week, look back and see if any patterns emerge.

	Assessment	Care Received
Monday		
Tuesday		
Wednesday		
Thursday		
Friday		
Saturday		
Sunday		

5

Community Around the Word

I once threw a "What I Like About You" surprise party for my husband, Jon. I contacted his friends, colleagues and church community, asking them to send me short phrases that describe what they like about Jon. I printed out these words and phrases on colored paper and used them as the decorations for his party. It was so much fun to see what other people wrote about him. Most of them were the kinds of things you would expect: "thoughtful," "wise," "generous," "steady," "loves his family" and so on. But there were also some odd ones: "throws a great 'hammer'"; "deadly accuracy with a Frisbee"; and my favorite, "heart of gold, feet of lead."

The last grouping came from my husband's Ultimate Frisbee team. A random assortment of graduate students, professors and others have been playing together for almost twenty years, and Jon has been a central member of the team for the last eighteen. Week in and week out, whether in the heat of a humid Iowa July or the icy cold of January, they spend part of their Saturday afternoon together running, throwing and catching a plastic disc.

As with any sports team or musical group, the love of the game brought them together, and the experience of playing together has created friendships. They have inside jokes, nicknames and shared history. Jon is teased about his speed (thus the "feet of lead" comment) but admired for his skill in throwing. Many of the folks who play on Saturday have played together so much that they can anticipate each other's moves, completing elaborate plays with very little communication.

Without this group, Jon wouldn't be able to enjoy the game he loves. Playing Frisbee by yourself just doesn't work.

God wired us for community. It has often been noted that in well-functioning teams the sum is greater than the parts. The apostle Paul would definitely agree, as seen in his use of the image of a body to describe the church. A Christian leader I respect puts it this way: "We're better together." Life lived or tasks accomplished in community are both more enjoyable and more effective.

Though I am a strong advocate for regular personal Bible reading and study, I am convinced that every believer needs to regularly study the Bible with others. In this chapter we will consider three reasons that we are "better together" in Bible study and why communal Bible study is essential to the health of the body of Christ.

> "They devoted themselves to the apostles'
> teaching and fellowship, to the breaking
> of bread and the prayers."
>
> ACTS 2:42

BETTER TOGETHER: *Amplification*

Amplification is any technique that makes sound louder and clearer. In a large room or a setting with a lot of white noise, a microphone enables the primary speaker to be heard and understood by a greater number of people. In Luke 5 Jesus amplifies his voice by getting into Simon's boat and speaking from the lake rather than the shore. Communal Bible study similarly amplifies our experience of the Scripture. Like a P.A. system, the process of studying together enables every element of inductive Bible study to come across louder and clearer.

All six primary elements of inductive Bible study—cultural context, historical context, attentiveness, curiosity, understanding and response—

are strengthened and deepened when studying the Bible in community. It is amazing how much more can be seen when six or eight pairs of eyes look closely at the text, rather than just one. Small group Bible studies are able to ask more penetrating questions, pool insights, challenge assumptions, and create an environment that is dynamic and lively.

Furthermore, when we study in community we are helped to sit longer with one passage. Too often our personal reading is a quick read through. On our own it is too easy to let the Scripture go "in one ear, out the other." But a passage that can be read in three minutes can also be discussed for two hours. Members of groups that have had extended discussion, even arguments, about the interpretation of a passage come away with a sharper understanding and a higher retention rate.

In inductive manuscript study, the more diverse the community the better. Through seeking to approach the text inductively we attempt to lay aside our preconceptions and bias, but it is impossible to do so thoroughly. We bring our experiences and presuppositions with us to the text. We all have blind spots that cannot be exposed without the help of others. Diversity increases the variety of perspectives and enables a group to consider the text from different angles.

Some of my best experiences in the Bible have been with non-Christians. They don't take a lot for granted. They ask questions of the text that had never occurred to me, and those questions prove to be deeply fruitful. By wrestling with the perspectives and questions of those who don't have allegiance to Jesus, my faith is deepened and my understanding expanded. It's likewise invaluable for men to study with women, older folks with teens, wealthy with poor, Westerners with those from the global south and so on.

I recently spent several days participating in a dig-in of the Gospel of Luke. The group was comprised of people from all over North America (including Saskatchewan and Montréal). The ages ranged from the twenties to the fifties, and four different ethnicities were represented. When studying the parable of the great banquet in Luke 14, someone read verse 23 and asked, "Why does the master tell his servant to *compel* people from the roads and lanes to come to the banquet?" We struggled for a while trying to answer this question from the text, wondering if the master even cared about the people in the roads and lanes or if he only cared about numbers. We felt very uncomfortable with the possibility that this scripture in some way supported forced conversions.

In the midst of our wrestling with the text, a man who was born and raised in the Middle East shared a story about his parents and hospitality. In their culture, the value of reciprocity requires that any gift or invitation be matched in the coming months. With this information, the meaning of the text jumped out at us. The servant must *compel* the poor farmers and travelers to come to the banquet because they are in no position to *repay* the invitation. Those who represent the master must assure them again and again that the master wants them to enjoy his feast even though they cannot reciprocate.

For those who gather around God's Word with a common desire to grow as Christians, experiences of communal Bible study can produce deep joy. Over our four days of studying Luke, the joy and energy level in the room built day by day. There was joy when a new insight emerged or a connection was made with earlier passages that had never been considered. There was the joy of seeing something built (our understanding of Luke), like the feeling of satisfaction you have when building a new deck or restoring an old car. Each day we found more to laugh about as we played with language and the text, and as our relationships grew we found ways to lovingly tease each other.

Group Bible study amplifies insight, understanding, perspective and joy. "Turning up the volume" through studying together enables us to hear and enjoy the beauty and power of the Scriptures.

BETTER TOGETHER: *Friendship*

My closest friends are those with whom I have studied the Bible. This might be because I like the Bible so much, and we tend to develop friendships with those who share the same interest. But I think it is more than that. I think those friendships are deep and lasting because of the way that manuscript Bible study creates a setting for shared experience with Jesus.

Cedar Falls, Iowa, is in the north-central part of the state and home to the University of Northern Iowa (UNI). One Saturday night, a group of UNI students were hanging out, trying to decide how to spend their evening. Someone suggested that they drive to the Minnesota border. Soon the idea had grown and expanded until the group had made plans to cross the border of every state that touches Iowa. Each Saturday night they would go a different direction—north, south, east, southeast and so on—until they had visited all six neighboring states. (*Visit* is probably too strong a word; in many cases they would cross the border, find the nearest gas station, buy a snack and get back in the car to drive home.) As the semester progressed and the group of friends told stories of their "border runs," others asked if they could join them. Eventually, the weekly road trip became a caravan of three or four cars.

On one level these were pointless trips; the destination was of no particular consequence. The value was in the road trip itself, the time in the car talking, laughing, listening to music and snacking. Manuscript Bible study with a consistent group of people is a lot like a road trip (though unlike a trip to the border, the destination of spiritual growth and deepened understanding is inherently valuable). Group Bible study creates a context for time spent together talking, discussing, thinking, laughing and praying. It is amazing how a group who begins without knowing each other well can come to feel bonded after eight weeks of digging into the Scriptures together, or a few days of intensive study at a dig-in. This is because a manuscript study nurtures great conversation, provides ground rules for discussion, encourages self-disclosure and cultivates shared ownership.

When I was dating my husband, the thing I enjoyed most was the quality of our conversations. We could talk for hours, sharing stories from our childhood, discussing big ideas, dreaming about a future together. I came away from those conversations feeling satisfied, like having eaten a really good meal. We all yearn to have good conversations, but too often we have to settle for snippets or predictable conversations about weather, health, children's activities or movies. Sometimes I long for the time and space to have deeper, more substantive conversations, but an interesting topic doesn't present itself, or not everyone knows enough about the topic to join in. Gathering around God's Word gives us something to talk about that is interesting, substantive and accessible.

We've all been in conversations that aren't very satisfying, not because the content wasn't interesting but because of the dynamic between the participants. Inductive Bible study creates a relatively even playing field, provides tools for everyone to participate and uses ground rules for a healthy group dynamic. For example, I used to teach student groups a silly hand sign to use when someone was on a tangent. An enthusiastic member of the group might begin to talk at length about something that wasn't central to the text at hand; around the room the "tangent" sign would go up. We would laugh together and then get back on course. (See chapter twenty-one for a list of ground rules for small group Bible study.)

Small groups that build friendship must promote vulnerability and self-disclosure. This can happen at any phase of the study, but it is particularly important during the discussion of application. As noted in chapter one, application is integral to inductive study. We don't gather together to just discuss something "out there." We also gather to share what's happening "in here" (our hearts, lives and relationships) and let the Holy Spirit speak into our present reality. Good application questions help a group to discuss personally and specifically (see chapter eleven). If the group dynamic has been good, the small group becomes a safe environment to share vulnerably. Often the sense of community shifts to a new level as people open up about their lives and how the Scripture speaks to current challenges. Weekly small group Bible studies become places of support and encouragement as members seek to grow in response to God's Word.

In addition to nurturing great conversation, healthy group dynamics and self-disclosure, communal Bible study builds friendships by creating the opportunity to share ownership of something valuable. Just as a married couple who buys a home shares ownership of that home, so groups that have devoted themselves to studying a book of the Bible share ownership of their understanding of that text.

A friend of mine uses the analogy of building a house to describe the process of inductive Bible study.[1] Imagine a group that receives a pile of lumber, tresses, doors and windows and is asked to build a house together. No blueprint or instructions are provided. They have to keep trying various arrangements until all the materials provided fit together in a coherent and stable structure. At the end of inductive study, if the group has put in the hard work of observing, asking questions, answering them from the text and synthesizing their answers into a coherent whole, there is something akin to a house that they can then point to, inhabit and enjoy: shared understanding and convictions about the text.

I have had the good fortune of being a part of a group of people who have been profoundly shaped by the Gospel of Mark. Together, over years and years of communal study of Mark, we have developed deep insight into its themes, its structure, and its relevance to discipleship and mission. I feel a bond with those who have shared in the construction of this house. It is a beautiful house and I love living there, but I am always aware that my understanding of Mark comes from the community around the Word and is not by my own doing. In the process of building our home in the Gospel of Mark, lifelong friendships were created and convictions about Christian life and ministry were developed that are still bearing fruit worldwide.

BETTER TOGETHER: *Launch Pad*

The third benefit of communal study (besides amplification of the text and friendship) is the foundation it creates for common mission. Big endeavors require a foundation, a footing on which the rest can build. The bigger the endeavor, the greater the foundation needed. Think about a launch pad. If you are shooting rockets in a grassy park with your son's Cub Scout troop, the rocket only weighs a few ounces and the "blast" is minimal. A flat piece of cardboard is sufficient to provide a stable launch pad. For a NASA space shuttle, by contrast, the launch pad needs to be large enough and strong enough to handle the weight of the shuttle (about 55,000 pounds) and the intense heat created at liftoff.

The church is created for mission. Collectively we have been given the general mission of incarnating Jesus' presence to our hurting world. We flesh out that mission in countless specific ways, whether it be running a free medical clinic, translating the Bible for minority language groups, planting churches or something else. All of these endeavors require a foundation—a launch pad—to support their weight and withstand the strain of forward momentum. Communal Bible study provides that foundation.

When a group of people give themselves to studying the Scripture together, they lay the foundation for common action. The process of inductive study trains them *how* to function as a team. The content of the inductive study provides direction on *what* they can do together. And hearing from Jesus together through the Scriptures gives the *motivation* for creating new ministries.

Many years ago a group of college seniors participated in a manuscript study of the book of Amos. They had a powerful time in the Scriptures and heard God's injunction to "let justice roll down like waters, / and righteousness like an ever-flowing stream" (Amos 5:24). As they scanned their context, they realized that there was a very poor neighborhood only a few miles from their affluent university. In response to Amos, they began to explore that neighborhood, build relationships and see if there was some way they could serve the poor. They soon discovered that the local schools were understaffed, that adults in the neighborhood often worked multiple jobs to make ends meet and that most of the kids performed well below grade level. The group of college students created an after-school tutoring program, enlisting members of their campus fellowship to give three hours a week to tutor inner-city kids in reading, writing and math. They shared the gospel with teens and invested in their lives.

By the end of the school year, it was obvious that God was up to something. Several of the members of the original Amos study decided to change their after-graduation plans and move into the neighborhood to continue and expand the ministry. Over thirty years later, Bay Shore Christian Ministries continues to be used by God to disciple youth and build leaders. Communal study of Amos provided a substantial launch pad for a big endeavor of mission.

I am convinced that the Holy Spirit speaks to whole communities through the Word, and not just to individuals. In fact, every book of the Bible (with the exception of 1-2 Timothy, Titus, Philemon and 3 John) was written to a community, whether the people of God at large (most of the Old Testament and the Gospels) or the people of God in a specific location (e.g., Romans and Ephesians). The authors intended to shape the beliefs and behavior of those communities—to influence them collectively, not just individually. It is invaluable for local congregations and communities to seek to hear God's voice by letting themselves be shaped by a common text.[2] Thus, when we gather to study we must ask, "What does this mean for *us*?" as diligently as we ask, "What does this mean for *me*?"

ESSENTIAL PRACTICE

Community around the Word isn't just beneficial; it's essential. Throughout church history, periods of growth and vibrancy are marked by devotion to the Scriptures. It is no wonder that when we gather together on Sundays God's Word is given center stage through reading and preaching (and in churches with a traditional liturgy, praying and singing).

When Nehemiah and Ezra led the returned exiles in the process of restoration, they focused on three objectives: rebuild the Temple and the city wall, reestablish the Law at the center of God's people, and recommit the people to holiness. These three objectives represent central components of any healthy Christian community: a *context* for gathering, the *content* of God's Word, and a *commitment* to obedience and discipleship.

Nehemiah 8 is a wonderful snapshot of how the Law was reestablished at the center of Israel. After the successful completion of the wall around Jerusalem (thus providing safety from their many enemies), Ezra led an ancient dig-in. Everyone capable of understanding (not just adult men) was gathered in the city's largest square. A platform was built (there's that issue of amplification again), and Ezra stood before the people and opened the book of the Law of Moses. For over six hours Ezra read the Scripture and the people listened attentively (Nehemiah 8:3). The Levites spread out among the people, holding small discussion groups to make sure that everyone understood what they were hearing. On the second day, specific communal application was given: the people were instructed to celebrate the festival of booths. For seven days there was great rejoicing as they obeyed God by having a citywide camp-out and celebration. Ezra's daily reading of the Law continued throughout the entire festival.

It wasn't enough that the exiles had returned to their promised land physically; they needed to return to the Lord as well, through learning and obeying the Scriptures. Without being shaped by God's Word, their covenant and unique relationship with God was meaningless. And just as Israel needed to engage with the Scriptures communally, so does the church. Communal study is essential to know the Word collectively, to bring maturity to the body of Christ and to be directed by the Word.

Know the Word collectively. I knew a South African woman in college who had previously spent six months in jail. Her crime was traveling around the country reading labor laws to workers in their own language. (She spoke thirteen of them!) This act was a threat to the apartheid government, for ignorance is a powerful tool of oppression. When people know the law, they can evaluate their situation and determine if those in authority are wielding their power appropriately. (Knowing the Bible is similarly helpful in evaluating culture.)

Small group Bible study *for* the laity *by* the laity protects the church from false teachers and authoritarian leaders. During the years of rapid church growth just after the dissolution of the Soviet Union, the International Fellowship of Evangelical Students worked tirelessly to train students in small group inductive Bible study. They knew that many cults would take advantage of the newfound open access and spiritual hunger. For the sake of the health and integrity of the church long-term, believers needed tools to discern truth from heresy. Community around the Word equipped a generation of church leaders to keep the Bible in the center and judge all other teaching and practice by its plumb line.

When calling God's people back to himself, the Lord said to the prophet Amos, "See, I am setting a plumb line in the midst of my people Israel" (Amos 7:8). Plumb lines are essential in construction. Plumb lines give builders a vertical reference point which, used alongside a level (for the horizontal reference point) allows them to build straight and true. Tall buildings, such as cathedrals and skyscrapers, must follow the plumb line exactly so as to not lean. Even a sixteenth of an inch off from the plumb line on the first floor spells disaster by the time the building reaches the height of fifty feet. The Bible is the plumb line God has given his church; it must be known broadly, and not just by a few, if it is to fulfill its purpose.

Bring maturity to the body of Christ. The body of Christ cannot mature as "one new humanity" (Ephesians 2:15) without the nourishment of the Word. Just as individuals have an immaterial dimension that needs to be fed with God's Word, so groups have an immaterial dimension that can get sick or weary. As Eugene Peterson puts it, "Holy Scripture nurtures the holy community as food nurtures the human body."[3] Local expressions of the church might grow numerically, but they won't gain maturity without feeding on God's Word together.

At Cape Town 2010, the third global congress of the Lausanne Movement for world evangelization, the gathered community feasted on the book of Ephesians daily through small group inductive Bible study and expository preaching. The themes of Ephesians informed the program topics and discussions. The content of Ephesians challenged the group to increase the quality of organizational partnerships. Furthermore, studying the Bible together inductively brought about many new crosscultural friendships. The health and fruitfulness of that international gathering was, in large part, a result of being in community around the Word.

Directed by the Word. Finally, community around the Word is essential for the church because it is through the Word that God leads and directs his people. During the exodus, the people of Israel made their way through the wilderness by following a pillar of cloud by day and a pillar of fire by night (Exodus 13:21-22). Through the pillars they knew that God was present guiding them. As we have seen in chapter three, God's Word mediates God's presence today. When a church seeks the Lord's will and asks him, "What are you up to, Lord? How do you want us to be involved in your mission of redeeming the world?" both prayer and communal Bible study must be employed. The evangelical relief and development organization World Vision understands that any Christian organization, in order to maintain its Christian ethos and character, "needs to have a way of encountering God."[4] At one point, World Vision pursued that communal encounter with God by bringing together sixteen of their staff in leadership positions for a week-long manuscript study of the Gospel of Matthew. God met them and gave direction and correction that has kept them vibrant as a Christian organization.

When we gather together, with the Scripture at the center of our communal life, something beautiful develops. Studying the Bible in community grounds us, feeds us, weaves us together and launches us out into the world to take our part in God's mission. We can't be who we were created to be as the church without it.

REFLECTION EXERCISE:
Better Together

Make a list of the various small group Bible studies you have experienced.

Which was your favorite? Why?

To what extent in that group study did you experience the benefit of amplification?

To what extent did you experience friendship through that group?

Are there any ways that your experience of community around the Word became a launch pad for common mission? If not, why not?

Part Two

BUILDING BLOCKS

6

Honor the Author

Humorist A. J. Jacobs set out to read the *Encyclopaedia Britannica* (all thirty volumes) in one year. His witty account of that experience is chronicled in *The Know-It-All: One Man's Humble Attempt to Become the Smartest Man in the World.*[1] It is possible that no other person in history has read every article in that world-renowned encyclopedia, and for good reason. Everyone knows that you don't read even a single volume of an encyclopedia from cover to cover. That's not how an encyclopedia is meant to be read.

An encyclopedia is made up of thousands of smaller articles, written by experts on a wide variety of subjects. According to Wikipedia, the *Encyclopaedia Britannica* is the work of over four thousand independent expert contributors compiled by more than one hundred editors. Readers select individual articles according to their interest.

It is strange to read an encyclopedia as if it were an epic novel, beginning at the beginning and reading straight through. That doesn't fit its nature. Likewise, it doesn't fit the nature of the Bible to read it cover to cover.[2] It looks like a single-volume book and is the size of many of the books on your shelf, but it is actually a library, comprised of sixty-six different books that were written over the span of over one thousand years by many authors. In this respect, the Bible is more like an encyclopedia than an epic novel. Though it contains an overarching plot and narrative (more about that in the next chapter), not all of the books of the Bible fall in chronological order.

In fact, halfway through the Old Testament individual books cease to have clear connection to the books that come before and after, just as encyclopedia entries for *elementary school* and *elephant* aren't related even though they come next to each other. Furthermore, the Bible contains passages that break up the flow of the overall story: genealogies, census records, contracts, laws, building specifications, songs, aphorisms, personal letters and so on.[3] This is why so many of us who make a New Year's resolution to read straight through the Bible slow down toward the end of Exodus and come to a screeching halt when we hit Leviticus. Reading those instructions on how to build and accessorize the tabernacle (Exodus 36—40) or the proper way to offer a bull, ox or turtledove (Leviticus 1—7) can feel like running through wet cement.

A major difference between the Bible and an encyclopedia (besides the obvious one of divine inspiration) involves the significance of its authors. An encyclopedia has thousands of authors, but by and large we don't take notice of them. (It doesn't help that the printer uses the tiniest letters possible for the author's name at the end of each article.) The authors and compilers of the various books of the Bible, especially the New Testament, play a much more prominent role. Many of their names are used as the titles of the books they penned. These men were selected by God to be partners with him in creating the sacred Scriptures. Taking the Bible seriously requires that we honor the human authors God has chosen to work through.

PARTNERSHIP

Theologian Donald Bloesch writes, "Scripture has two sides—the divine and the human, but we have the divine only in and through the human."[4] It shouldn't come as a surprise that the God who came in the flesh through Jesus Christ would favor incarnation as his *modus operandi*. When setting out to redeem the universe, he chose to create a nation through which he could reveal himself to the rest of the world. Likewise, followers of Jesus are considered his body, intended to incarnate the presence of God and bear witness to him. Thus, it is in keeping with God's character that he chose to involve humans intimately in the creation of Holy Scripture. (This stands in stark contrast to the Book of Mormon, which Joseph Smith claimed was a translation of golden plates created by God himself and involved no human authorship.)

> **"So also our beloved brother Paul wrote to you according to the wisdom given to him, speaking of this as he does in all his letters. There are some things in them hard to understand, which the ignorant and unstable twist to their own destruction, as they do the other scriptures."**
>
> 2 PETER 3:15-16

The Bible is divine because God inspired it. "The Scriptures were recorded by human beings but inspired by the Spirit of God. In them the Spirit continues to speak to people today and every day."[5] However, divine inspiration does not imply dictation. It isn't as if Jeremiah or Luke were put into a trance and made to write down whatever God told them. The Holy Spirit guided their thinking and gave them wisdom and insight, but they nonetheless made choices about content, form and style, just as you or I do whenever we write. They were people of faith, often leaders in their communities, who wrote to encourage and evoke faithful living among the people of God. "It was the biblical writers' conviction the God had involved himself in history, and that he governed its whole course, which gave the historical books of the OT their theological quality and content."[6] Biblical authors functioned in partnership with the Holy Spirit.

The Bible is not partly human and party divine but fully human and divine, just like Jesus. Bloesch rightly describes this as "the paradoxical mystery of the divinity of the Bible shining through its true humanity."[7] God is the ultimate author of the Bible (that's why we call it "God's Word"), but the human writers and editors that created the Bible are actual authors, not merely stenographers.

REAL PEOPLE

I sometime fantasize that if I had a time machine, I'd invite a group of biblical authors to my house for dinner. I'd have to hire an interpreter, though, one who knew Hebrew, Aramaic and Greek, for it to work. It would be fascinating to watch them compare notes and try to understand each other's worlds. Let us consider a handful of the men who were partners with God in writing the Bible. David, Nehemiah, Luke and James each come from a different culture and time in history, and their perspectives on the world vary tremendously, yet each is used by God to communicate to God's people then and now.

> "God gives himself as a companion to particular
> and very real people, people who must speak
> about and to God in the very particular and
> real language that is their own."
>
> H. M. KUITERT, *Do You Understand
> What You Read?*

David. David was the famous king who started life as a lowly shepherd boy and received God's promise to be father of the Messiah. He was the epitome of a "renaissance man." A valiant soldier and charismatic leader, David also sponsored the building and development of Jerusalem, making it Israel's capital. Additionally (contrary to my presuppositions about military leaders and politicians), David was an accomplished poet and musician (1 Samuel 16:14-23). David's personality, position and place in Israel's history are all reflected in his psalms. Psalms 23 and 28 draw on David's days as a shepherd. Other psalms are replete with military images (e.g., Psalm 4; 7; 18; 20). Likewise, Jerusalem figures prominently in David's psalms (e.g., Psalm 24; 26; 27; 51; 122); his delight in and yearning for the city is conveyed vividly.

The psalms are a prime example of the blending of human and divine. David brought his own language, insights and concerns to the compositions. The Holy Spirit inspired, and continues to speak through, this beloved section of the Bible.

> **"The whole Bible from Genesis to Revelation is culturally conditioned. It is all written in the language of particular times, and evokes the cultures in which it came to birth."**
>
> **N. T. WRIGHT,** "How Can the Bible Be Authoritative?"

Nehemiah. Nehemiah lived more than five hundred years after David. Though he eventually became the governor of David's beloved city Jerusalem, he was born in Persia, not Israel. As the cup bearer to the Persian king, Artaxerxes, Nehemiah lived a life of privilege in the king's court. People of the various cultures and races controlled by the Persian Empire filled the capital city Susa. It is likely that Nehemiah was fluent in multiple languages and was privy to imperial documents and decrees. Nehemiah shared David's devotion to the Lord, but the world he led and wrote about was tremendously different from David's.

Luke. Luke is the Scripture's sole Gentile author. Nonetheless, his two-volume work (Luke-Acts) comprises one quarter of the New Testament. Only the apostle Paul contributed more material to the New Testament than Luke. As a traveling companion to Paul, Luke had a front-row seat to the spread of the church across the Roman Empire. As a well-educated member of Greco-Roman society (a physician by occupation), he saw the world through a different set of eyes than some of the other Gospel writers who lived their entire lives in Palestine. He wrote using the Greco-Roman styles to which his audience was accustomed.

James. The book of James was written by Jesus' younger brother, who came to faith in Jesus as the Messiah sometime after Jesus' resurrection (1 Corinthians 15:7). James eventually became the leader of the church in Jerusalem (see Acts 12:2, 17; 15:13; 21:18; Galatians 1:19; 2:12). His letter has a profoundly Hebraic style, including aphorisms (short phrases that express truth), picturesque illustrations and prophetic diatribes against the rich. Unlike Luke, who wrote for a predominantly Gentile audience, James wrote to encourage and exhort Jewish Christians who had been driven out of Jerusalem by persecution.

As authors, David, Nehemiah, Luke and James each had a distinct style. Their particular experiences, place in history and personality are incorporated into their writing. They did not set out to write "timeless truth." They wrote for real communities, with real problems and challenges. They used images and forms that spoke powerfully to their readers.

CONTEXT MATTERS

We cannot read the books of the Bible in a vacuum. To honor the Bible, we must honor its human authors by making their intended meaning the goal of our interpretation. Inductive Bible study requires that we identify the author of the particular text we are considering and take that author seriously, on his own terms. Even in a book such as Hebrews, whose author is unknown, some characteristics of the author can be surmised from the text itself. One of the first steps of inductive Bible study involves learning about the book's author, audience and date of composition—its historical context. The author, the audience and their respective settings provide the context for understanding the meaning of a particular book.

The context of 1-2 Chronicles provides a great illustration. If you have ever been reading the Old Testament and thought you were experiencing déjà vu, you were probably in 1-2 Chronicles. Originally just one book, 1-2 Chronicles cover all the same material written about in 1-2 Samuel and 1-2 Kings, which were also written as a single book but split into four parts when the Hebrew Bible was translated into Greek. When they were first divided, they were referred to as 1-4 Reigns. For the sake of ease, I'll refer to them that way and to 1-2 Chronicles just as Chronicles.

Both Reigns and Chronicles were written anonymously. In four books, Reigns traces Israel's political history from the creation of the monarchy, through the civil war that created the two nations of Israel and Judah, and finally to the destruction of both kingdoms by the Assyrian and Babylonian empires, respectively. First Samuel covers the lives of Samuel, Saul and David, thereby providing explanation of the origins of the Davidic monarchy. Second Samuel is entirely about the exploits of King David and his family. First and Second Kings narrate the history of the kings that followed David, toggling back and forth between the kings that reigned over Israel and Judah. Second Kings closes with a poignant image of defeat: Judah's King Jehoiachin in exile, dependent on the provision of King Evil-merodach of Babylon (2 Kings 25:27-30).

If the people of God already had a written record of their monarchs in Reigns, why did the author of Chronicles decide to write another one? The answer is found by considering the audience and date of each. The four books of Reigns were written during the Babylonian exile, sometime between 587 and 538 B.C. "The function of King's review of history . . . is to explain why the Exile came about and to express an admission that there was ample cause for God to judge Israel."[8] Like the books Jeremiah and Lamentations, 1-4 Reigns is an attempt to make sense of the recent devastation. Those who were deported, and their children born in exile, are the audience. The narrative account is theologically laden and intended to bring the people of Israel to repentance and reliance on God's grace so that they might be restored to their land.

One half of the text in Chronicles is repeated word for word from Reigns. It covers the same period of history and subject matter, but it provides a new viewpoint and perspective. "The dominant theological emphasis of Chronicles is the constant concern for the temple, its worship, and its officials, the Levites."[9] The author provides a condensed version of the history of the monarchs, giving less coverage to the kings of the northern kingdom and providing selective coverage of the rest. (For example, the famous stories about David slaying Goliath or committing adultery with Bathsheba are not included.) Kings who were faithful to the Lord (David, Solomon, Hezekiah and Josiah) and invested in the Temple are highlighted.

Chronicles was written between 400 and 350 B.C., 150-200 years after 1-4 Reigns, and well after the exiles had returned to Judah and rebuilt the Temple. It is written from Jerusalem, not Babylon, and it addresses those who neither experienced life in Israel prior to the Babylonian conquest nor life in exile. The author of Chronicles wished "to bring a specific message from God applied to the people of his own day, and it is this that leads him to his extensive reworking of his text, omitting what was now irrelevant, adding material that was now newly relevant, changing what was now misleading and so on."[10] The writer of Chronicles "longs for and seeks to contribute to a recovery of the glorious days of David and Solomon—not by reestablishment of the monarchy but by a return to obedient worship."[11] Chronicles provides vision and motivation for faithful worship and obedience to a new generation facing a new set of challenges and temptations.

Knowing the approximate date of the writing and considering where that falls in Israel's history gives us a sharper understanding of Chronicles. It enables us to envision the audience and the author(s), and consider their concerns and questions. Similarly, the Gospels each cover the same history but bring different emphases to the fore.

There is much more to studying these overlapping accounts in the Bible than merely comparing the various renditions of the same stories. A fruitful approach is to continually ask, "Why did this author choose to include this?" and "How does this author put this story together, and what would that communicate to the original audience?" Understanding historical context enables us to be alert to the unique message of each book of the Bible and to feel at least some of the force of its impact.

KEEPING THE TEXT CENTRAL

The author and audience had common frames of reference that affect the interpretation of the text. The biblical authors could not have imagined life in the twenty-first century. Computers, plastics and air travel were inconceivable to them. Let's admit it: They didn't have us in mind when they were writing. (God, of course, had us in mind, but he chose to communicate by embedding his story in time, space and culture.) In one very real sense, then, the books of the Bible weren't written for us. When we keep the original author and audience in mind, we are faithful to the text. By keeping the books of the Bible rooted in their context, their stories come to life in our imagination, and we encounter God alongside our ancestors in the faith. Studying the Bible becomes an adventure, like traveling overseas. Characters become three-dimensional and memorable.

In the world of literature studies, understanding the author's meaning to the original audience is referred to as "authorial intention." Secular literary criticism has little respect for authorial intention; postmodern philosophy has argued that truth is relative and that meaning is controlled by the reader, not the author (a position referred to as "reader response"). Whether reading Shakespeare or J. K. Rowling, the meaning of a text, according to reader response, is what it means to you. The quest for the "true meaning" is irrelevant, since all meaning is constructed.

While the issues surrounding postmodern literary criticism are much more complex than I can summarize here, reader response has raised some valuable questions and pushes us to recognize that we bring our own lens to anything we read. However, the reader response position has undermined many people's confidence in the truth of the Bible and our ability to know that truth.

> "We do not create the meaning. Rather, we seek to discover the meaning that has been placed there by the author."
>
> J. SCOTT DUVALL AND J. DANIEL HAYS,
> *Grasping God's Word*

One of my primary reasons for being committed to the Bible's authorial intention is the nature of God. God is a communicator and he desires relationship. Real relationships must be built on truth. God has inspired the Scriptures and he continues to lead us into his truth by the active work of the Holy Spirit. "When the Spirit of truth comes, he will guide you into all the truth" (John 16:13). As the authors of *Grasping God's Word* write, "If you read the Bible merely as great literature, merely for its aesthetic value, or merely for its suggestive moral guidance, not as communication from God, then you can interpret it any way you choose."[12] If we believe the Bible is communication from God, then the text, not the reader, must be central in determining meaning.

The current trends in literary theory can help us to hold our interpretation of the Bible lightly, recognizing that we always bring our personal and cultural lenses to the text. But those trends, with their assumption that there is no truth outside of us, will not help us to understand the Bible more fully or to build a secure life. The solid rock of God's Word on which we seek to build our lives is solid because it has meaning and truth in and of itself. It is a force to be reckoned with; something completely solid and other than us. In it we meet the real God who created the universe and is active in human history. The Bible will not be reduced to "This is what it means to me."

Inductive Bible study takes seriously the nature of the Bible: both divine and human, transcendent and historically grounded. We approach it with great expectations of meeting God, actively speaking to us through the Holy Spirit. When we recognize that the Bible is a collection of books and that each book has its own historical context, we honor the human coauthor through whom God worked. Thus, as we study we must continually ask ourselves, "What was the author trying to communicate?" and "How would this sound to the original audience?" In focusing on that line of communication first, we are able to hear more fully from God speaking to us as well.

PRACTICUM
Researching Historical Context

Background information on the books of the Bible can be found in most study Bibles. I recommend reading a few different sources to get a better sense of what is widely recognized and what is speculative. I regularly use the IVP *New Bible Dictionary* and *Nelson's Complete Book of Bible Maps and Charts.*

Instructions

- Using a Bible dictionary, fill in the following grid with background information on the Gospel of Matthew and the Gospel of Mark.

- Put yourself in the shoes of the audience for each. What challenges might they have faced?

	Matthew	Mark
Author		
Audience		
Date		
What challenges might the audience have faced?		

7

Respect for the Story

To celebrate my daughter Mary's eleventh birthday, I took a group of fifth grade girls to a matinee. Mary had selected the film *The Lightning Thief,* which follows the adventures of Percy Jackson, a teen who is thrown into a modern rendition of the Greek myths when he learns that his father is the Greek god Poseidon. The movie was based on a five-book series very popular among kids in Mary's class. Both Mary and I had read the first book of the series and enjoyed it.

On the way out of the theater, I asked the girls what they thought of the movie. Most of them said, "It was good" or "I liked it." However, while we were driving to my home for cake and ice cream, I overheard two of the girls in the back of my mini-van expressing some displeasure. Both were avid readers and great fans of the Percy Jackson series. One of them was offering her critique of the movie and was displeased about the ways the filmmakers had diverged from the storyline of the book. She was particularly offended that the two primary female characters had been melded into one, effectively undermining the significance of each in the plot. Her seatmate agreed, and for at least ten minutes the two of them highlighted the differences between the book and the movie.

I was amazed at how bothered these two young readers were. From their perspective, the story of Percy Jackson had been violated by the film about Percy Jackson. (I don't anticipate that a job adapting screenplays from literature is in either of their futures.)

My daughter's friends demonstrate an important value for those of us who study the Bible: respect for the story. Faithful biblical interpretation requires that we take the fullness of the biblical narrative seriously, rather than edit it and simplify it to fit our agendas. As theologian Donald Bloesch points out, "God has acted decisively in the particular history of biblical Israel culminating in Jesus Christ."[1] When we truncate the story of God's work in history as attested to in the Bible for our own purposes, we put ourselves at the center and are at risk of creating a god in our own image.

Consider the story of Noah's ark. Noah's floating menagerie is standard fare in preschool Sunday school classes. It's fun to sing the "arky, arky" song with young children, make the noises of the various animals that joined Noah on his boat and draw rainbows. The problem is that the story of Noah is actually a story about genocidal judgment. The context of Noah's building project is God's great displeasure with utter wickedness of the human race and his use of natural disaster to accomplish his judgment. It is a tragic story, not a fun or whimsical one. When we teach our children the story of Noah, seldom do we mention all the dead bodies floating in the water. We sanitize the story and cut it down to the parts we like, but in doing so we violate the text.

I understand why Bible stories must be adapted for a young audience, of course, but most of us never get beyond a Sunday school understanding of the biblical narrative. No wonder so many young adults have little interest in studying God's Word. They don't realize that there is so much more to the biblical stories of their childhood than zoo animals on a boat or "the wee little man" in a sycamore tree. Even small children can be taught how these stories demonstrate God's gracious salvation.

To honor the Bible as the Word of God, we must be faithful to the Bible's rendition of each story as well as respect the larger story of which they are a part. This big story that stretches from Genesis to Revelation is often referred to as the "metanarrative," the overarching plot line of God's work in the world. I prefer to call it "redemptive history," the story of how the world came to be so messed up and what God is doing to put it to rights again.

THE BIG STORY

A Bible publisher recently told me, "If you want to ensure that someone will have a bad experience reading a book, tell them to only read one page a day." Whether it is a murder mystery, a romance novel or a book on your favorite hobby, limiting yourself to one page at a time will suck all the enjoyment from reading. But this is what most of us do when reading the Bible. We are used to reading one chapter[2] at a time, which amounts to just a page or two. In doing so, we undermine our ability to get a feel for the drama of the narrative and the inherent connectedness of the various stories. I remember as a teenager staying up late to read the last one hundred pages of *Gone with the Wind* because I was so caught up in the drama. Why not read the Bible in the same way? Set aside a few hours to curl up with a cup of coffee and the book of Revelation. If you read it straight through (as the original audience would have listened to it), the depth of struggle of the God's faithful witnesses and grandeur of Christ's ultimate triumph over evil will engulf you and you will be moved to worship with the angels. In a "big read" of Revelation, all the confusion over signs, seals and beasts fades away; Jesus, the Lamb who was slain, is magnified.

We can remedy our tendency to break the Scriptures into tiny pieces by learning the outline of the big story of the Bible. When the broad strokes of redemptive history are committed to memory, we are able to hear the particular parts within the larger context. One way that I have found to do that is to think of it as a five-act play. Remember being introduced to Shakespeare in high school English class? All of Shakespeare's plays are structured in five acts, with predictable plot development in each act. If you know which act you are reading in, it is easier to interpret particular scenes.

The Bible can also be divided into five acts.

> Act 1: Creation and Fall
>
> Act 2: Israel
>
> Act 3: Jesus
>
> Act 4: The church
>
> Act 5: Redemption

Learning these five acts is an excellent way of understanding the ultimate meaning of world history: God is at work to redeem and restore his good creation.

Act 1. Act 1 is tragic. It begins with God's magnificent work of creation, but the story quickly takes a dark turn as humanity plunges into alienation, discord and violence. Act 1 answers the question "What went wrong?" The answer to the question "What is God doing about it?" is found in the remaining acts. The passages of Scripture that provide understanding of Act 1 are Genesis 1—11 and Proverbs 8:22-31.

Act 2. Act 2 is the story of the nation of Israel, created by God so that "in you all the families of the earth shall be blessed" (Genesis 12:3). Genesis 12 through the end of the Old Testament provides the content for Act 2. It is worth noting that there is more biblical material about Act 2 than any of the other acts. The value of the Old Testament is immeasurable in understanding who God is and how he works in the world. The apostle Paul made the remarkable claim that the Jewish Bible is "able to instruct you for salvation through faith in Christ Jesus" (2 Timothy 3:15).

Act 3. Act 3 is the dramatic turning point of the entire story, as God himself comes to earth and the promises made in Acts 1 and 2 are fulfilled. Jesus' life, death and resurrection are the center of redemptive history. Thus, the four Gospels take pride of place in the Bible as a whole. It is only through Jesus that the rest of the Bible can be fully understood. The redemption of his cross and the power of his resurrection catapult the story forward into Act 4—the act in which we find ourselves.

Act 4. Act 4 is the story of the church, beginning with its birth at Pentecost in Jerusalem and spreading out to the ends of the earth with the gospel (Acts 1:8). The book of Acts and all of the epistles are part of this Act, but church history and our current experience are also found here.

Act 5. Act 5, the return of Jesus to vanquish evil and death and restore the world to right, is yet to come. Act 5 is the culmination of history and the doorway to an eternity of intimacy with God in the new creation. In Act 5, all that went wrong in Act 1 is resolved, and the significance of Acts 2, 3 and 4 is made clear.

Ultimately, the Bible is a story about God and what he is up to. We are invited to find ourselves in the story, but never as the protagonist. Each of us has but a cameo in this epic tale. The real hero is the Trinity—Father, Son and Holy Spirit—relentless in their pursuit to restore what has been broken and to establish the kingdom of God. It is a wonderful story, a true story—a story that makes sense of our tragic world and fills us with hope.

LANDMARKS

Studying any book of the Bible requires us to consider where the particular book falls in the grand narrative of redemption history. Each act has its own pivotal events that are important reference points. I like to think of these as landmarks along a highway. If you are driving along the American west coast, to be properly oriented you need to know that San Diego is the city closest to the Mexican border in the south, that there is a famous bridge about halfway up at San Francisco, and that when you reach Seattle you are still two hours away from the Canadian border. If you know where you are in relation to San Diego, San Francisco or Seattle, you'll have a pretty good sense of how long it will take you to your destination.

When reading the Old Testament, it is important to know where you are in relation to its landmarks—if the passage you are reading, for example, comes before or after the parting of the Red Sea, or before or after Israel's civil war. Likewise, in reading a text from Act 4 (the church) you should ask yourself "Was this written before or after the Temple in Jerusalem was destroyed?" If you don't have a good grasp of the "landmarks" in the Bible, consider taking an Introduction to the Bible class at church or reading a book that provides an overview of the Bible's big story.[3]

Reading the prophetic books of the Old Testament in historical context is particularly necessary, since the words of each prophet were addressed to Israel (and its neighbors) at significant points of national history. One of the best ways to do this is to read about the contemporary kings of that prophetic book. Isaiah's call to repentance, warning of judgment and promise of restoration make much more sense in light of the sections of 2 Kings and 2 Chronicles that depict Israel just before being conquered by Babylon. Likewise, Haggai's biting words from the

Lord, "Is it a time for you yourselves to live in your paneled houses, while this house lies in ruins?" (Haggai 1:4), must be paired with the narration of Ezra 1—6, in which the returned exiles give up on rebuilding the Temple because of opposition. Table 7.1 provides a chart of the prophets in chronological order, the ruler at that time, and what part of the historical books of the Old Testament cover that period.

THE STORY WITHIN THE STORY

Respect for the story involves understanding where a particular passage you are studying falls within the narrative of a particular book. Each book was crafted intentionally, and the ordering of material is one of the strategies the authors and compilers used to communicate meaning. Placing a text within the narrative context involves looking at the passages immediately before and after, but it also entails considering the narrative sweep of the whole book.

I like to illustrate this using a favorite New Testament passage, Luke 19:1-10, in which Jesus invites himself to Zacchaeus's house. In each of the next four chapters, I will be using this story to demonstrate the concepts of the chapter and will illustrate my findings on a manuscript (see figure 7.1). At the end of each chapter, you will have an opportunity to do the same using a manuscript of Mark 4:35-41, the story of Jesus and the disciples in a storm.

Let's start with the immediate context. Just prior to the Zacchaeus passage, Luke describes Jesus healing a blind beggar (Luke 18:35-43). Even a quick reading of that text reveals several striking similarities and differences between the two stories. One happens as Jesus is approaching Jericho, the other as Jesus leaves Jericho. Both the beggar and Zacchaeus are outcasts and considered unclean. One is desperately poor, the other is exceedingly rich. Both of them take initiative in the interaction with Jesus, the first through shouting and the second through climbing a tree. Both receive a transformation or healing: recovery of sight and salvation. Both are publically affirmed by Jesus: "Your faith has saved you" and "He too is a son of Abraham." In light of all these parallels, it appears that Luke intended for these two stories to be understood in tandem. Might it be that salvation is the spiritual equivalent of having physical sight restored? Is Luke intending to communicate that Zacchaeus's tree climbing was an act of faith? Certainly we can conclude that Jesus responds positively to those who seek him.

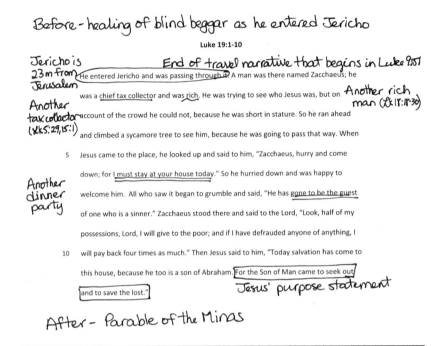

Figure 7.1.

If we look back just a little further, we find the story of the rich ruler who asked Jesus about eternal life (Luke 18:18-28). The common themes of riches and salvation invite us to consider reading the story of Zacchaeus with the story of the rich ruler in mind. When comparing the two men's encounters with Jesus, the most obvious difference is that the rich ruler sadly departs from Jesus because he is too attached to his money, but Zacchaeus welcomes Jesus and enthusiastically divests himself of his wealth. Since the issue of money and discipleship is such a strong theme in Luke's Gospel, it is telling that Luke gives us two stories of rich men, one that responds positively and one that doesn't. In Luke 18:24-35, Jesus said, "How hard it is for those who have wealth to enter the kingdom of God! Indeed, it is easier for a camel to go through the eye of a needle than for someone who is rich to enter the kingdom of God." Through the story of

Table 7.1. Approximate Dates of the Ministries of Old Testament Prophets.

Name of Prophet	Approximate dates of ministry	Rulers of Judah	Rulers of Israel	Rulers of Babylon/Persia	Historical setting
Joel	c. 810-750 B.C.	Joash (=Jehoash), Amaziah, Uzziah (=Azariah)			2 Kings 11:1—15:7
Amos	c. 760 B.C.	Uzziah (=Azariah)	Jeroboam II		2 Kings 14:23—15:7
Jonah	c. 760 B.C.		Jeroboam II		2 Kings 14:23-29
Hosea	c. 760-722 B.C.		Jeroboam II, Zechariah, Shallum, Manahem, Pekahiah, Pekah, Hoshea		2 Kings 14:23—18:37
Micah	c. 742-687 B.C.	Jotham, Ahaz, Hezekiah			2 Kings 15:32—20:21; 2 Chronicles 27:1—32:33; Isaiah 7:1—8:22; Jeremiah 26:17-19
Isaiah	c. 740-700 B.C.	Uzziah (=Azariah), Jotham, Ahaz, Hezekiah			2 Kings 15:1—20:21; 2 Chronicles 26:1—32:33
Nahum	c. 664-612 B.C.	Josiah			2 Kings 22:1—23:30; 2 Chronicles 34:1—36:1; Zephaniah 2:13-15
Zepha-niah	c. 640 B.C. onward	Josiah			2 Kings 22:1—23:34; 2 Chronicles 34:1—36:21
Jeremiah	c. 626-587 B.C.	Josiah, Jehoahaz, Jehoiakim, Jehoiachin, Zedekiah			2 Kings 22:1—25:30; 2 Chronicles 34:1—36:21
Habakkuk	c. 560 B.C.	Jehoiakim			2 Kings 23:31—24:7
Daniel	c. 605-535 B.C.	Jehoiakim, Jehoiachin, Zedekiah		Nebuchadnezzar Belshazzar, Darius, Cyrus	2 Kings 24:1—25:30; 2 Chronicles 36:5-23
Ezekiel	c. 593-570 B.C.			Nebuchadnezzar	2 Kings 24:8—25:26; 2 Chronicles 36:9-21
Obadiah	c. 587 B.C. onward			Nebuchadnezzar	2 Kings 25; 2 Chronicles 36:5-23
Haggai	c. 520 B.C.			Darius	Ezra 5:1—6:22
Zechariah	c. 520 B.C. onward			Darius onward	Ezra 5:1—6:22
Malachi	c. 433 B.C.			Artaxerxes I	Nehemiah 13

From *New Bible Dictionary,* 3rd ed., ed. I. Howard Marshall, A. R. Millard, J. I. Packer and D. J. Wiseman (Downers Grove, Ill.: InterVarsity Press, 2008), p. 968.

Zacchaeus's salvation, we have an illustration that "what is impossible for mortals is possible for God" (Luke 18:27).

When we look to the passage immediately after the Zacchaeus story, we learn that Jesus is very close to Jerusalem (Luke 19:11), which makes his interaction with Jesus the last event in Jesus' long journey to Jerusalem and his impending death. The parable Jesus tells is another one about money. Without unpacking the meaning of the parable, we can safely say that the relationship between money and response to Jesus is being heavily underlined by Luke as his telling of the gospel narrative turns toward Jesus' passion.

As we have seen, paying attention to immediate context can bear a lot of fruit. It is also valuable to consider the larger narrative context of any passage. This can be more difficult to do if you haven't spent much time in the book you are considering. In chapter seventeen, I'll provide a little training on determining the structure of a book, which helps to bring the narrative of the whole book into view. For now, let me share a few thoughts about Luke 19 in its larger context.

I'll start with location, since physical movement is often an indicator of narrative structure. We've already noted that the Zacchaeus story happens just outside of Jericho (about twenty-three miles from Jerusalem) and is the last public event before Jesus enters Jerusalem. Luke introduces the theme of Jesus traveling toward Jerusalem ten chapters previously (Luke 9:51). Jesus' public ministry began in Luke 4:16, which means that the vast majority of Luke's telling of the story happens in the context of an extended travel narrative. All that is covered between Luke 9:51 and Luke 19:27 is meant to be understood in the context of "Jesus set his face to go to Jerusalem" where he would be rejected and crucified. Why might the story of Zacchaeus's salvation be the final story of this section? Could Luke be using structure to make the point that Jesus is able to save even the worst of sinners, like a chief tax collector, because of what will happen in Jerusalem?

Another element of the larger structure involves the repeated theme of eating and dinner parties. In the Gospel of Luke, we learn as much about the content of Jesus' teaching from these "table fellowship" scenes as we do from scenes set in the synagogue or Temple. In Luke 5:27-32,

Jesus' new disciple Levi gives a great banquet in Jesus' honor. The guest list is dominated by tax collectors and other kinds of sinners, garnering the criticism of the Pharisees. At the end of that scene Jesus declares, "I have come to call not the righteous but sinners to repentance." That statement of purpose parallels the one made at the end of the Zacchaeus story, "For the Son of Man came to seek and to save the lost" (Luke 19:10). Luke seems to be using this story to underline the purpose of Jesus' incarnation. Salvation for those sick with sin drives his mission.

Considering a text's location in relationship to the surrounding material and the flow of the overall narrative within which it is found both anchors and illuminates it. Rather than Luke 19:1-10 being "just another" story of Jesus and a tax collector or a humorous interlude (short men climbing trees is pretty funny) before the intensity of Jesus' passion, looking at this story within its larger story reveals the depth of Jesus' commitment to bring salvation to those who are sick and lost, and the beauty of Luke's craftsmanship as a writer.

THE WHOLE STORY

Respect for the biblical stories also involves working with each story as a whole. It can be tempting, especially for those who are teachers, to cut up or leave out parts of the story. A missions conference planning team of which I am a part made the decision to open the conference with the scene in Luke where Jesus comes to his hometown of Nazareth and announces his mission (Luke 4:16-30). There, Jesus makes a beautiful declaration: "The Spirit of the Lord is upon me, because he has anointed me to bring good news to the poor. He has sent me to proclaim release to the captives and recovery of sight to the blind, to let the oppressed go free, to proclaim the year of the Lord's favor" (vv. 18-19). He punctuates these ringing words by saying, "Today this scripture has been fulfilled in your hearing" (v. 21). What a wonderful beginning for a conference! It sets just the right tone and vision.

However, the story doesn't end there. Jesus' next move is to pick a fight with the audience and to remind them of times when God's blessings went to Gentiles rather than the people of Israel. The audience becomes so enraged that they attempt to throw Jesus off a cliff.

Yikes! I found myself struggling. *Do we really want to start opening night with this heavy element of Jesus' rejection? It isn't exactly the tone we were looking for.* But submission to the text won out. In our choice to use the whole passage, and not the most convenient part, we chose to bend our purposes to God rather than seek to bend him to ours.

PRACTICUM
Examining Narrative Context

Take some time to place the story below within the context of the larger story of Mark as a whole. Use the manuscript below to record your thoughts and findings.

Practical Steps

- Read Mark 4:35-41 a few times.

- Now read the stories immediately before and after, looking for similarities and differences. Do those stories shed any light on this one?

- Take a look at the passages within Mark 4—5. Are there any obvious points of connection? What might the significance of those mean for your understanding of this text?

- Now flip through the Gospel of Mark as a whole, considering:

  » Where does this passage fall in the overall flow of the book?

  » Are there any other scenes similar to it, or is it unique?

  » Why might Mark choose to tell this story at this point in his narrative?

Mark 4:35-41

On that day, when evening had come, he said to them, "Let us go across to the other side." And leaving the crowd behind, they took him with them in the boat, just as he was. Other boats were with him. A great windstorm arose, and the waves beat into the boat, so that the boat was
5 already being swamped. But he was in the stern, asleep on the cushion; and they woke him up and said to him, "Teacher, do you not care that we are perishing?" He woke up and rebuked the wind, and said to the sea, "Peace! Be still!" Then the wind ceased, and there was a dead calm. He said to them, "Why are you afraid? Have you still no faith?" And
10 they were filled with great awe and said to one another, "Who then is this, that even the wind and the sea obey him?"

8

Attentiveness

I have mixed feelings about video links sent by friends. I don't want to waste my time, even though there are many funny or interesting videos online. Perhaps I was bored or in a more relaxed mood when I received an email that said, "You've got to see this." The link took me to a YouTube video called "Awareness Test." The video began with a lineup of young people, half dressed in white, the others in black. A pleasant male voice said, "How many passes does the team in white make?" Each team had a basketball and passed it to their teammates while the players wove in and out of one another like a complicated dance. I concentrated on the game and tried to count, but the ball was passing quickly and I soon lost track. Twenty seconds later, the narrator said calmly, "The answer is thirteen. But . . . did you see the moon-walking bear?"

What in the world is he talking about? I thought as the footage of the basketball game was rewound to the beginning lineup. This time, rather than concentrating on the ball and trying to keep track of how many times it changed hands, I allowed myself to look at the scene as a whole. Sure enough, from the right side of the screen, a person dressed in a bear costume stepped into the game. The bear did the moonwalk, a dance move made famous by the late Michael Jackson, while the ball whizzed by him on every side. It was a ridiculous sight: a costume you might see at a children's fair, a dance step from the 1980s and a frenetic basketball game played by a group of urban youth.

The video ended with a plain black screen and the statement, "It is easy to miss something you aren't looking for." My determination to do well on the awareness test caused me to miss an obvious feature of the scene. The moonwalking bear was in plain view the whole time, and yet I had failed to see it.

The video had been made to promote bicycle awareness, but its point is broadly applicable. When driving in a new place, we miss beautiful landscape because we are preoccupied with finding the right turnoff. In visiting an art gallery, we barely notice remarkable pieces lining the halls as we find our way to the gallery of a famous painting. Our preoccupations limit what we are able to see or notice.

I believe this is particularly true when reading the Bible. Unless we train ourselves otherwise, most of us will come to the Bible looking to reinforce what we already think. When we read it, most often we are looking for a word of comfort, an illustration of a point we want to make or evidence of a dearly held theological position. This tendency has had tragic consequences, enabling Western Christians, for example, to uphold and defend the practice of slavery for centuries. They came to the Bible with preconceived notions of racial superiority, and they found narratives and verses to support it. They seemed to be blind to the many other passages and ideas that would challenge both the practice of slavery and the worldview that undergirded it. Perhaps they were so focused on looking for justification of slavery that they missed the moonwalking bear.

It's easy to point fingers at believers in other times and other places, and criticize them for their blindness toward issues that we think are obvious. But before we take the speck out of another's eye, we must first take the log out of our own. All of us are guilty of using the Scripture to reinforce our dearly held views and practices.

It takes humility before God and other Christians to come to the Bible fully open to being challenged or corrected. Rather than approaching the Word seeking to justify ourselves, a humble posture assumes that we are ignorant and blind to many of God's truth and values. "If one is to see things as they really are in a given passage, his mind must first be turned away from all preconceived ideas and biases as to the meaning of that passage. The way this is done is to become a lover of truth, regardless of the consequences."[1] This will involve holding our convictions in an open hand, allowing the Bible to have its full authority in our lives. Truth must be our goal, even if seeing that truth threatens dearly held convictions.

The murder mystery novelist Agatha Christie's character Hercule Poirot embodies a commitment to truth at all costs. This makes him both invaluable and dangerous. Poirot is able to identify criminals that stymie the police, but in doing so, he inevitably uncovers family secrets and incriminating evidence about the rich and powerful. Christians who, like Poirot, are committed to truth at all costs are likewise both invaluable and dangerous to the church and the world. The Gospels make it clear that religious people and institutions do not always take kindly to those who challenge long-held practices and assumptions. Too often, stability and the status quo win out over truth.

In *The Murder of Roger Ackroyd*, the deceased's wife becomes frustrated with the inefficiencies of the local law enforcement and decides to call in Poirot. During his initial interview, Poirot makes sure she knows what she is getting herself into.

> "If I go into this, you must understand one thing clearly. I shall go through with it to the end. The good dog, he does not leave the scent, remember! You may wish that, after all, you had left it to the local police."
>
> "I want the truth," said Flora, looking him straight in the eyes.
>
> "All the truth?"
>
> "All the truth."
>
> "Then I accept," said the little man quietly. "And I hope you will not regret those words. Now, tell me all the circumstances."[2]

THE ART OF SEEING

Inductive Bible study requires a commitment to the truth and a teachable, humble posture toward the Scripture. Without them, we aren't able to do justice to the first step: observation.

Observation is "the art of seeing things as they really are,"[3] the ability to recognize all the elements in a scene or text. Skillful observers, whether they are bird watchers or sports enthusiasts, have developed the ability to pay attention to a wide range of details. For example, my husband sees a hundred times more than I do in just ten minutes of a football game. He has learned the various plays, strategies and positions. He loves the complexity of the game. Thus, when Jon watches football on Sunday afternoon, he is able to observe dynamics and movements to which I am oblivious. I, on the other hand, can only recognize when a thrown ball is caught or dropped. The rest of the action on the screen is meaningless to me. After a few minutes of watching, I usually pick up a magazine and tune out the television. Jon is happy to teach me more, but honestly, I'm not that interested in paying close attention. Both Jon's enjoyment and my lack of enjoyment are directly related to the quality of our observing.

As we consider how to observe the Scripture fully, I find it helpful to think in terms of "attentiveness." Attentiveness is a posture, a way of carrying yourself in relationship to the world. Attentiveness implies careful observation, awareness and perception. It involves being emotionally present and engaged, thoroughly conscious of what we are experiencing or reading. Robert Traina, author of a classic work on inductive Bible study, wrote that "to truly observe is to be mentally aware of what one sees. Observation transcends pure physical sight; it involves perception."[4]

Have you even been driving on the freeway and lost track of time? Your eyes have been open and you have seen enough of your environment to successfully stay between the lines and not rear-end the car in front of you, but you haven't been consciously aware of the act of driving. This often happens to me as my mind wanders to a problem at work or I begin planning tonight's dinner. I might notice mile marker 178 and then the next mile marker I am aware of is 194. Sixteen miles have passed but I haven't been consciously aware of my driving. I've been on "automatic pilot" and have failed to be attentive to my driving. I hate to admit it, but I have this experience when reading the Bible just as often as when I'm driving.

When driving on "automatic pilot" my eyes are open and my optical synapses are firing, but I'm only seeing in the most basic way. It's a risky way to drive because I'm not alert to potential obstacles on the road ahead or aware of my escalating speed. (Most of my speeding tickets are the result of being in auto-pilot mode.) Driving (and life) requires more than basic seeing.

Attentiveness goes beyond basic seeing by adding the will. When your will is activated, the "automatic pilot" switch has been turned off and you are fully present. Attentive reading enables us to grasp the depth and beauty of a skilled author. "Get a will behind the eye, and the eye becomes a searchlight, the familiar is made to disclose undreamed treasure."[5] One of the reasons people are so excited about inductive Bible study when they first encounter it is the discovery of "undreamed treasure" in familiar passages. Once they learn how to observe well, they find that the Bible is incredibly rich. They might even be baffled that they have read it for so many years and yet missed so much.

A few years ago, I was teaching John 1—4 to a group of about a hundred Christian leaders. I pressed them to push themselves further in observation and to not be content with what they already know about familiar stories like the conversion of Nathanael, the wedding at Cana or the woman at the well. One often ignored element of observation is counting, and so I encouraged them to pay attention to how John uses numbers. While we were studying the story of the Samaritan woman in John 4, someone observed that she had been married five times. Another noticed that her jar is the seventh water jar in John's Gospel (there were six at the wedding in Cana). I asked, "Why might these numbers be significant?" The group pondered a while, and then a woman in the back of the room raised her hand. She said, "We've mentioned that several famous Old Testament characters met their wives at a well. She's living with a man who isn't her husband, so that means she's been with six men. When Jesus offers her living water, is he offering to be the seventh man, the completion of what she's been looking for and hasn't found?" At this point, the room erupted. We were so excited to see that the living water that quenches all thirst wasn't just an abstract offer, but was fleshed out immediately in her experience with

Jesus "courting" her. Through that insight, the Holy Spirit spoke to our hearts of the fullness and completeness of Jesus' love for each of us. Being more fully attentive to the details in the text led us into a powerful experience with Jesus.

TOOLS

In the observation phase of inductive Bible study, we work hard to look beyond what already know. We "bring the mind to the place where it is actively engaged in observing details."[6] Rather than a quick read through, we sit before the text and focus on it at length.

In any endeavor, whether it is fixing a flat tire or making candy, the right tools make a huge difference. In InterVarsity Christian Fellowship, the campus ministry organization for which I work, we've developed a simple tool that makes observing easier and more fun. We call it the "manuscript." A manuscript is a section or entire book of the Bible printed on regular white paper formatted in a particular way. All of the formatting found in a typical Bible is stripped away: no chapter or verse numbers, no section headings, no paragraphs. Rather than the text being in columns (like a phone book), it is printed like a novel or a letter. The margins are made extra wide and the text is double-spaced to provide lots of room for marking the text and writing notes. Figure 8.1 is an example of a manuscript of Luke 19:1-10, the story of Zacchaeus. (In chapter thirteen you will find instructions for how to create a manuscript.)

A manuscript is printed without chapter or verse numbers because they were not part of the original text. They were added later to make it easier to reference different parts of the Bible regardless of the size of paper on which it was copied or printed. (Tradition says that the person who added the verse numbers did some of his work while riding a horse on his way to the printing house; this bumpy ride explains why some verses begin in the middle of a sentence.[7]) Likewise, paragraphs and section headings are removed since they have been added by the publisher and contain an element of interpretation. Their presence can be a stumbling block in "seeing things as they really are."[8] Using a manuscript is an attempt to get as close as possible to the original text in the form the audience received it.

Though it is convenient to have a long book broken down into smaller pieces, the places where the Bible has been broken doesn't always reflect the flow and structure created by the author. For example, the chapter break at Ephesians 6 comes in the middle of Paul's explanation of what mutual submission looks like in household relationships. He commands in Ephesians 5:21, "Be subject to one another out of reverence for Christ," and then provides three parallel relationships (wives/husbands, children/fathers, slaves/masters) to flesh out the implications of his command. This section goes from 5:21 to 6:9. The chapter break and heading at 6:1 undermines our ability to see the structure of Paul's argument. We are more likely to read Paul's commands to wives and husbands on its own, rather than using the parallel examples to shed light on one another. Likewise, we can easily fail to recognize that the husband, father and master in any particular household is the same man and thus ask how the section as a whole

Luke 19:1-10

He entered Jericho and was passing through it. A man was there named Zacchaeus; he was a chief tax collector and was rich. He was trying to see who Jesus was, but on account of the crowd he could not, because he was short in stature. So he ran ahead and climbed a sycamore tree to see him, because he was going to pass that way. When

5   Jesus came to the place, he looked up and said to him, "Zacchaeus, hurry and come down; for I must stay at your house today." So he hurried down and was happy to welcome him. All who saw it began to grumble and said, "He has gone to be the guest of one who is a sinner." Zacchaeus stood there and said to the Lord, "Look, half of my possessions, Lord, I will give to the poor; and if I have defrauded anyone of anything, I

10   will pay back four times as much." Then Jesus said to him, "Today salvation has come to this house, because he too is a son of Abraham. For the Son of Man came to seek out and to save the lost."

Figure 8.1.

speaks to him—what does it look like for a householder to live in mutual submission with his wife, children and slaves?

A table and colored pens or pencils are also helpful tools. Studying at a table makes it possible to lay out multiple pages side by side in order to see larger chunks of a book and trace themes between sections. We tend to be more alert and able to concentrate when we are seated at a table than on a couch. The physical posture of working on a manuscript at a table reflects the active mental and spiritual posture required by attentiveness. I keep a package of colored pens on my desk for use when doing a manuscript study. Using different colors enables me to trace repeated words and themes.

It's fun to use a variety of colors and shapes to mark a manuscript. I find it easier to remember what I have seen if I have taken the time to select a color and shape and to search for every instance of that particular element.

TRAINING

If you were to take a golf lesson, the pro would instruct you in how to hold the club, how to stand and how to swing. Your training would include learning to check each of these things every time you hit the ball and then lots and lots of practice. If you learn the things to pay attention to (grip, stance and swing), you can go back and check your form when the ball doesn't go where you want it to. Breaking the golf swing down into parts enables you to learn all the elements that eventually become a fluid motion. After practicing the form taught by the pro, you make small adjustments to make it your own and soon what might have felt stiff or rigid becomes natural.

Knowing what types of things to look for when observing a passage of the Bible will help you to be attentive to the text and to see more than you normally do. All observations fall into one of three categories: context, content and connections.

> ### Categories of Observation
>
> 1. Context
> 2. Content
> 3. Connections

The next three sections will cover each of those categories in detail, including charts with explanations and examples. When you are first learning to studying the Bible inductively, you may want to go through each of the three charts systematically. But eventually you will develop your own style and incorporate the various elements of observation from all three categories. If you have experience with manuscript study, working through the charts methodically will enable you to be more thorough in observing God's Word.

CONTEXT

Have you ever walked into a movie theater fifteen minutes after the movie started? It can be confusing because you don't know who the characters are, how they are related to one another or the problem driving the plot. Sometimes you can figure it out over the course of the movie, but often you need to whisper with your neighbor to get enough information to understand what you are watching. Those first fifteen minutes provide the context of the story.

Context sheds light on the meaning and significance of a statement, event or story. We all hate it when our words are taken out of context and used to say something different from what we meant. When politicians quote one another maliciously, the most common retort is, "I was quoted out of context." The setting of a statement is necessary to grasp its significance and intended force. N. T. Wright explains the importance of context with the example of a simple statement: "It's going to rain." Whether or not the hearer responds to that statement with rejoicing or disappointment depends on the context. If the context is a farming community that is suffering from prolonged drought, then the announcement of rain is wonderful news. But if the setting is a family vacation to Disney World, "It's going to rain" will be met with groans. In this scenario, the degree to which it is bad news will intensify based on other elements of the narrative, such as whether or not it has rained every day thus far or if this is the last day of the vacation. "The context supplies an implicit narrative, and the force of the statement depends on the role that it plays within those different potential narratives."[9]

I once visited a church on a Sunday when the topic was how God has made us each uniquely and given us gifts, abilities and interests that he wants to use. The pastor used the acronym S.H.A.P.E. and provided a few Bible verses to support each of his five points. *H* stood for "Heart." The pastor quoted Revelation 17:17: "God has put it in their hearts to carry out his purpose." I didn't recognize that verse, but it sounded encouraging and something I might want to underline in my Bible and share with friends. But when I flipped to Revelation 17 to read the verse in context, I was shocked. The pastor had only quoted half of a sentence. The full verse says, "For God has put it into their hearts to carry out his purpose by agreeing to give their kingdom to the beast, until the words of God will be fulfilled." Rather than offering a beautiful promise about God's work in our hearts, the verse describes God's sovereign work in the hearts of his enemies. It comes in the midst of a passage about Babylon personified as a "great whore" who will soon be overcome by the beast. The people referred to in verse 17 are ten kings who will unite with the beast and make war on God's people. The context of the verse made it clear that we don't want what they have in their hearts!

"When we disregard literary context, we run the risk of forcing the Bible to say what we want it to say."[10] In doing so, we set ourselves over the Scriptures rather than submitting to its authority.

Every passage of the Bible has a narrative, historical and cultural setting. The narrative setting is its place within a particular book of the Bible. The historical context is the setting of that book of the Bible in the grand sweep of history as God redeems our broken world and abolishes death and sin. (See chapter seven for a five-act outline of redemptive history.) The cultural setting is the particular culture of the author and the audience of a particular book. Since the Bible was written over a thousand years by people speaking different languages and living in different parts of the Middle East, there are many different cultural settings represented. Author and audience sometimes share the same cultural context, but sometimes they don't.

Observing context often involves a little research. Good study Bibles provide information about the author, audience and date of each book. I recommend that those who study the Bible inductively buy a Bible dictionary, which can provide all that information and more.[11] Table 8.1 shows how to determine narrative, historical and cultural context.

Table 8.1. Observing Context

Context Element	How to Determine	Example
Narrative context	Note the stories immediately before and after. Look for major repetitions or contrasts with those stories. Where does this passage happen within the course of the book?	The healing of the blind man as Jesus enters Jericho (Luke 18:35-43) immediately precedes the story of the restoration of Zacchaeus as Jesus is leaving Jericho (Luke 19:1-10).
Historical context	Where does this passage fit within the metanarrative of the Bible? To which act does it belong? A particular book of the Bible might have passages about different acts. Proverbs is primarily Act 2, but Proverbs 8:22-31 is Act 1. Many of the Prophets and all of the Gospels contain passages regarding Act 5. Locate the passage in relationship to key events of that act. If reading a prophetic book, read about the history of Israel at that time in the historical books of the Old Testament. (See table 7.1.)	Jesus' comments about the fall of the Temple in Mark 13 happen forty years before the destruction of the Temple by the Roman army (Acts 3—4). First John is written late in the first century by one of the last remaining eyewitnesses of Jesus' life, death and resurrection (1 John 1:1-3).
Cultural context	Research author, audience, and time and purpose of writing in a Bible dictionary. Continually ask, "What did the author intend to communicate to the original audience?" Look up key or confusing words and concepts in a concordance or Bible dictionary. Put yourself in the shoes of the audience to feel the weight of a passage. Ask the questions the audience might ask, rather than twenty-first-century questions.	*Baptism* (Mark 1:5): "Non-Jews who were converting to Judaism would immerse themselves in water, probably under the supervision of a religious expert. John's baptizing activity fits this model." (Craig S. Keener, *The IVP Bible Background Commentary: New Testament* [Downers Grove, Ill.: InterVarsity Press, 1993], p. 135.) *Knowledge of good and evil* (Genesis 2:9): A Jewish idiom for independent moral choice (Deuteronomy 1:39; 2 Samuel 19:35). (John Goldingay, *Old Testament Theology: Israel's Gospel* [Downers Grove, Ill.: InterVarsity Press, 2003], p. 132.)

CONTENT

Content refers to the basic elements that make up a story. When studying the Bible, we need to get the story straight by answering the questions of who, where, when, what and how. These observations are facts that anyone who reads the passage could agree upon. Some find it helpful to catalog this information to bring details you might otherwise overlook into view.

Table 8.2 provides some direction on how to get the most out of observing content elements. I suggest using a different color to mark everything you observe about different characters. After you have identified all the basic elements of the story, notice changes in any of the

Table 8.2. Observing Content

Content Element	Example	Pay Attention
Characters	A blind man, crowds, Simon Peter, the Pharisees	Note both individuals and groups; note which are major and minor.
Descriptors of characters	Short, angry, rich, muttering	Note adjectives, verbs, adverbs and emotions for each.
References to any member of Trinity	God, Father, Jesus, Lord, Holy Spirit, Son of Man, Rabbi, etc.	Note the different titles used and who uses them; include pronouns. Particularly notice everything Jesus says and does.
Character interactions and relationships	Peter to Jesus: "Go away from me, Lord" (Luke 5:8); Jesus touches the leper (Mark 1:41)	Note when dialogue or monologue; note speaker for each.
Places and setting	Jericho, sycamore tree, house, wilderness, synagogue, a banquet	Look up each place on a map; note distance between locations.
Time references	Now, in those days, later, in the year of, immediately	Notice the length of time passed between actions and events since the preceding story.
Primary event(s)	Miracle, confrontation, teaching, travel	Note if there is one primary event or a few woven together. If so, ask yourself how these events are related to each other.
Action (verbs)	Mark 1:17: "Follow Me" (command in present tense) "and I will make you become fishers of men" (NASB) (promise in future tense)	Note imperatives; notice shift between past, present and future tense.
Old Testament allusions or quotations	"Clothed with camel's hair, with a leather belt around his waist" (Mark 1:6/2 Kings 1:8); "eat bread in the kingdom of God" (Luke 14:15/ Isaiah 25:6)	Use a Bible with cross-references or a Bible background commentary to find exact references in Old Testament; read the context of the Old Testament reference.
Numbers	"He summoned ten of his slaves and gave them ten pounds" (Luke 19:13); "He was in the wilderness forty days, tempted by Satan" (Mark 1:13)	Calculate size or amount into a modern unit of measurement. Some numbers, such as 6, 7, 12, 40 and 70, have symbolic overtones and indicate an Old Testament allusion.

content elements. How much time passes in the narrative? Do the characters move or change? How do the characters respond to one another? If you notice several similarities in the description of the characters, making a chart to compare and contrast them will enable you to see even more (e.g., the comparison between the blind beggar and Zacchaeus in chapter seven could have been made using a chart).

For an example of a manuscript marked with content observations, see figure 8.2.

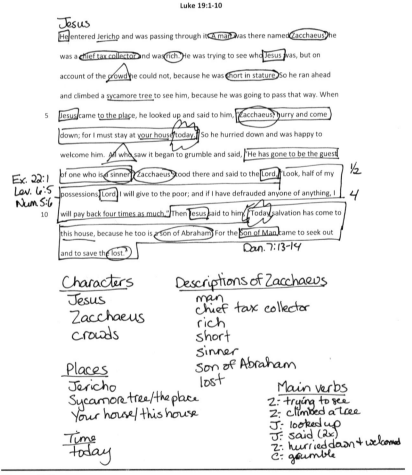

Figure 8.2.

CONNECTIONS

In addition to context and content, it is useful to observe connections between words and phrases. Observing connections enables us to notice the author's style in writing. Authors make choices of *how* they communicate as well as *what* they communicate. Consider the four Gospels. Each of them describes Jesus' arrest, trial and crucifixion. The content elements are basically the same in all four, but each tells the story uniquely. Matthew arranges the material and weaves in different themes to the passion narrative than Mark, Luke or John, in line with the particular goals and concerns of his Gospel. The choices authors make are what we observe in the connections category.

Authors use a variety of strategies of communication. These strategies involve varying forms of connection between different words, phrases and narrative elements. For example, repetition is a common strategy for communicating emphasis. In Genesis 2, the word *man* is repeated much more than any other word (seventeen times). The next most frequent repetitions are the synonyms *earth*, *ground* and *land* (twelve times). Without even looking at the plot of the story, then, we can already tell that a theme of Genesis 2 is the relationship between humans and the environment.

Repetition is an effective strategy for communicating emphasis and is employed by most of the biblical authors. However, emphasis and significance can be communicated in many other ways by creating different types of connections. By learning these strategies (sometimes called "Laws of Composition") we can observe the text more fully. Table 8.3 describes the most common connections found in biblical text. A more extensive table of the Laws of Composition can be found in appendix D.

For an example of a manuscript marked with connections, see figure 8.3.

Those new to inductive study might find in helpful to use each of these three categories—context, content and connections—in a defined order when working on observing the text. When I am pressing myself to observe more thoroughly, I pull out my content chart and check to see that I have located all references to characters, setting,

Table 8.3. Observing Connections.

Connection Element	Definition	Example
Repetition	Reiteration of the same term	"Holy" (Leviticus); "seed" (Mark 4:1-20)
Continuity	Repeated use of similar terms, phrases, ideas	Three lost and found parables (Luke 15)
Series or progression	The relationship between parts of group with common characteristics; can be indicated by use of *and, moreover, furthermore, likewise* or *then*	"In the beginning was the Word, *and* the Word was with God, *and* the Word was God" (John 1:1)
Contrast or alternative	Association of opposites; often indicated by use of *but, some . . . others, not . . . but, although . . . yet, though . . . yet* There are two different Greek words for *but.* One is weaker than the other; it can be translated as *and* or *but.* The weaker word doesn't indicate a sharp contrast. A primary interpretation should not be based on a logical argument using *but* unless you have checked which Greek word is used. This can be done by using an interlinear Bible (described in chapter sixteen).	The righteous *and* the wicked (Psalm 1); "*Some* were convinced by what he had said, while *others* refused to believe" (Acts 28:24)
Comparison	Association of things that are alike but vary in some way; sometimes indicated by use of *even as, as* or *so*	Four kinds of soil in parable of the sower (Mark 4:1-20); "*As* the Father has sent me, *so* I send you" (John 20:21)
Images, symbols, metaphors	Expression of a secondary idea distinct from the original meaning of the term	"Olive tree" (Romans 11:24); "living water" (John 4:11)
Cause to effect	Progression from the reason for an action or condition to the result; a situation that leads to a response; sometimes indicated by use of *so that, that* or *immediately*	Paralytic obeying Jesus' command to stand up (Luke 5:24-25); "Suddenly there was an earthquake, so violent that the foundations of the prison were shaken; and *immediately* all the doors were opened" (Acts 16:26)
General to specific	Movement from a general idea or activity to particulars about that idea	"The LORD is my shepherd, I shall not want" followed by specific ways the author is cared for by the Lord (Psalm 23)
Climax	Progression from lesser to greater to greatest	Tempted by desire, desire conceived, sin birthed, sin fully grown, sin gives birth to death (James 1:14-15)

Connection Element	Definition	Example
Reason	Words such as *for, because, since, as* and *whereas* reveal reasoning or explanation	"Blessed are the poor in spirit, *for* theirs is the kingdom of heaven" (Matthew 5:3); "I heard the sound of you in the garden, and I was afraid *because* I was naked" (Genesis 3:10)
Inference	A conclusion based on an event or statement; often indicated by use of *therefore, wherefore, consequently* or *accordingly*	"Many of the Jews *therefore,* who had come with Mary and had seen what Jesus did, believed in him" (John 11:45); "Be perfect, *therefore,* as your heavenly Father is perfect" (Matthew 5:48)
Condition	A statement that is only true or will happen if something else is true or happens; indicated by *if, if . . . then* or *provided that*	"*If* you love me, you will keep my commandments" (John 14:15)
Temporal statements	The relationship between an action and the time the action can come to pass; indicated by *when, then* or *whenever*	"Blessed are you *when* people revile you and persecute you" (Matthew 5:11)

Adapted from Robert Traina, *Methodical Bible Study* (Grand Rapids: Zondervan, 1980), pp. 50-52.

time, primary events, action, Old Testament allusions and numbers. Being methodical in this way always brings to light valuable information. However, most people don't naturally work like that. When sitting down to study a fresh manuscript, they look for elements of all three simultaneously. This usually works quite well, especially in a small group setting where observations are pooled by a group.

OBSERVING FROM WITHIN

Another way to observe a passage is to use your imagination. By imagining being in the story as one of the characters or a bystander, we are able to use more of our senses in the task of paying attention. I think of this as "observing from within." Envisioning a scene or putting ourselves in the shoes of a character enables us to be alert to the drama of the story and to feel its significance.

People have been created by God with the ability to be both analytical and creative (left- and right-brained). Too often in approaching the Bible we use only one side of our brain. Inductive study has the

Luke 19:1-10

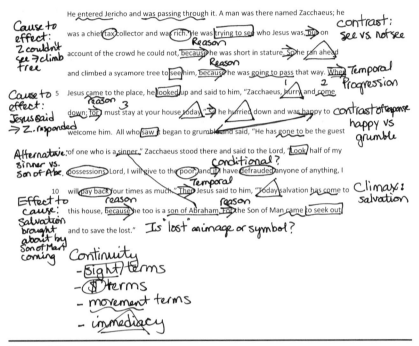

Figure 8.3.

reputation of being highly analytical, but there is no reason it has to be exclusively so. We perceive and learn best when all of our minds (and hearts too) are fully engaged. So learning to use our imaginations when studying the Bible is imperative. Chapter eighteen provides further explanation of the value of engaging our imagination in inductive study and suggests some creative exercises that aid that process.

PRACTICUM
Pay Attention

Using this manuscript and some colored pens, look closely at this passage and mark your observations. Make sure to observe context, content and connections, and refer back to tables 8.1, 8.2 and 8.3.

Mark 4:35-41

On that day, when evening had come, he said to them, "Let us go across to the other side." And leaving the crowd behind, they took him with them in the boat, just as he was. Other boats were with him. A great windstorm arose, and the waves beat into the boat, so that the boat was
5   already being swamped. But he was in the stern, asleep on the cushion; and they woke him up and said to him, "Teacher, do you not care that we are perishing?" He woke up and rebuked the wind, and said to the sea, "Peace! Be still!" Then the wind ceased, and there was a dead calm. He said to them, "Why are you afraid? Have you still no faith?" And
10 they were filled with great awe and said to one another, "Who then is this, that even the wind and the sea obey him?"

9

Curiosity

I noticed the moving sale sign out of the corner of my eye while I was running through my neighborhood on a Saturday morning. I usually try to avoid stopping at yard sales because I inevitably bring home some great "bargain" that soon finds its way to the Goodwill store. But this sign was in front of a classy home that I've often admired from the curb. I hesitated to stop in the midst of my run, but I reasoned with myself that the owners of that beautiful house might have some great treasures. Honestly, more than my desire to find a bargain, my curiosity about what their home looked like on the inside and what very wealthy people might be getting rid of is what propelled me up their long driveway in all my sweaty glory.

Curiosity has that effect on us. It causes us to override other objections and venture a little further to investigate. Curiosity is the reason that Wikipedia is one of the top websites in the world. Curiosity fuels inquisitive behaviors such as exploration, investigation and learning. Scientists, artists, inventors, creative writers, journalists, explorers and others driven by the desire to know new things enrich our world with their discoveries, innovations and insights. Likewise, social gatherings and travel tours are made more lively and interesting when curious people are present.

Posing a question about our surroundings or the people we encounter often leads to rich discoveries. I recently found myself on a road trip with a group of women from my church. One woman, April, was relatively new to the church, and this was my first opportunity to interact with her. I asked her a few questions. "I can tell you have an accent, but I don't recognize it. Where did you grow up?"

"Kenya," she replied.

"What brought you to the United States?"

I expected that she would say, "I have family here," or "I came for college." Instead I was mildly shocked when April said, "Commercial pilot school." When I picture the pilots in the cockpit of my plane, I have never envisioned an African woman behind the controls.

As the mile markers on the interstate sped by, April and I engaged in animated conversation. My initial questions led to many more—about flight school, her life in Kenya and her other interests. I learned that April is an avid soccer player; she sings in a gospel choir and acts in community theater. The more I asked, the more I discovered about this talented, smart, confident young woman.

At its root, curiosity is an emotion. It is the desire to know or learn, an urge to seek and find, a drive to know new things.

> Deeply curious people put themselves in the posture of a learner almost all of the time. They are full of questions, always wanting to know more and constantly expanding their understanding of all kinds of subjects. They listen and absorb information, thoughts, and perspectives different from their own.[1]

I am convinced that curiosity is fundamental to a vibrant life, meaningful relationships and transformative Bible study.

GOOD LITTLE MONKEY

Children are inherently curious. Through exploring their surroundings, they come to make sense of the world. Some maintain that God-given quality into adulthood, but too many of us let curiosity languish. We are subtly (and sometimes explicitly) taught that curiosity is bothersome or even dangerous. The folk saying "Curiosity killed the cat" belies this attitude.

Remember Curious George, the cartoon monkey in children's books? Curious George inevitably gets into trouble because he explores the world around him, often making a mess in the process. Every book in the series begins with "George was a good little monkey, but always very curious." When reading these books to my children, I changed the sentence to "George was a good little monkey *and* always very curious" because I wanted my children to grow up with a sense of wonder about the world and the expectation that their "why?" and "how?" questions would be greeted warmly by adults, rather than brushed off.

> "What distinguishes humans from all other species is that capacity to formulate questions—and to find answers that lead to more questions."
>
> RONALD KOTULAK, "Answering the Big Questions"

Curiosity is an asset than can be developed by anyone, regardless of their economic, educational or social status. Here are some of the benefits of curiosity:

1. It makes your mind active instead of passive.
2. It makes your mind observant of new ideas.
3. It opens up new worlds and possibilities.
4. It fuels creativity.

The mind is like a muscle which gets stronger with exercise. Those that proactively exercise their mind through active learning, stimulating experiences and problem solving have a vibrancy that is attractive. Curiosity brings excitement into life. Furthermore, learning is more enjoyable to those who are curious. As Albert Einstein reportedly said, "The important thing is to not stop questioning. Never lose a holy curiosity."

"GOD SAID IT. I BELIEVE IT. THAT SETTLES IT."

Tragically, this is not the message that many of us have received from the church. Those that ask questions are viewed as troublemakers. Historically, questions have been regarded as a challenge to the church authorities. In religious systems that are hierarchical, those in positions of leadership are viewed as speaking for God, and their interpretations of the Scripture are sacrosanct. The clergy and theologians determine what is true and right; the faithful are those who accept the teachings of the church without question. This attitude can be found in every form of Christianity whether it be Eastern Orthodox, Roman Catholic, Protestant or Pentecostal. A popular fundamentalist bumper sticker in the 1970s captures the sentiment: "God said it. I believe it. That settles it."

In medieval Europe, priests and monks were viewed as the only trustworthy mediators of biblical truth because the vast majority of people were illiterate. Even in denominations that trace their roots to Martin Luther, the man whose questions catalyzed the Protestant Reformation, there can be an overemphasis on learning from experts rather than asking genuine questions and seeking for answers. Christians are encouraged to study the Bible, but this often boils down to reading commentaries or the notes in a study Bible rather than studying the text directly. When I was in college, a relative criticized me for leading a Bible study with my peers. She believed that if I didn't have a theology degree, I wasn't qualified to teach the Bible. Her challenge reflected the unspoken assumption of many Christians: it is best to leave Bible interpretation to pastors and theologians.

One of the great untold stories of modern missions is the Christian movement among the poor in Bangladesh who have been taught to study the Bible for themselves and not rely solely on the teaching of pastors. Though predominately illiterate, inductive Bible study has been found to be widely successful. As oral learners, they are skilled at remembering what they hear. Thus, after a Bible passage is read aloud a few times, a leader can ask, "What did you observe?" and the congregation can recall all the salient details of the passage. They are invited to ask questions and then discuss together how to answer their questions from the text. Just as in a manuscript study, the leader keeps the text at the center and lets the group develop its interpretation, rather than telling the group what the "right" answer is. Their capacity to listen, ask significant questions and think critically enables them to engage God's Word for themselves, even though they can't read.

HOLY CURIOSITY

Many believers have little confidence in their ability to faithfully interpret the Scripture. This lack of confidence (or fear of getting it wrong) shuts down curiosity and undermines vibrant Bible study. Is this what God intended? Does God view curiosity as threatening or impertinent? Were people meant to leave their innately inquisitive nature at the door when they join the church? I believe emphatically that this is not the case. God loves it when we ask questions of him (and the Scripture) if we are asking with a sincere and seeking heart.

Consider Abraham, who received a powerful sign of God's covenant of grace when he asked God the question, "O LORD God, how am I to know that I shall possess it?" (Genesis 15:8-17). Likewise, Moses' relationship with God went deeper at two crucial points in the exodus story: when he asked God, "What is your name?" (Exodus 3:13), and when he asked God to "show me your glory" (Exodus 33:18). The psalmist, who lived close to God's heart, was full of questions (e.g., Psalm 10:1; 74:1). The book of Habakkuk is structured as a dialogue between the prophet and the Lord. Habakkuk voices his complaints through a series of questions, then waits in faith for God's reply (Habakkuk 1:3, 13; 2:2). Evidently, asking questions is a means of seeking God.

In the New Testament, Peter's great sermon at Pentecost was launched by two questions from the crowd: "How is it that we hear, each of us, in our native language?" and "What does this mean?" (Acts 2:8, 12). When reading from the scroll of Isaiah, the Ethiopian eunuch asked Philip, "About whom . . . does the prophet say this, himself or someone else?" (Acts 8:34). Much of Paul's letter of 1 Corinthians seems to be a response to a series of questions the church has asked him (1 Corinthians 7:1, 25; 8:1; 12:1; 16:1). In the early church, question asking led to salvation and spiritual growth.

> "One cannot simply read the Bible, like other books. One must be prepared really to enquire of it. Only thus will it reveal itself. Only if we expect from it the ultimate answer, shall we receive it."
>
> DIETRICH BONHOEFFER

Of all the characters in the Bible, the one who seemed to love questions the most was Jesus. He commended those that stayed after public lectures and asked him about the meaning of his parables, saying that the questioners had found the secret of the kingdom of God (Mark 4:10-11). In fact, he got angry at the Pharisees when they stopped asking questions and were silent (Mark 3:5). He often answered a question with a question, moving the discussion deeper to the heart of the matter (Mark 2:18-19, 24-25). Jesus summarized his view of questions when he told his disciples specifically and clearly to "ask, and it will be given you; search, and you will find; knock, and the door will be opened to you" (Matthew 7:7-8). Jesus not only welcomed asking and seeking, he commanded it.

POSTURE OF THE HEART

Questions are invaluable to the spiritual life. However, there is a type of question asking that is not honored by God: the question that is not accompanied by a willingness to learn or change. In the Garden of Eden, the serpent asked the woman, "Did God say, 'You shall not eat from any tree in the garden'?" (Genesis 3:1). His intention was to undermine God's credibility, not to know God better. The Pharisees asked Jesus, "Is it lawful for a man to divorce his wife?" not out of sincere motives but as a way of testing him (Mark 10:2).

Jesus always discerned the difference in a person's motivations as they asked him questions, and he responded accordingly. After clearing the Temple courts, he refused to answer those who asked angrily, "By what authority are you doing these things?" (Mark 11:27-33). But to the teacher of the law who asked, "Which commandment is the first of all?" he engaged in dialogue and publicly affirmed him by saying, "You are not far from the kingdom of God" (Mark 12:28-34). The difference is the state of the heart behind the question.

The Bible places great importance on the heart. Moses urged the people of Israel to "circumcise . . . your heart . . . and do not be stubborn any longer" (Deuteronomy 10:16). When the Lord instructed Samuel to anoint the young shepherd boy David, he said, "[Mortals] look on the outward appearance, but the LORD looks at the heart" (1 Samuel 16:7). God promised his people that a day would come when he "will give them one heart" (Jeremiah 32:39). When challenging the religious leaders of his day, Jesus quoted Isaiah 29:13: "These people . . . honor me with their lips, while their hearts are far from me" (Mark 7:6).

In the Synoptic Gospels (Matthew, Mark, Luke), the quality of the heart is a central concern. Those that are unteachable and opposed to Jesus are described as having hard hearts. In the Gospel of Mark, this assessment is made of both the Pharisees (Mark 3:5) and the disciples (Mark 6:52). The image is filled out more extensively by Jesus' parable of the sower, which we have already considered in chapter one. Hard hearts are like the path. The seed of God's Word can't even begin to grow, much less bear any fruit, because the soil is packed hard. Conversely, the good soil stands for "the ones who, when they hear the word, hold it fast in an honest and good heart, and bear fruit with patient endurance" (Luke 8:15). This soil is soft and receptive to the Word. Because of their willingness to respond and change, people with soft hearts are able to be fruitful in their Christian lives. If we examine our hearts as we ask questions, we can weed out cynicism and self-protection, and open ourselves to sincere learning.

SHARPEN UP

Once we give ourselves permission to be fully curious and have sought the Spirit's help to approach the Bible with a soft heart, the next step is to strengthen our ability in question asking. Learning to ask good questions is a valuable skill in inductive Bible study (and in the rest of life). To grow in our question asking involves learning how to hone our questions and how to ask a broader range of questions. We will consider honing first; in the following section, we will look at various types of questions and reflect on their value for Bible study.

Honing is the process of sharpening or smoothing. Knives and swords can be honed on a whetstone to sharpen their edge and make them more effective. A stand-up comedian becomes funnier when she hones her comedic timing. In Bible study, honing our questions is the process of making them more effective. Well-formed questions unlock a passage so much more effectively than poorly formed ones. In Bible study, honed questions capture the tension of the text, are open-ended and are relevant.

Often, a question first emerges in our minds as "Huh?" or "I don't get it." Imprecise or abstract questions indicate that we have found a point of intrigue in the text but that we haven't thought about what troubles us long enough to identify what is at the core of our interest. For example, when we read at the beginning of the Gospel of Mark, "Now John was clothed with camel's hair and wore a leather belt around this waist and ate locusts and wild honey" (Mark 1:6) we wonder, "What's up with this guy?" The text practically begs us to ask a question here. There is something strange about this character.

But "What's up?" is a very fuzzy question. To turn our curiosity into a really good question, we must identify more precisely what is strange about this description of John the Baptist. Learning how to ask sharp questions involves putting your finger on what specifically intrigues, perplexes or is unclear to you. The strange element in this verse is the camel's hair (sounds itchy) and the locusts (yuck). Our attention has been caught about how he dresses and eats. So, more helpful questions about John the Baptist would be, "Why are these details about John's clothing and diet included in the story?" or "What would this description of his appearance and eating habits mean to the people of his day?"

Exploring the answer to either of those questions will lead us to discover that Elijah was described in exactly the same way (see 2 Kings 1:7-8). And once we discover that Mark is pointing out some connection between John and Elijah, a whole host of fruitful questions present themselves: Are there other aspects of this passage that allude to Elijah in some way? What is similar about the ministries of John the Baptist and Elijah? What do the prophecies about Elijah and the Messiah say? (In the coming chapters we will consider how to find the information that will enable us to answer these questions, so I won't cover that yet.)

One thoughtful, well-articulated question leads us further down the path on our treasure hunt through the Scriptures than a handful of vague and imprecise questions. If we take the time to ponder a troubling phrase, sentence or passage long enough for the problem to become clear in our mind we can unlock the meaning of the text. Let me offer another example from a few verses further in Mark's Gospel.

Mark 1:14-15 is an important transition between Jesus' temptation in the wilderness and his public ministry. We might ask, "Why does Jesus say, 'The kingdom of God has come near; repent and believe in the good news'?" This is a fine question on a basic level. In fact, "Why?" questions make up a large percentage of the questions we ask in Bible study. But our basic "Why?" questions can be made more helpful if we ponder the text a little more. Rather than asking "Why does Jesus say this?" we could ask "Why would 'repent and believe in the gospel' be the appropriate response to the kingdom of God being at hand?" In doing the work of honing our question, we have had to notice that Jesus' proclamation is made of two parts: an announcement and a command. The question is stronger because we are considering the causal relationship between parts of Jesus' statement. When we ask about the response Jesus asks for, we are much better situated to explore what his proclamation of the kingdom of God connotes and implies.

Notice that the examples of good questions we have considered are open-ended, meaning that the answers will be beyond a simple "yes" or "no." Questions that can be answered with a simple affirmative or negative bring our thinking to a halt rather than pushing us further. Good questions press us deeper into the text. For example, if I asked, "Is John the messenger prophesied by Isaiah?" (Mark 1:2), the answer "yes" doesn't unlock more of the text. But if I turn it into an open-ended question (such as "Why does Mark begin the Gospel with this quote from Isaiah?"), there are five or six reasons that can be drawn from the passage.

Another characteristic of good questions in Bible study are ones that are relevant to the story or line of reasoning. Irrelevant questions are tangential rather than central to a passage. You can tell if a question is a tangent if thinking about it takes you away from the text rather than into it. For example, in your curiosity about John's diet, you might wonder, "What do locusts taste like?" or "How long could a man survive eating only locusts and honey?" To satisfy your curiosity, you could read about cultures that eat locusts by doing a quick Google search or listen to someone in your small group share about a wilderness survival show on the Discovery Channel. However, answering those questions won't actually help you dig further into Mark 1. When a tangential question is asked in a small group, it's best to chuckle together, name it as a tangent and move on to a more relevant question.

So effective students of the Bible open the flood gates of their curiosity, but then they direct their exploration through honing their questions. They clarify the tension and make sure their questions are open-ended and relevant. This might seem like a lot of work, but putting the effort in at this point of the study will pay off later.

The process of turning so-so questions into really good ones can be done when studying by yourself when you go back to your first set of questions and rewrite them as needed. It can also be done communally. This can be a lot of fun as someone throws out an initial question and then the group hones it together. The process of sharpening your questions will begin to bring understanding of the text, even before you attempt to answer them.

BROADEN OUT

In addition to well-honed questions, Bible study is aided by having a sufficient *range* of questions. In a woodworking shop, different tools accomplish different tasks. The same is true of questions in Bible study. Developing our skills in Bible study includes learning to use a broader selection of tools. Questions about a passage of the Bible can be sorted into four different categories, as seen in table 9.1.

Table 9.1. Question Types in Bible Study

Question Type	Goal	Description
Type 1	To SEE the text more fully	Questions that help us to envision the scene.
Type 2	To RELATE the text to our lives	Questions that make a connection between ourselves and the characters.
Type 3	To UNDERSTAND a part of the text	Questions that explore the tension or points of intrigue in the text.
Type 4	To UNDERSTAND the text as a whole	Questions that reveal how different sections of the text relate to each other.

People are often more drawn to one of the types than another. Consider a hypothetical small group Bible study whose members are named Joe, Amber, Clint and Joan. The first question out of Joe's mouth always begins with "Why?" Joe asks things like, "Why is Jesus so harsh toward the Pharisees?" or "Why does Jesus answer the man's question with a question?" Joe's "Why" questions are type three questions.

Amber, on the other hand, asks type one questions. She wants to know, "Who are the Herodians?" or "At Jesus' baptism, could the crowd hear the voice from heaven, or only Jesus?"

Clint is most interested in the implications of a passage for our lives. He is eager to ask type two questions, like "Does Jesus really expect us to turn the other cheek?" or "Does this passage mean that I will receive anything I pray for?"

Joan likes to step back and ask broader questions like, "Why would the author put these two stories next to each other?" or "How is Mary's experience with the angel different than Zechariah's?" Joan's questions are type four questions.

All four types of questions are needed in inductive Bible study, but we don't always ask all four types unless we are being intentional about it. Part of the benefit and blessing of studying the Bible in community is that a group is more likely to cover a broad range of questions and thus explore a passage more thoroughly. However, individuals can have extensive personal study if they pay attention to the type of questions they are asking and press themselves to ask all four types of questions every time they sit down to do inductive Bible study.

Notice the quality and the range of questions in the manuscript of Luke 19:1-10 as shown in figure 9.1. I have written them near to the part of the text they refer to and have included a number to indicate their type.

Growing in Bible study involves learning to ask honed questions of the text and becoming more thorough in our question asking. Just as a competitive tennis player needs to develop their backhand swing as well as their forehand, it is invaluable to develop your question asking skills. As you formulate questions, your curiosity will grow and the process of discovery will be all the more rewarding. As noted by social psychologist Robert Cialdini, "The *Aha!* experience is much more satisfying when it is preceded by the *Huh?* experience."[2]

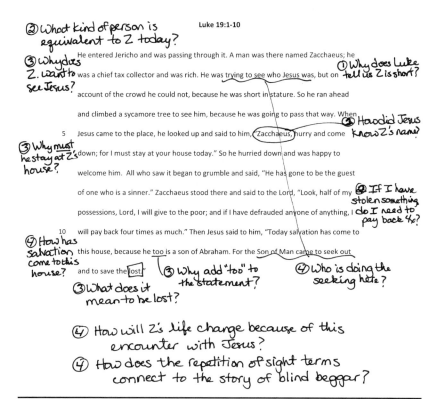

② What kind of person is equivalent to Z today?

Luke 19:1-10

③ Why does Z. want to see Jesus?

① Why does Luke tell us Z is short?

He entered Jericho and was passing through it. A man was there named Zacchaeus; he was a chief tax collector and was rich. He was trying to see who Jesus was, but on account of the crowd he could not, because he was short in stature. So he ran ahead and climbed a sycamore tree to see him, because he was going to pass that way. When Jesus came to the place, he looked up and said to him, "Zacchaeus, hurry and come down; for I must stay at your house today." So he hurried down and was happy to welcome him. All who saw it began to grumble and said, "He has gone to be the guest of one who is a sinner." Zacchaeus stood there and said to the Lord, "Look, half of my possessions, Lord, I will give to the poor; and if I have defrauded anyone of anything, I will pay back four times as much." Then Jesus said to him, "Today salvation has come to this house, because he too is a son of Abraham. For the Son of Man came to seek out and to save the lost."

③ How did Jesus know Z's name?

③ Why must he stay at Z's house?

④ If I have stolen something do I need to pay back 4x?

④ How has salvation come to this house?

③ Why add "too" to the statement?

④ Who is doing the seeking here?

③ What does it mean to be lost?

④ How will Z's life change because of this encounter with Jesus?

④ How does the repetition of sight terms connect to the story of blind beggar?

Figure 9.1.

PRACTICUM
Curiosity

Using this manuscript, write eight well-honed questions. Try to write at least one question of each type listed in table 9.1.

Mark 4:35-41

On that day, when evening had come, he said to them, "Let us go across to the other side." And leaving the crowd behind, they took him with them in the boat, just as he was. Other boats were with him. A great windstorm arose, and the waves beat into the boat, so that the boat was
5 already being swamped. But he was in the stern, asleep on the cushion; and they woke him up and said to him, "Teacher, do you not care that we are perishing?" He woke up and rebuked the wind, and said to the sea, "Peace! Be still!" Then the wind ceased, and there was a dead calm. He said to them, "Why are you afraid? Have you still no faith?" And
10 they were filled with great awe and said to one another, "Who then is this, that even the wind and the sea obey him?"

10

Understanding

My daughter recently asked me to rent an action/adventure movie to watch while she lay on the couch recovering from a cold. I wasn't planning on watching it with her, but after the first five minutes I was hooked. My curiosity had been piqued. What was happening to the main character? Why did he see someone else's face when he looked in the mirror? Why did the woman next to him on the train consider him a friend when he clearly didn't recognize her? Why did he claim to be a helicopter pilot, when the identity card in his wallet showed that he was a history teacher? I was confused but interested, and so I kicked off my shoes and curled up on the couch alongside my sniffling teen.

Like most good stories, *Source Code* had caught my interest through confusion and intrigue. It showed me an appealing character in an odd situation and gave me enough information to get my attention, but not enough to be self-explanatory. Like a trail of crumbs through the forest, new bits of information and a slowly growing understanding pulled me throughout the story line until finally, at the end, there was clarity. (Well, at least the central questions were answered. Several new questions were left for the audience to ponder.)

The Bible is full of great stories. Most of them are dramatic, intriguing and unexpected. Just imagine reading the book of Genesis for the very first time. If you had never heard the story of Adam and Eve, your attention would be caught by the presence of two mysterious trees, a talking serpent and the Lord's ominous statement, "In the day you eat of it you will surely die." What happens next? Why don't they drop dead when they eat the forbidden fruit? What will happen to the man and the woman once they are expelled from the garden? Just like a good movie, our interest is caught and we want to read more.

Unfortunately, many of us have lost the sense of the drama and intrigue of the Bible. Our basic familiarity with the stories has become an obstacle. We think we already know what happens and what it means. We read because we know we should, but if we are honest, we are already a little bored before we begin. One of the reasons inductive Bible study is so powerful is that it wakes us up to the intrigue of the biblical narratives. If you pay attention to the text by observing closely, and if you let your curiosity go to town on what you see, by the end of the observation stage you should be more confused (and more interested) than when you started.

Once you are confused enough or are asking real questions, your mind is engaged and you are ready to pursue understanding. As my friend Shawn Young says, "Questions lead to understanding and understanding leads to a deeper faith. Probably the most crucial thing you can do to develop a stronger faith in God is to ask lots of questions."[1]

PATH OF UNDERSTANDING

The interpretation phase of inductive Bible study is the process of moving from confusion to clarity. It involves putting together all the small bits of information that have been observed and working toward

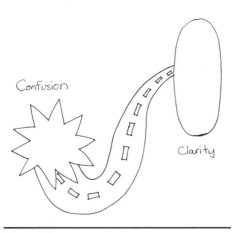

a general conclusion about the text. The goal of interpretation is to discover a coherent whole that holds together the various parts in a harmonious unity. As renowned ichthyologist Dr. Agassiz once said to his student, "Facts are stupid things . . . until brought into connection with some general law."[2]

Figure 10.1.

Imagine yourself on a journey, setting out from a starting place, walking down a winding road and arriving at your destination. In inductive Bible study, the process of observation creates the starting place; interpretation happens as you define terms, envision the drama, answer questions using the text and summarize the core message. The starting place is characterized by confusion, the destination by clarity. (See figure 10.1.)

In this chapter we will consider how to take the context, content and connections of the text (see chapter eight) and use your well-honed questions (see chapter nine) to engage the text and create a coherent summary of the core message. The following sections will provide a step-by-step explanation of the process. At the end of the chapter I will describe the "guardrails" along the path to understanding that help us from driving off the road.

On the path to understanding we attempt to answer the question, "How do the things we've observed relate?" A good interpretation of a passage of the Bible is coherent and whole. It takes into account all of the details and makes their relationship to one another clear. Like assembling a jigsaw puzzle, our interpretation makes sense if there aren't any holes or pieces left over.

> "People never think until they are faced with a problem. The essence of inductive Bible study, in fact, is to look at statements in Scripture long enough until one becomes troubled about something and then to try out various possibilities until one is found that makes things cohere."
>
> DANIEL P. FULLER, *Unity of the Bible*

This process of synthesizing the various parts into a clear whole takes time. It requires patient listening to the text, to the community gathered around the text and to the voice of the Holy Spirit. Our understanding of the text is often incomplete, shallow or just plain wrong because we haven't taken time to linger with the text, trying out various arrangements and staying with it until a coherent picture emerges. This poem from the nineteenth century captures the spirit of this process.

> Who sees a truth must often gaze
> Into a fog for many days'
> It may seem very sure to him
> Nothing is there but mist-clouds dim.
> Then, suddenly, his eyes will see
> A shape where nothing used to be.
> Discoveries are missed each day
> By men who turn too soon away.[3]

ROADMAP

When learning how to interpret passages from the Bible, it can be helpful to follow a step-by-step process. This is a little like using training wheels on a bicycle. Helpful at first, they can be discarded when no longer necessary. This seven-step "Interpretation Roadmap" will train you in the elements of the interpretative process. The actual experience, particularly in a group discussion, is much more fluid and the first six steps are often interwoven.

> ## Interpretation Roadmap
>
> 1. Identify units of thought
> 2. Define the genre
> 3. Define words and concepts
> 4. Look up OT references
> 5. Envision the drama
> 6. Answer remaining questions
> 7. Identify core message

Step 1: Identify units of thought. One way of paying attention to the way the author is building a story or argument is to recognize the units of thought (akin to paragraphs) that make up a larger section. In a printed Bible, an editor arranges the text into paragraphs to ease the reading experience. However, these are implicitly interpretative and not a feature of original biblical manuscripts. Manuscript study helps us to not be artificially influenced by the editorial decisions of others. (For more explanation about the features of a manuscript and how to format one, see chapter thirteen.) "Re-paragraphing" rather than having it done for us provides an opportunity to discover the structure and flow of a passage.

A new unit of thought is indicated by a clear *change* in location, time, characters or topic. After you have observed as much as you can and have written several good questions, take another look at the text and break the text into smaller units. Your proposed thought breaks may or may not correspond to traditional paragraph breaks; for example, in inductive study a change of speaker isn't necessarily an indication of a new unit of thought, as in John 4:7-26, where a back-and-forth interaction between Jesus and the Samaritan woman would conventionally require thirteen paragraph breaks. I would break this dialogue into three units of thought based on shift of topic in the discussion: thirst/water (vv. 7-15), husbands (vv. 16-18) and true worship (vv. 19-26).

As you mark breaks in the text (on a manuscript they can be drawn as a dark line between sections), write a short name for each unit. The name should capture the central action or theme of the paragraph. Identifying the change explicitly helps us to see the scene more clearly and to observe elements of content we might have overlooked. Noticing the progression of Jesus' conversation with the woman at the well—from water to her relational history to true worship—sheds light on Jesus' intentions in asking her for a drink. The process of marking and labeling units of thought presses us further in observing and helps us to begin seeing how our various observations relate to one another; it is the bridge step between the observation and interpretation phases of inductive Bible study.

I find it helpful to make a distinction between major and minor thought breaks. Major breaks generally come between scenes. For example, chapter 19 of Luke's Gospel has four major breaks. They come between verses 10 and 11 (change of topic but not of location or audience), between verses 27 and 28 (change of location and primary action), between verses 40 and 41 (change in characters and topic), and between verses 44 and 45 (change in location). By tracking the various shifts in the text and labeling them, you will be able to see how the sections relate or build on one another.

Luke 19:1-10 is a complete unit, but I see two minor breaks: one when Jesus arrives at the base of Zacchaeus's tree, and another after Zacchaeus's pledge of restitution. In the opening lines, Jesus is on his way but not actually present. The characters in this section are Zacchaeus and the crowd. The primary event is Zacchaeus's tree climbing. I'd name the paragraph "Z. is eager to see Jesus."

The change on line five is indicated by the phrase "When Jesus came to the place . . ." The paragraph is comprised of Jesus' request and the various responses it garners. I might name the paragraph "Jesus' initiative elicits responses." I would make another minor break just before Jesus makes his closing statement—"Today salvation has come . . ."—because I see that as a summary of the entire scene and not merely the close of his dialogue with Zacchaeus. I'd choose the title "Jesus gives interpretation." (See figure 10.2.)

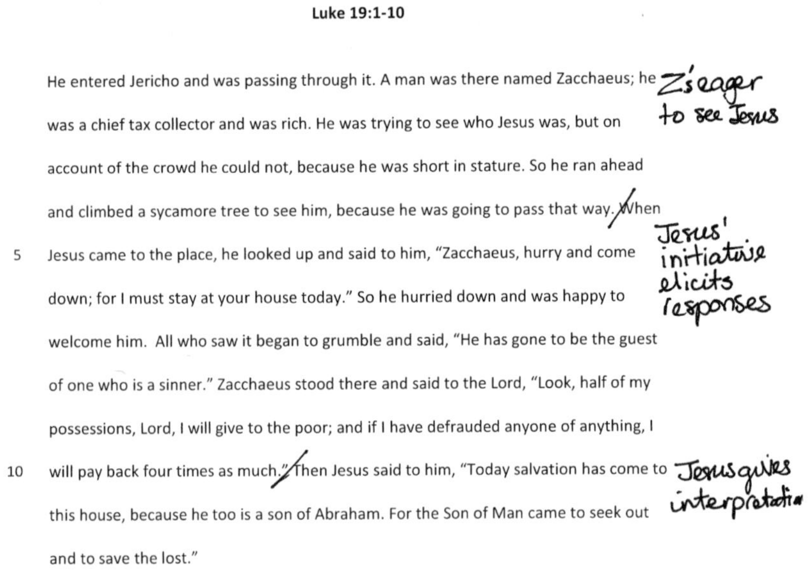

Luke 19:1-10

He entered Jericho and was passing through it. A man was there named Zacchaeus; he *Z's eager to see Jesus*

was a chief tax collector and was rich. He was trying to see who Jesus was, but on

account of the crowd he could not, because he was short in stature. So he ran ahead

and climbed a sycamore tree to see him, because he was going to pass that way. When *Jesus' initiative elicits responses*

5   Jesus came to the place, he looked up and said to him, "Zacchaeus, hurry and come

down; for I must stay at your house today." So he hurried down and was happy to

welcome him. All who saw it began to grumble and said, "He has gone to be the guest

of one who is a sinner." Zacchaeus stood there and said to the Lord, "Look, half of my

possessions, Lord, I will give to the poor; and if I have defrauded anyone of anything, I

10   will pay back four times as much. Then Jesus said to him, "Today salvation has come to *Jesus gives interpretation*

this house, because he too is a son of Abraham. For the Son of Man came to seek out

and to save the lost."

Figure 10.2.

Step 2: Define the genre. Genre is a literary term that means "form of writing." Genres "constitute more or less formal and implicit 'contracts' between authors and their audiences, launching certain expectations for interpreting particular texts."[4] Once form is recognized, a reader adjusts his or her expectations about how to read and understand the text at hand.

Thinking about genre might sound academic, but the reality is that we encounter different genres every day: advertisements, magazines, children's books, grocery labels, blogs, text messages and so on. We instinctively know how to adjust our reading and interpretation when switching between a Wikipedia article and a magazine at the dentist's office. We know that the poetry used in a song on the radio will be repetitive and lyrical. We expect the instructions in a recipe to be arranged with the list of ingredients at the beginning, followed by ordered instructions. We know to take all signs claiming "World Famous" with a grain of salt because overstatement is a normal part of advertising. We make these adjustments without even thinking about it because we are familiar with these various genres. When we encounter a genre with which we are less familiar—a Shakespearean play or a legal document—we tend to feel uncomfortable until we learn how this particular form of writing "works."

In chapter fifteen I will describe how to determine the genre of a passage and some of the implications for understanding different genres used in the Bible. Most good study Bibles or Bible dictionaries will include comments about the genre in the background notes for each book of the Bible. The classic book *How to Read the Bible for All Its Worth* is an excellent resource for explaining the implications of genre for interpreting different parts of the Bible.[5]

How does genre affect our understanding of Luke 19:1-10? Since it is a narrative, we might be tempted to skip the step of determining genre. However, doing a little research in a Bible dictionary will bear good fruit in our inductive study of Jesus' encounter with Zacchaeus. The Gospel of Luke is the first of a two-volume work by Luke, a Gentile who joined Paul's missionary band. The genre he used was a little different from that used by the other Gospel writers. His account of the life of Jesus and the growth of the early church was a common genre in his day: the Greco-Roman historiography.

Greco-Roman histories were both entertaining and instructive. Genealogical records, instruction given in the context of meals, travel narratives, speeches and dramatic episodes are their hallmarks. Rather than merely recording historical events, the writer of Greco-Roman histories highlighted their significance. Historiographies were designed to demonstrate the connection between the past and the present, thus providing validation and instruction for a contemporary view or practice.

As previously mentioned, Luke 9:51—19:27 is one long travel narrative and comprises the bulk of Luke's rendition of Jesus' public ministry. When Luke chose to place Zacchaeus's encounter with Jesus at the end of the travel narrative, he was signaling his audience to pay particular attention to this story. As we saw in chapter seven, the story of Zacchaeus is the climax of the larger narrative and in it is found the heart of the entire travel narrative: "For the Son of Man came to seek out and to save the lost" (Luke 19:10).

Since Greco-Roman historiographies were intended to teach and to promote particular practices or values, the original audience would have been asking themselves, "What is it about this story that we should imitate?" When Jesus invited himself over to a known sinner's house, he violated all sorts of social taboos. Perhaps the early church needed this model to help them break through the barriers of fellowship between Jewish and Gentile believers. Indeed, this a dominant theme of Acts, the sequel to Luke.

Step 3: Define words and concepts. Identify any words, phrases or concepts that you don't understand clearly or that might have particular significance for the original author or audience. Many of the questions generated when first looking at a text are of the definitional sort: "What is an ephod?" "Where is Susa?" "How long is a cubit?" Those types of questions are valuable in enabling us to gather the data we need to build an understanding of how the passage would have been heard by its original audience.

Because the Bible was written in a different period of history or uses language that may not be common today, it is important that we identify the words or references we don't understand fully. Look for other places that word is used within the book you are studying. Then consult a Bible dictionary or background commentary.[6] If multiple definitions are given, use the immediate context to help you discern which one seems to be what the author intended here. Immediate context always carries greater weight for discerning a word's meaning than data gathered from more distant contexts (such as general culture of the time).[7]

In studying Luke 19:1-10, the words and phrases I selected to define were *chief tax collector, sycamore tree, Son of Man* and *the lost*. I picked these because *chief tax collector* and *Son of Man* aren't common phrases in contemporary American society, so I want to make sure I understand what those meant to the original hearers. I picked *sycamore tree* because it is a major prop in the drama; knowing more will help me to envision the scene more clearly. Finally, *the lost* seems important, since it is part of Jesus' closing purpose statement and might mean more than merely a misplaced object.

From a Bible dictionary I learn that tax collectors were local men who agreed to work for the occupying Roman government. The system was known as tax farming and was used across the Roman Empire, not just in Israel. Tax collectors in each town were commissioned to turn in a certain amount of money periodically. How they collected that money was up to them (toll taxes, per capita taxes, custom taxes, etc.). Whatever was collected beyond the quota went into their pockets. The citizens had no recourse, since tax levels were set locally rather than by a central government, and since the Roman military was present to back the demands of the tax collector. A *chief* tax collector was akin to a district manager, overseeing many tax collectors and interacting more directly with the Roman government. Since Jericho was at the crossroads of several trading routes, the position of chief tax collector there was particularly lucrative. Tax collectors were despised as traitors who got rich at the expense of their kinsmen and participated in oppression.

A little research reveals that the sycamore tree referred to here is not the same as the North American sycamore or European-Asian sycamore maple.[8] A relative of the fig tree, this sycamore had a sturdy trunk and low branches, making it easy to climb. Its large leaves made it a convenient place to find some privacy, thus it was that the sycamore fig was often used as a place of prayer and meditation.

By using a concordance, I can see that *Son of Man* is used twenty-four times in Luke. Every time it is used by Jesus to describe himself. I find this very interesting. Why would Jesus choose to use this phrase when nobody else does? Under the heading "Jesus Christ, Titles of" in the *New Bible Dictionary* I discover that the significance of the phrase *Son of Man* is derived from Daniel 7:13-14, which describes the figure at the last judgment who is given authority over all nations and peoples: "His kingship is one that shall never be destroyed" (Daniel 7:14). It is a messianic title but since it was a lesser-used phrase, it didn't carry the same assumptions and associations that accompanied the term *Messiah* (which might be why Jesus preferred it).[9]

In English, *lost* has multiple meanings. A lost object is overlooked, no longer possessed or known, not appreciated or understood. A person can be lost in the sense of being ruined, hardened, or physically and morally destroyed. *Lost* can also mean helpless, unable to find the way, no longer visible, or lacking assurance or self-confidence. When Jesus refers to Zacchaeus as an example of *the lost*, which sense does he have in mind? Using a concordance and a Greek dictionary, I learn that the Greek word for *lost* used in Luke means "destroyed" or "perished." This bit of information seems to point to the sense of being ruined or destroyed rather than overlooked or misunderstood.

Step 4: Look up Old Testament quotations or allusions, and consider how the author is using them. A Bible with cross-references is a useful tool in identifying Old Testament references or allusions. When you look up an Old Testament reference, make sure to read the surrounding verses or chapter to understand its context. Ask yourself, *What are the similarities between the passage referenced and the passage I am studying?* and *Is there something implied but not said directly through using these references?*

For example, when Jesus was criticized by the Pharisees for his disciples' gleaning practices (Mark 2:23-28) Jesus told a story from 1 Samuel 21:1-6, in which David asks Abiathar the high priest to give him the bread of the Presence to feed his troops. Jesus doesn't cite this merely as an example of someone else who broke the law for good purpose. The context of the 1 Samuel story is David's flight when King Saul is attempting to murder him. By comparing the context of the two passages, we can see that Jesus is claiming to be like David, the new king anointed by the Lord. He subtly communicates to the Pharisees that their spiritual authority over Israel has been retracted like Saul's, and that he knows of the murderous intentions in their hearts.

When studying Luke 19:1-11, a Bible with cross-references shows that there are Old Testament allusions in reference to Zacchaeus's statement, "Look, half of my possessions, Lord, I will give to the poor; and if I have defrauded anyone of anything, I will pay back four times as much" (Luke 19:8). Exodus 22:1 states that the thief "shall pay five oxen for an ox, and four sheep for a sheep." The context is a list of laws about making restitution for stealing. Likewise, Leviticus 6:5 and Numbers 5:6-7 are laws about restitution and say that if fraud is committed, the principal is to be repaid with an additional 20 percent. Thus, we can now understand that Zacchaeus is taking full responsibility for his sin against his fellow Jews and that he is promising to go over and above the requirements of the law in making restitution.

Additionally, "to seek out and to save the lost" resonates with Ezekiel 34, that great messianic passage promising that God himself will be the just and righteous shepherd his people have been lacking. "For thus says the Lord GOD: I myself will search for my sheep, and will seek them out" (v. 11). Verse 16 begins with, "I will seek the lost." By using the exact same phrases, Jesus is making a claim of being the fulfillment to Ezekiel 34. Many of the Jewish crowd present would have heard that. In using the phrase "Son of Man" and the language of Ezekiel 34, Jesus is asserting himself to be the Messiah and true Shepherd of the people of Israel.

Step 5: Envision the drama. Inductive study is often viewed as being primarily academic and dry. This is unfortunate as there is no reason why inductive study has to be this way. There is no inherent contradiction between rigorous thinking and vibrant experience. If a study feels stale or abstract, it probably is because we have lost sight of the drama of the text.

I find it helpful to stop periodically in the midst of defining and analyzing to envision the narrative and let the drama come to life. This is done by using your imagination to describe the scene at various points along the story line using the details of the text.

Let's begin by imagining the primary character of our passage. Picture in your mind a short, wealthy, powerful Jewish man in the ancient world. Imagine his expensive robes, flowing beard and perhaps an ostentatious signet ring. Now picture the crowds lining the streets to get a look at Jesus, the traveling rabbi. Remember that earlier this day Jesus restored sight to a loud-mouthed beggar in this very city. Surely the story about that miracle has spread, and the streets are full of people wanting to see Jesus. In fact, those with sick relatives are probably crowded around, hoping Jesus will stop and heal.

One of our questions was "Why does Zacchaeus want to see Jesus?" By envisioning the scene we can answer that now. *Everyone* wants to see Jesus. He has quite a reputation and he has just performed a public miracle. It is probable that Zacchaeus has heard through his networks about Jesus' positive relationships with tax collectors and that he had invited one of them to join his inner circle of disciples (Luke 5:27). At the least, his curiosity has been piqued, but perhaps his sense of spiritual need was also being awakened.

How do you imagine the scene as Zacchaeus climbs the tree? I see him standing on tiptoe, trying to see over the crowd. When that doesn't work, he tries to push his way through to get to the front of the crowd. But that doesn't work either, because no one would want to be courteous to him. I picture Zacchaeus looking around for another option when he notices a sycamore tree a little further up the road. Line four tells us that he ran ahead and climbed up (probably lifting up his expensive robes in the process). In most cultures men don't climb trees, but especially not in the ancient Middle East. Zacchaeus is making an utter fool of himself, and he doesn't seem to care. It is likely that he hasn't cared what other people think about him for a very long time, as seen by his choice of profession. He's already viewed as a sinner (line nine), so why not be viewed as undignified as well?

Then comes my favorite part. Jesus and his group of disciples make their way down the street, followers and onlookers crowding around on every side and then, all of a sudden, Jesus stops. (If I were portraying this in a cartoon, I'd show a massive pile-up behind Jesus as one person after another hit the brakes on a busy freeway.) Why does he stop? His eye has caught sight of something in the tree, perhaps a flicker of cloth or a high-quality sandal hanging down from one of the branches.

What is most amazing to me is that Jesus called Zacchaeus by name: "Zacchaeus, hurry and come down" (line six). How does Jesus know his name? Is this a demonstration of omniscience? Or has Jesus overheard people in the crowd mocking Zacchaeus? ("Look at Zacchaeus in that tree. What a bozo. Doesn't he have any self-respect?")

What must Zacchaeus have felt when he heard his name and the famous rabbi inviting himself over for dinner? I imagine a huge grin spreading across his face, a quick jump out of the tree, and lots of bowing and hand shaking. Meanwhile, the crowd turns their judgments on Jesus, grumbling to one another about Jesus' choice in friends. They are offended, thinking, *What kind of a holy man would associate himself with someone as despicable as Zacchaeus?*

Before Jesus even set a foot in his home, Zacchaeus expressed his desire to repent and make restitution. Not a single religious word has come out of Jesus' mouth. Though all Jesus has done is single him out and express his desire to dine at his house, Zacchaeus's response is wholehearted. The scene closes with Jesus publicly affirming Zacchaeus (calling him a son of Abraham) and interpreting for the crowd that the encounter they have just witnessed should be understood as salvation.

Step 6: Answer remaining questions. By this point the passage has become so much clearer than when we began. However, not all of our questions have been addressed. To answer the remaining questions, look back to the text and develop theories that hold multiple observations together. Refrain from the temptation of saying, "My study Bible says it means . . ." or "In a sermon I heard, the pastor said . . ." Referring to other people's interpretations undermines the process of thinking hard and continually looking back to the text. In inductive study we keep the text in the spotlight and make our own interpretations supported directly by the text itself.[10]

It is useful to create two or three options for answering your significant questions. Compile evidence from the text for each option. To build evidence, look to see whether words, phrases, logical connectors, literary features, immediate context, cultural information and so on support one option more heavily than another. Some questions almost answer themselves, since there is so much clear evidence for one option; other questions take more work.

In our study of Luke 19:1-10, eight of our original questions (see figure 9.1) remain unanswered:

- What kind of person is equivalent to Zaccheaus today?
- Why *must* Jesus stay at Zaccheaus's house?
- Why does Jesus add "too" to his interpretation statement?
- What does it mean to be lost?
- Who is doing the seeking in this passage?
- How has salvation come to this house?
- How will Zaccheaus's life change because of this encounter with Jesus?
- How does the repetition of sight terms connect to the story of the blind beggar in Luke 18?

I'll address four of these questions to demonstrate how to answer them using the text. The question *What kind of person is equivalent to Zaccheaus today?* is a type two question and helps bridge the gap between the author's world and ours. I don't see many men walking around in expensive robes, and I have never met an actual tax collector, but in our world there are also people with power who have made a lot of money at others' expense. So perhaps Zaccheaus is like a Las Vegas casino owner or an unethical slum landlord. Definitely not the kind of person you would expect to be interested in Jesus. If we focus on the element of Zaccheaus being a traitor, we could imagine a black policeman in apartheid-era South Africa.

The text says that Jesus' initial statement was, "Zaccheaus, hurry and come down; for I must stay at your house today." Why *must* Jesus stay at Zaccheaus's house? Let's generate a few options. First, Jesus may be in need of a place to stay, and no one else has invited him in. Second, Jesus sees Zaccheaus in the tree and recognizes that Zaccheaus has taken initiative toward him; Jesus is eager to interact with someone with genuine spiritual interest. The third might be that Jesus can tell Zaccheaus is a tax collector, and since his ministry is so successful with tax collectors he decides to take the initiative and see what will happen.

There isn't any evidence in the text that Jesus was intending to stay in Jericho that day (in fact, the first line says he was passing through it), so it doesn't make sense that Jesus was in need and Zacchaeus's house was the best he could do. So option one seems to be ruled out. Option three seems plausible in light of the entire book of Luke, but it doesn't use the details that Luke has provided about Zacchaeus's height challenges or the repetition of urgency in passage (Zacchaeus ran ahead, Jesus told him to hurry down, Zacchaeus hurried down, and the use of "today" in lines seven and eleven). Option two better uses those details, and so Jesus' eager response to Zacchaeus's genuine spiritual interest is the best answer.

Why does Jesus add "too" to his interpretation statement ("Today salvation has come to this house, because he too is a son of Abraham")? "Too" is another way of saying "also." "Sons and daughters of Abraham" is an expression meaning "the people of Israel"—those who have a special covenant with God. This statement is intended to be heard by the crowds. It reminds them that Zacchaeus is one of them. Through his interaction with Jesus, Zacchaeus—who had been a traitor to his people by working for the Romans as a tax collector—isn't only being restored to relationship with God, he's being restored to the family of God as well.

What does it mean to be lost? In step four, we learned that the Greek word means "destroyed" or "perished." Jesus uses it to describe Zacchaeus. The only other time the word *lost* is used in this Gospel is in Luke 15 (vv. 3, 5, 6, 8, 9, 24, 32). I found this out by looking up the word *lost* in a Bible concordance and identifying the places it is used in Luke. (For instructions on using a concordance, see chapter sixteen.)[11] In Luke 15 Jesus tells three parallel parables to describe the state of a sheep, a coin and a son before they are found and restored to their rightful place. Here in Luke 19, for the first time Jesus describes an actual person, not just a character in a parable, as lost. In Luke 15, the younger son asked for his share of the family inheritance, disgraced his Father and ended up starving in a Gentile land. Zacchaeus is not poor, starving or living far from Israel, but *morally* and *spiritually* he has gone far from his God and his people. He is a successful version of the younger son. The father in the parable equates lostness with being dead and being found with restoration to life. In Luke 19:9-10, Jesus interprets his encounter with Zaccheaus as salvation of the lost. Using the context of Luke 15 it becomes clear that Luke uses *lost* to described someone estranged from God and his family, a state of spiritual death.

This comparison to the younger son in the parable invites another question: *What other parallels might we find between Zaccheaus in Luke 19 and the younger son in Luke 15?* Both are Jewish males and identified as a "son" (though Zaccheaus isn't called "son of Abraham" until the end of the story). Both associate themselves with Gentiles: the younger son works for a man who raises pigs, Zaccheaus works for the Romans. This works out well for Zaccheaus but not so well for the prodigal. Both take initiative and indicate a desire to draw near to the authority figure in the story. Furthermore, in both stories the one turned toward responds with greater initiative and grace than is expected. The Father *runs* through the town to welcome his son with an embrace and a feast. Likewise, Jesus changes his plans, stops his journey and calls Zaccheaus by name to invite himself over to his house. In both stories, grumbling (from the older son and the crowds, respectively) is one of the responses to the demonstration of extravagant grace. Both are restored to their family, though Zaccheaus's restoration is to the covenant community, not a biological family.

Step 7: Identify the core message. In this last step along the path of interpretation, we work to draw together all the threads of our study and write a statement that integrates what we have come to understand. What overriding theme or purpose has the author been trying to communicate? This step is incredibly important in crystallizing our insights into a coherent whole. Your statement of the core message will enable you to remember the significance of a passage and provides a hanger for the rest of your insights about the passage. It should use the language of the text and have some punch, rather than being merely a summary of the action.

Start by looking at the titles you gave each paragraph in step one and see if a theme emerges. I labeled the three paragraphs of Luke 19:1-10 "Zaccheaus is eager to see Jesus," "Jesus' initiative elicits responses," and "Jesus gives interpretation." The core message involves the movement of Zaccheaus toward Jesus and of Jesus toward Zaccheaus, and Jesus' understanding of their encounter.

Go back to your manuscript and remind yourself of places you observed climax or reason.[12] By returning to my Luke 19 manuscript (figure 8.3), I'm reminded that the climax of the interaction between Zacchaeus and Jesus was stated by Jesus as "Today salvation has come to this house." The use of the word *for* in the final sentence indicates that Jesus is giving the reason for his entire mission, not just the immediate event: "For the Son of Man came to seek out and save the lost." Putting the themes from our work on *lost* together with these elements, I might state the core message like this: *Jesus demonstrates the Father's heart for the lost by bringing salvation to a man who is both undeniably sinful and yet profoundly repentant.*

There are myriad ways the core message can be stated. Some people enjoy taking the time to wordsmith the core message and create something pithy and memorable. My statement isn't particularly sleek, but it captures the central elements of Zacchaeus's sin, Jesus' initiative and motivation, salvation, and Zacchaeus's repentance. It uses some of the language of the text (*lost* and *salvation*) while also bringing in the tie to Luke 15 by using the phrase "the Father's heart." Writing a summary statement helps you to articulate the clarity of understanding gained through all your hard work and enables you to share your discovery succinctly when discussing the Bible with others.

GUARDRAILS

In inductive Bible study we use some guardrails to keep our interpretation on track. I will note them here without extensive comment, as the principles have been woven throughout this handbook. To check that an interpretation of the text is legitimate, we should be able to answer the following questions affirmatively.

1. Does the text support this interpretation?
2. Does this interpretation take into account all the elements of the text, including its historical and narrative context?
3. Would the original audience agree with this interpretation?

Misinterpretation occurs for primarily two reasons. The first is lack of discipline in paying attention to the text. The second is sifting the text through personal or philosophical assumptions out of the need to protect a vested interest which the text, its meaning or its application might challenge. One of the great benefits of studying the Bible in a diverse community is the challenge of people with other worldviews or assumptions than our own. Our worldviews by their nature are the unexamined framework through which we understand reality. Bringing our worldviews into the process of interpretation without an openness to let our assumption be challenged leads us to read *in* something not in the text or to read *out* something that *is* in the text. We usually aren't even aware that our assumptions are coloring our understanding of the text until someone else makes an observation or asks a question to which we have been blind.

ARTISTS AND SCIENTISTS

Students of the Bible must hold their interpretations lightly but with confidence. Although there is no such thing as infallible interpretation, there is no need to doubt that we can better and better approximate the meaning of the given text. Keeping the spotlight on the text will keep us moored in the truth. If we have been faithful to the inductive process, the Holy Spirit will have plenty of space to shine his light and bring us understanding. Paul Byer, the creator of manuscript study, taught that the probable meaning of the text is both an art and a science. As any artist or scientist would confirm, we never "master" our subject. We come back to it again and again, each time learning, seeing and understanding more. Sometimes earlier interpretations will be amended by a new insight or the exposure of a blind spot. But the process of lingering with the text and working toward a clear understanding will always be a life-giving experience.

PRACTICUM
Path of Understanding

Using your notes from the practicums at the end of chapters seven through nine, follow the steps of the interpretation roadmap to study Mark 4:35-41. When you are done, share your statement of the core message with a friend.

Interpretation Roadmap

1. Identify units of thought
2. Define the genre
3. Define words and concepts
4. Look up OT references
5. Envision the drama
6. Answer remaining questions
7. Identify core message

Mark 4:35-41

On that day, when evening had come, he said to them, "Let us go across to the other side." And leaving the crowd behind, they took him with them in the boat, just as he was. Other boats were with him. A great windstorm arose, and the waves beat into the boat, so that the boat was
5 already being swamped. But he was in the stern, asleep on the cushion; and they woke him up and said to him, "Teacher, do you not care that we are perishing?" He woke up and rebuked the wind, and said to the sea, "Peace! Be still!" Then the wind ceased, and there was a dead calm. He said to them, "Why are you afraid? Have you still no faith?" And
10 they were filled with great awe and said to one another, "Who then is this, that even the wind and the sea obey him?"

11

Response

The book of James uses a striking image to illustrate the choice we face each time we encounter God's Word. When we study the Bible, we have the option to be doers or merely hearers (James 1:22-25). If we hear the Word but do not act on it, we are like those who can't remember what we look like shortly after standing before a mirror. In the Greco-Roman context, "the image of looking into a mirror is a metaphor of moral improvement."[1] James uses this metaphor to illustrate the folly of not responding to God's Word and letting it transform us.

Unless you are particularly vain and enjoy admiring yourself, the main reason to look in a mirror is to make some kind of improvement to your appearance. I use a mirror to apply make-up or when styling my hair. My husband checks his reflection in a mirror to ensure that his tie is straight and his collar is smooth. Mirrors are useful to show us reality. Without them, we might go hours with a piece of spinach stuck in our teeth or with our hair rumpled.

Each time I see myself in a mirror, I make an appraisal and then have a choice of whether or not to act. If my hair doesn't need to be brushed, my make-up isn't smeared, and I have no food in my teeth, my choice is simple: I leave my face just as I see it. If my assessment of my appearance is that there is something out of place, I will probably choose to fix it. It would be very odd if I passed by a mirror and saw mud on my face but chose to leave it there. Yet we often make that choice when we study the Bible.

It is much too easy to have a great time studying the Bible but walk away unchanged. We might be busy, or eager to get on to our next activity, or we might just be uninterested in letting the Word expose what is really going on in our hearts and lives. The Scriptures are like a mirror; they make it possible to see truth about ourselves that we cannot see without them. But having stood in front of the mirror, we are faced with a choice.

> "But be doers of the word, and not merely hearers who deceive themselves. For if any are hearers of the word and not doers, they are like those who look at themselves in a mirror; for they look at themselves and, on going away, immediately forget what they were like."
>
> JAMES 1:22-24

When we choose to leave the mud on our face and then quickly forget that it is there, we deceive ourselves. Willfully maintaining a mental picture of ourself that is different from reality is self-deception. When I spend some time before the mirror of God's Word I realize that my Christian character is stronger in my mind than in reality. Unless I am deliberate about acting on the Word, the insight about myself from God's mirror slips away, and I am left with only the idealized view of myself. I have the opportunity for truth, transformation and genuine encounter with God, but I can just as easily miss it when I step away from the mirror.

Seeing ourselves rightly isn't intended to shame or burden; it's intended to bless us. "But those who look into the perfect law, the law of liberty, and persevere, being not hearers who forget but doers who act—they will be blessed in their doing" (James 1:25). God wants to transform us and lead us into the fullness of life. It is a law of liberty, an instrument of freedom. But the blessing is not automatic. We are blessed as we obey and respond.

There is a simple rule at the Olesberg house. If someone uses up something when cooking or snacking, they are to add it to the shopping list on the refrigerator. It is an easy "law": use up the peanut butter, write it on the list; use up the brown sugar, write it on the list. Those who obey this law are "blessed in their doing." When my family applies this simple rule, the staple items that we use regularly are always available. We don't have to make a special run to the grocery store for one ingredient when we are in the middle of making cookies. But the blessing of this house rule is only possible if it is obeyed. Knowing the rule is not sufficient; it must be applied to bring about its benefit.

INVITATION

Application is the final step of inductive Bible study, but it is in no way the least important. As we discussed in chapter one, God's Word is powerful. Through the Bible we experience God and draw close to him. Studying the Bible gives the Holy Spirit space to speak into our lives. When we are responsive to God's Word and apply it to our lives, we participate with God in the transformational power of the Word.

Perhaps one of the reasons it is difficult for us to consistently respond to the Bible is that application isn't a part of most of the other reading we do. When you take an English or history class, most teachers do not ask, "How will you live differently because of this book?" But, as we've seen, the Bible isn't an ordinary book. God is present in a very real way and eager to interact with us through it.

I find it helpful to think of application as an invitation from God. An invitation is a small gift that, if responded to, leads to greater gifts. They are inherently fun to receive. Whether it be a wedding, a dinner party or a game of softball, an invitation is a way of providing an opportunity to spend time with someone or to enjoy an activity. Even if you choose to decline, it's nice to have been included. When my husband says, "Let's go for a walk," he is inviting me to spend time with him, to talk, to share about our days, to enjoy holding hands. Extending each other invitations, whether large or small, is a way that we communicate love and desire for relationship.

God expresses his love and interest in our lives by extending invitations to obey, repent, trust or receive from him. I recently studied Luke 10:1-24 with a group of friends. In the story, Jesus sends out thirty-six pairs of followers to proclaim the kingdom of God and to heal in his name. I was attracted to the theme of joy in the text, and I thought to myself that I'd love to experience more of the joy exhibited by Jesus and those followers. When considering how to apply the passage, I sensed the Holy Spirit inviting me to apply the passage by believing that the kingdom of God comes near to people through me. My boldness in evangelism ebbs and flows, so I knew that this was an invitation to be on the alert for evangelistic opportunities.

A few days later, a woman I had only recently met told me that she was intrigued by a sentence from the Bible quoted in the novel she was reading. I began to ask her questions and soon learned that she was interested in the Bible, but had read very little of it. In fact, she had no idea where to buy one and was surprised to learn that you can get them at Walmart. By the end of our conversation, she had agreed to meet me at a coffee shop to study a passage of the Bible with me. I was filled with joy and excitedly told my family and friends about our conversation. Joy flooded me again on the afternoon that she and I studied Genesis 2 and she began to understand a little more about God's goodness.

The Holy Spirit was clearly already at work in my friend's life. He could have used any Christian in our town to speak with her, but he chose me. He extended an invitation to me for a front row seat of his work of seeking the lost. He responded to my desire for greater joy by letting me watch him at work drawing someone into his kingdom. It is possible that I wouldn't have been bold enough to ask her further questions or offer to meet for a Bible study if I hadn't been looking for a way to apply Luke 10. Just as James 1 promises, I was blessed in the doing.

When we view application as an obligation or a duty rather than an invitation, we make it harder than it needs to be. We don't expect blessing when fulfilling an obligation. My daughter takes out the trash on Thursday nights because it is her duty as a member of the household. She doesn't look forward to it, she usually needs to be reminded to do it, and when she finally gets around to doing it, she does it as quickly as possible so that she can get back to talking to her friends on the phone. It is a huge mistake to view applying a Bible study in the same category with household chores. Doing so reveals that our view of the Bible and our relationship with God has become twisted.

HEARING FROM GOD

How do we go about discerning what God's invitation is to us from a particular Bible study? What's involved in recognizing the voice of the Holy Spirit speaking to us through the Word? It starts with bringing our whole selves to the Bible study—not just our heads, but our hearts too. It requires a posture of trust that says to God, "Here I am. You are welcome to show me anything I need to see. You are welcome to say to me anything I need to hear." As Richard Foster writes in his book *Life with God,*

> Reading the Bible for interior transformation is a far different endeavor than reading the Bible for historical knowledge, literary appreciation, or religious instruction. In the latter case we learn head knowledge; in the former, heart knowledge. To allow the Bible to infiltrate us with the Life God offers—piercing us like a two-edged sword dividing "soul from spirit, joints from marrow . . . [judging] the thoughts and intentions of the heart" (Heb. 4:12)—we must bring to the Bible our whole selves, expectantly, attentively, and humbly.[2]

When we draw near to God through the Scriptures with soft hearts, he is only too willing to speak to us in a way we can understand.

Applying the Bible involves change. Sometimes that change is shown in action; sometimes it is a change in heart or mind. But if we haven't been impacted in some way as a result of studying the Bible, we have missed God's invitation.

To begin the process of hearing God's invitation, start by consid-

Table 11.1. Application Questions

Area of Life	Application Questions
God	What does this passage show about God's character and purposes? How does my view of God need to change in light of what I learn here? How would my relationship with God be different if I fully believed what this passage says about him?
Self	With which of the characters do I most identify? Why? Does that character provide an example to follow or avoid? How does this passage challenge me to repent, trust or act?
Relationships	What problem between people is addressed in this passage? In which of my relationships is that problem present? How does this passage call me to treat people differently?
Mission	What does this passage reveal about God's purposes in the world? How does it invite me to participate with what God is doing?

ering the core message of the passage you're studying. How is this message different from how you think about the world? How are you being invited to think, feel or act differently? Critically reflecting on our own views and practices in light of the core message gives the Holy Spirit room to expose our limited or distorted views of life.

It can be helpful to consider four general areas of life when listening for God's personal invitation: God, self, relationships and mission. Table 11.1 offers a few application questions for each of those areas that can be applied to most passages.

There are many possible ways to apply any passage of the Bible. Most passages lend themselves to application in three or four areas. It is wise to pick one to focus on so we are sure to follow through (it's too easy to become overwhelmed by all the ways we need to grow and end up not responding to any of them). In a group of six to eight people, it is possible that the participants will be led to a variety of applications. The Holy Spirit tailors his invitation to each of us specifically in light of our unique situation and stage of discipleship. A faithful response by one member of the group often spurs others to trust God in more significant ways. Table 11.2 offers four potential application questions for Luke 19:1-10, followed by responses from four different people.

Table 11.2. Sample Responses to Application Questions of Luke 19:1-10

Area of Life	Application Question	Response
God	What do you learn about Jesus?	"Jesus takes initiative with me! That makes me feel loved. God isn't distant; he draws near."
Self	How eager are you to get near Jesus? To what extent are you willing to make a fool of yourself to know him more?	"I feel self-conscious during worship. I realize that when I'm singing, I'm nervous about what the people around me might think of me. This Sunday, I will close my eyes, focus on Jesus, and sing from my heart."
Relationships	Are there any ways you have taken advantage of someone? If so, what will it look like to make restitution?	"A few years ago, I regularly took small amounts of petty cash from the office where I worked. I've confessed that to God but never to the office manager. I want to estimate how much I took, write a check for more than that amount and take it to him."
Mission	How can you join with Jesus in seeking the lost?	"I've never gotten to know the guys at the end of my hallway because they are heavy partiers. I'm going to knock on their door tonight and suggest we have lunch together in the dining hall sometime this week."

FOCUSED REFLECTION

I've learned that if a friend says, "Hey, we should get together sometime," but a specific date and time isn't set, the meeting doesn't happen. As much as we like one another, a general intention to spend time together isn't sufficient to make hanging out a reality. We need a particular plan: "6 p.m. this Friday, your house."

Application to Bible study is similar. Transformation doesn't happen if we don't move from the general idea to a particular plan. Discerning God's particular invitation to us requires a process of focused reflection.

Focusing involves narrowing our sights and selecting a target. Olympic archers shoot for the center of the bull's-eye every time they release an arrow. It isn't sufficient to shoot in the general vicinity of the target. They aim to hit the heart.

Application to Bible study is most transformative when we focus our attention and actions on something particular. Just as honing our questions leads to deeper understanding, focusing our application increases its impact. Focused application has four characteristics: prayerful, real, risky and specific. (See figure 11.1.)

The process of discerning the Holy Spirit's particular invitation to us begins on the outside of the circle with prayer and works in until we have a specific plan.

Be prayerful. We begin with prayer because, though spiritual growth is a natural process, it is not an automatic one. The parable of the sower makes it clear that there are many obstacles facing the seed sown in our hearts. Whenever the Word goes out, Satan looks for the opportunity to snatch it away (Mark 4:15). Without the help of the Holy Spirit, our hearts remain hard, rocky or thorny. Only God has the power to soften the human heart (Ezekiel 11:19; 36:26), and so we rely on him not just when we are acting on the Word but even to the point of discerning the specific response he his calling us into.

Self-deception is a formidable impediment to transformational application. We cannot deliver ourselves from it because its very nature is to hide itself from our awareness. We are dependent on the Holy Spirit to shine God's light on our hearts and break through any blindness or resistance.

I recently led a group in a manuscript study of Genesis 3, the tragic story of Adam and Eve's choice to disobey God. We had a powerful time of interpretation and were able to identify the process that led the first couple to doubt the goodness of God and choose independence from him. As the teacher, I had been thinking about how God might use the study to convict the participants of their own sin and distrust of God, but my heart was far from examining my own life. In fact, I was feeling pretty good about myself. It wasn't until the next day that I finally prayed, "Lord, how does this passage

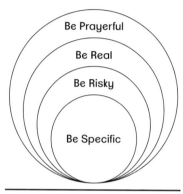

Figure 11.1.

apply to me? Please open my eyes." I soon realized that, like Adam and Eve, I was blaming my husband for something that was my fault. A discussion he and I had been having was at an impasse because of my inability to see my sin. The work of the Holy Spirit through the Word brought me to repentance. If I had sought to identify personal application without praying, I would have missed what I most needed.

Be real. You've probably all been in a Bible study where someone says "I learned I just need to trust God." Though this is true and the Scripture will always direct us to trust God, this response is superficial and overly simplistic. Application responses must be about real areas of our life. Genuine transformation isn't possible without transparency and vulnerability. If a theme of the passage is trust, then being real would mean admitting a way in which you are currently struggling to trust God, such as your finances or in a strained relationship. If you find yourself struggling to identify specific areas of our life for application, then ask the Holy Spirit to show you.

Being real involves identifying *current* struggles, not just referring to challenges we have faced in the past or ways we might respond in the future. Ask yourself questions such as, *What areas of my life are similar to one of the characters or the situation in this story?* or *How does the topic of this passage play itself out in my life?* Sometimes we haven't yet admitted to ourselves that we are struggling in a certain relationship or situation until we are asked, "How does this passage apply to you?" Thus, the process of application leads us into self-reflection and greater self-knowledge, enabling us to be met by God in areas we haven't yet brought before him in prayer. In naming and articulating live issues, and then letting the truth of the Scripture address them, Bible study becomes a direct encounter with the living God.

Be risky. Once we have prayerfully identified a current arena of life, the next step of discernment is to consider a response that requires trust of God. Deepening as a person of faith involves being stretched and challenged—just like muscles. Risk necessitates us to rely on God to come through for us in an identifiable way. If you are applying a passage about love for your neighbor, deciding to smile more when you walk down the street will not be transformational application. You don't need to rely on God to smile more. We must avoid general responses that any person could do even if they weren't a Christian.

Applying God's Word should stretch us in some way and increase our dependence on God. It is much more risky to show love for your neighbors by baking cookies for them and knocking on their door to deliver them. It might feel like a risk to take initiative with someone you don't know well. Perhaps the time involved to bake and deliver will require you to trust God to help you with other responsibilities. For many of us, the risk will involve being bold in identifying ourselves with Jesus if we are asked why we are taking this initiative. As we step out and choose responses that cause us to need God, we give the Lord opportunities to come through for us in amazing ways.

Be specific. Finally, transformational application is specific. After we have prayerfully decided on a real area of our lives and have identified a risky response, we must fill in the details. Making specific plans helps us to overcome possible obstacles to applying. For example, in studying James 3 about the significance of our words, I might become convicted that I have been harsh in how I speak to my children. The next step is to think of specific examples of when I was harsh. Which child did it involve? What did I say? What were the circumstances of the incident? (Often, this process of getting specific will deepen the conviction and clarify ongoing dynamics.) Once I have a particular incident in mind, I can decide how and when I will speak with the child. I might decide to pick them up from school on Tuesday and go to a favorite café to offer my apology and talk together about the dynamics in our relationship that contribute to frustration and tension.

It can be helpful to share your plans with someone else so that you can be held accountable to following through. The support and encouragement of a friend is a great boost when doing something risky or challenging.

R.S.V.P.

At the end of every inductive Bible study, consider how God is inviting you to respond. Take the time to move from the core message of the passage to discover how it intersects with your life in the here and now. The process of being prayerful, real, risky and specific will put you in the position for God to speak powerfully and lead you into transformation. Responding to God's invitation in concrete and specific ways enables you to receive the blessings that only come to those who are doers of the Word.

PRACTICUM
You Are Invited

Re-read your core message statement for the manuscript of Mark 4:35-41 from the end of chapter ten. Follow the steps discussed in this chapter (summarized below) to discern how God would have you apply this passage. Write your application plans at the bottom of the manuscript.

Practical Steps

- Pray for the Holy Spirit to lead you.
- Turn the core message into questions for reflection.
- Look for places in your life that are similar to one of the characters or the situation.
- Look for promises, commands, or an example to follow or avoid.
- Choose an action that you can take in the next two days.
- Share your plans with another.

Mark 4:35-41

On that day, when evening had come, he said to them, "Let us go across to the other side." And leaving the crowd behind, they took him with them in the boat, just as he was. Other boats were with him. A great windstorm arose, and the waves beat into the boat, so that the boat was
5 already being swamped. But he was in the stern, asleep on the cushion; and they woke him up and said to him, "Teacher, do you not care that we are perishing?" He woke up and rebuked the wind, and said to the sea, "Peace! Be still!" Then the wind ceased, and there was a dead calm. He said to them, "Why are you afraid? Have you still no faith?" And
10 they were filled with great awe and said to one another, "Who then is this, that even the wind and the sea obey him?"

Part Three

TOOL BOX

12

Selection

Since Scripture study is one of the primary ways we hear from God and are guided by him, it stands to reason that God should be involved from the beginning: even in the process of selecting what portion of Scripture to study. I view the selection process as an act of discernment. It's akin to deciding together with a friend where to go on vacation, rather than selecting a destination for vacation on your own and then inviting a friend to join you there.

When we ask Jesus, "What do you want us to study?" we are expressing our trust of him as our good Shepherd. Like sheep, we don't inherently know what we need to eat or which road to take, but our Shepherd does. As David said so beautifully, "He leads me in right paths for his name's sake" (Psalm 23:3). I function under the assumption that if the Lord clearly leads us to a particular book or passage to study, then what he intends to do in the individual's or the community's life is related to the content of that Scripture. For example, every three years InterVarsity Christian Fellowship hosts the Urbana Student Missions Conference. In the months preceding the event, the organization commits itself to immersion in the Scripture selected for the conference. Not only the Urbana planners, but leaders and students across the movement study that text, often repeatedly, and seek to live it out for the year prior to Urbana. Thus, when the Spirit led the Urbana 09 planners to select John 1—4, I knew that God intended to increase our commitment to and fruitfulness in evangelism. John 1—4 is filled with stories of one-on-one encounters with Jesus that lead to conversion, and it depicts a cycle of witness in which those who meet Jesus always turn around and tell someone else. Indeed, from 2008 to 2010 (before and after Urbana 09), InterVarsity recorded higher conversion rates than seen in over a decade. A greater level of passion and creativity was evidenced all across the movement. Students embraced the call to share the gospel with their friends, often doing so through evangelistic Bible studies from John 1—4. This was specific growth God wanted for us at that time in our organizational life, and he used John 1—4 as one of the catalysts.

Discernment in selecting Scripture for manuscript study can be done by an individual (for themselves or a group) or by a group (for communal study). Either way, the process is the same: prayer; reflection on current strengths, weaknesses or opportunities; brainstorming Scripture that has resonance with the individual or group's current reality; holding the various options before the Lord in prayer; and patient listening until there is clear confirmation about which Scripture to select.

The larger the group or greater the significance of the event to engage in this Scripture, the more space should be given to the discernment process. Thus, if I am choosing which book of the Bible to study next in my personal time with the Lord, I might take a day or two to decide; if I am making a selection for a weekend dig-in for a church that is in a time of transition, I might linger in the discernment process a week or two. Discerning the Scripture for an Urbana conference typically takes four to six months.

In addition to a posture of humbly seeking the Lord's will, there are various practical considerations that are good to bear in mind. Here are the questions I am typically asked about selecting Scripture, followed by my response and some suggested passages.

How do you decide whether to study a whole book or selected passages? Studying whole books is invaluable. By studying entire books, we learn how to discern a book's central message and deepen our understanding of the vision and personality of specific biblical authors. If new to inductive study, I recommend shorter books such as Ruth, Esther, Jonah, Amos, Mark, Ephesians, Philippians, Colossians, James, 1 Peter and

1 John. Once an individual or a group has some experience in manuscript study, they might try studying Genesis, Joshua, Nehemiah, Daniel, John, Acts, Romans, 1 Corinthians or Hebrews.

In general, though, there aren't many opportunities for Christians to study whole books together. Long books can take more than a year of weekly study.[1] If there are a limited number of study sessions scheduled, individual passages or portions of books might be preferable. Series, such as the parables or encounters with Jesus in the Gospels, are great for new small groups. Also, there are subsections of longer books that work well in manuscript study, such as Genesis 1—11, Exodus 1—15, Deuteronomy 1—11, Matthew 5—7, John 1—4, John 18—21, Acts 1—7 and Revelation 2—3.

When choosing a section, be careful to identify the beginning and end of a unit, so as to avoid truncating a scene or argument. I was recently asked to teach Jesus' inaugural address in his hometown of Nazareth in Luke 4. My first inclination was to select 4:16-22, ending with the people's (seemingly) positive response to Jesus' claim to be the fulfillment of Isaiah 61. However, the scene doesn't end there. The section from verses 23-30 is continuous with the part before; there has been no change in time, location or characters. By the end of the scene, the crowd is infuriated with Jesus and attempts to kill him. If I am convinced that the author determines meaning (which I am), then I must teach the whole scene as Luke wrote it and not just the part I like.

What about studying epistles? When an individual or group is first learning inductive study, I recommend that they begin with Gospel passages. Jesus is the center of our faith, and so studying about him and what he said and did should be central to our growth. Unfortunately, many Christians assume that the Gospels are "introductory" and the epistles are "advanced." Nothing could be further from the truth. Some think they already know the Gospels because of Sunday school lessons; however, it is quite different to study a passage as an adult than as a child (as our discussion of Jesus and Zaccheus has shown).

Others assume that manuscript study only works, or works best, when applied to a story or a poem, as in the Gospels or the Psalms. In reality, manuscript study works just as well on epistles. There are a few things to keep in mind, however, when digging into one of the letters.

First, remember that all epistles have a narrative context. What we have in the epistles is the equivalent of one side of a telephone conversation. When studying epistles it is particularly important to ask, "How would this have sounded to the original audience?" and "What might the author be responding to?" As discussed in chapter six, frame of reference affects interpretation. Thus, we keep in mind that Paul was writing not primarily for us but for the Corinthians, for example.

Second, epistles are intentionally crafted and ordered by the author, so observing structure is particularly important. Any interpretation of a part of the book must make sense within the larger outline of the book. (We'll look more closely at how to identify structure in chapter seventeen.) This means that we are asking, "How does this section's placement within the flow of the letter impact our understanding of it?" Furthermore, authors of epistles utilize logic and reasoning more extensively than the other books of the Bible. Make sure to identify all the logical connectors (*for, but, because, therefore,* etc.) and understand how they are being used. (Table 8.3 in chapter eight can help you with this.)

What length of passages work best? There is no passage too short for a powerful hour-long small group Bible study. As long as the unit can legitimately stand alone, then even two or three verses work well. For example, I have been in studies of Matthew 13:44-45, the parables of the treasure hidden in a field and the pearl of great price, in which the group was disappointed that our time was over because there was more they could have discussed.[2]

In their eagerness to cover a whole book in a limited number of weeks, some small group leaders attempt to cover entire chapters (or multiple chapters) that should be studied in smaller sections. Remember that chapters are an artificial marker and not a reliable indication of a book's structure. My rule of thumb is to not study more than two pages of manuscript (roughly thirty verses) at any one time. Our minds can't give careful attention to more than that, and so our observations and interpretation are bound to be weak if given too much text in one sitting.[3] For example, Mark 1 is forty-five verses long and covers three pages of manuscript. Rather than attempt to study the chapter as a whole, I study it in three sections: verses 1-13 (Jesus' inauguration), verses 14-34 (the first disciples' introduction to Jesus) and verses 35-45 (the spread of Jesus' ministry). Chapter thirteen goes into greater detail on creating a manuscript for study.

What Scripture works best for those who are new to the Bible? When studying the Bible with non-Christians or new Christians, start with passages from the Gospels. The most important thing for bringing someone to faith is to look at Jesus directly. Incidents of Jesus interacting with various people are particularly good. In introducing someone to Christianity, who Jesus is and how he interacts is more important than his speeches.

Sometimes a person's background is such that they don't even have a framework for looking at Jesus or understanding the significance of his incarnation, death and resurrection. For folks that are from highly secular environments (such as Chinese international students) or non-monotheistic religions (such as Hindus or Buddhists), Genesis 1—3 is a better place to start. That material reveals God as creator, the value of human life, his interest in relating to us personally, and the nature and consequences of sin. With that backdrop in place, passages about Jesus carry their appropriate force.

PRACTICUM
What's Next?

Follow these steps to discern which book or passage you might study next:

1. Prayer. Take time to express your love for Jesus and your desire to grow as his disciple, and to ask for his Spirit to show you what part of Scripture he would have you focus on.
2. Self-reflection. Take time to reflect on the following:
    a. Personal strengths and areas of life that are going well

    b. Personal weakness and areas of life that are currently difficult

    c. Opportunities before you for new ministry, responsibilities or relationships

3. Brainstorming. List three to five sections of Scripture that you think might connect with an element of your self-reflection.

4. Prayer. Over the next few days briefly hold these options before the Lord a couple times a day, asking him to highlight one of them.
5. Selection. Make a final decision in full confidence that you can't go wrong no matter which Scripture you choose. The Holy Spirit will work through all of them, whether or not you are sure you have heard God's voice.

13

Creating a Manuscript

The manuscript method of Bible study described in this handbook was created by InterVarsity campus staff Paul Byer in the 1950s. Paul had been taught to study the Bible inductively by Jane Hollingsworth, one of InterVarsity's first employees. Paul was visually oriented (his degree was in architecture), and he often studied the Bible at his drafting table.

> In my personal Bible study I used a pencil to mark up the text, and then got started using some colors to designate themes and key words, etc. But something bothered me, although I wouldn't have been able to verbalize this at first. It was just that every time I flipped a page the material I had worked on disappeared from sight and there was no way to relate it visually to the new pages. One morning it hit me; I had to buy two New Testaments and cut the pages out of both (I was working in 2 Corinthians) and then could put each page face up and work right through the whole text. So I did this, and discovered that this opened up meaning, as the internal structure and relationship within the text became apparent, thus the whole letter of 2 Corinthians took on new meaning.[1]

Paul and his ministry partner decided to try this method with students during summer camp. Rather than buying two Bibles per student and cutting them apart (seems a little sacrilegious, doesn't it?), they typed the entire book of Colossians on standard paper and made copies. They were amazed at how a simple change in format engaged the students and enabled them to see the Scripture with fresh eyes.

Additionally, their experiment created a means for communal study of the Scripture that was lively and highly interactive. (Previous to this, inductive Bible study was primarily associated with individuals studying in isolation.) Paul refused to explain the meaning of a passage and instead facilitated the process of discovery by continually asking, "How would you answer that from the text?"

Over the coming decades, manuscript study spread throughout Inter-Varsity Christian Fellowship/USA to other movements in the International Fellowship of Evangelical Students, and into the mission field as student leaders and campus staff mentored by Paul became missionaries in Asia, the Middle East and Africa.[2]

Lucky for us, we no longer have to type out whole books of the Bible. Online Bible sites and word processing software make it relatively simple to create manuscripts in less than ten minutes. However, whether downloaded or hand-typed, the format matters. Table 13.1 describes the features of a properly formatted manuscript, including an explanation of the significance of each feature. This format has been followed in creating the manuscripts used in earlier chapters of this book.

CHOOSING A VERSION

Manuscript study does not require knowledge of biblical Hebrew or Greek, but a good translation of the Bible is invaluable. All translation involves interpretation, so "in a certain sense, the person who reads the Bible only in English is at the mercy of the translator(s), and translators have often had to make choices as to what in fact the original Hebrew or Greek was really intending to say."[3] There are a plethora of English versions available (and strong opinions about which of them is more faithful to the original meaning). In general, all English Bibles can be classified in one of three categories. The first is known as "formal equivalence." These versions (such as KJV, NASB, NRSV and ESV) "attempt to keep as close to the 'form' of the Hebrew or Greek, both words and grammar, as can be conveniently put into understandable English."[4]

The second grouping (such as NIV, *Good News Bible* and *New Living Translation*) are known as "functional equivalents." They seek to overcome the historic and cultural distance in the text by restated words

Table 13.1. Features of a Properly Formatted Manuscript

Feature	Significance
Single sided, unbound	The genius of the manuscript method includes helping students of the Bible to make connections between various sections of a book and see bigger themes. Double-sided printing or binding in a handbook nullifies this benefit. I keep my longer manuscripts in three-ring binders, but I always remove them when I sit down to study. As a group (or individual) makes their way through a book, the unbound sheets can be spread out on a table to be viewed together. This is why a table and colored pens are listed in chapter eight as tools for manuscript study.
Chapter and verse numbers removed	Chapter and verse numbers were added to the Bible by Stephanus, a Parisian publisher, in 1551. They enable us to find a particular text regardless of version or edition. However, chapter and verse numbers are not inherent to the text. By printing the words and sentences only, we get closer to what the original audience saw. Many websites provide the option of omitting verse numbers.
Headings and footnotes removed	Section headings and explanatory notes or footnotes are the work of a publisher, not the biblical author. The headings and notes are inherently interpretive; keeping them undermines the inductive process.
Paragraph formatting removed	Ancient Hebrew and Greek texts were not formatted into paragraphs. (They didn't use punctuation either, but we can't eliminate that.) Publishers of the Bible often print the text in paragraphs, but unlike verse numbers, there is no universal agreement on paragraph breaks. Deciding on what to include in a paragraph is an important interpretative task; thus in manuscript study it is reserved for the studiers. (See chapter ten for instructions about identifying "units of thought.")
Double spaced	Double spacing provides room for circling and underlining words. The added white space makes paying attention easier, as well as giving room to write above and below particular words and phrases.
Wide margins	The margins should be increased to 1.25" or 1.5" to provide adequate space for labeling paragraphs, writing questions and taking notes on group discussion.
Title	The standard reference is used as the title. For entire books, the name of the book is sufficient (e.g. James). For manuscripts of a section, verses should be included (e.g., Mark 1:1-14).
Page numbers in the footer and line numbers in margins (by 5)	When studying in a group, giving the page and line number enables others to follow along: "I saw the words 'fear' or 'afraid' on page 9 line 27, page 10 line 26, page 11 line 26, and page 12 line 4." I recommend that the lines be counted by 5 so as to not unduly fill the margins. The counting should start afresh on each page.

and idioms into contemporary ways of speaking. These translations are easier to read and sound more natural.

The third category, "free translation," works to translate the *ideas* of the text with little concern about using the exact words of the original. Often known as paraphrases (such as *The Message* or *The Living Bible*), these versions provide fresh experience of the Word in devotional reading. They shouldn't be used for inductive study, since they are highly interpretative and obscure the voice of the biblical author.

I recommend using a "formal equivalence" version for serious manuscript study, especially when working on an entire book. (I have chosen the New Revised Standard Version for all examples in this book, unless otherwise noted.) However, when studying stand-alone passages or with groups that are new to manuscript study, I often use the NIV (New International Version) because the prose flows more naturally and is more broadly known among evangelicals than the NRSV.

One of the benefits of using a manuscript in small groups is that it provides a common translation to discuss. This helps a group from being sidetracked by comparing the passage in different translations. If there is a question about what a word means, rather than looking to an alternate English translation, it is best to look up the word in a concordance (see chapter sixteen) to learn about the original Greek or Hebrew word used.

In describing the impact of a week-long Mark manuscript study on students, Paul Byer writes, "Usually there is one or more places where the truth of the text breaks in upon them, and they are now aware that a particular change in actions, values, or relationships is called for."[5] That is because reading and marking a manuscript of a Bible passage enables us to interact with the text differently. Though a simple tool, using a manuscript puts both our inner and outer selves in a posture to drink in deeply from the life-giving Word of God.

PRACTICUM
I Spy . . .

Identify four things wrong with the formatting of the manuscript below. (If needed, see figure 8.1 for an example of a properly formatted manuscript.)

1.

2.

3.

4.

Mark 1:1-13

The Proclamation of John the Baptist

[1]The beginning of the good news[a] of Jesus Christ, the Son of God.[b]
[2]As it is written in the prophet Isaiah,[c]
"See, I am sending my messenger ahead of you,[d]
who will prepare your way;
[3]the voice of one crying out in the wilderness:
'Prepare the way of the Lord,
make his paths straight,'"
[4]John the baptizer appeared[e] in the wilderness, proclaiming a baptism of repentance for the forgiveness of sins. [5]And people from the whole Judean countryside and all the people of Jerusalem were going out to him, and were baptized by him in the river Jordan, confessing their sins. [6]Now John was clothed with camel's hair, with a leather belt around his waist, and he ate locusts and wild honey. [7]He proclaimed, "The one who is more powerful than I is coming after me; I am not worthy to stoop down and untie the thong of his sandals. [8]I have baptized you with[f] water; but he will baptize you with[f] the Holy Spirit."

The Baptism of Jesus

[9]In those days Jesus came from Nazareth of Galilee and was baptized by John in the Jordan. [10]And just as he was coming up out of the water, he saw the heavens torn apart and the Spirit descending like a dove on him. [11]And a voice

came from heaven, "You are my Son, the Beloved;[g] with you I am well pleased."

The Temptation of Jesus

[12]And the Spirit immediately drove him out into the wilderness. [13]He was in the wilderness forty days, tempted by Satan; and he was with the wild beasts; and the angels waited on him.

[a]Or *gospel*
[b]Other ancient authorities lack *the Son of God*
[c]Other ancient authorities read *in the prophets*
[d]Gk *before your face*
[e]Other ancient authorities read *John was baptizing*
[f]Or *in*
[g]Or *my beloved Son*

14

Prayer

For followers of Jesus, Bible study is fundamentally a spiritual activity, not an academic one. We don't study the Bible to satisfy intellectual fascination but out of a yearning to know God and be transformed by him. As seen in chapter four, engagement with Scripture is a primary means of caring for the soul. Through prayer, the heart opens itself to the work and presence of God's Spirit. Thus, a prayerful posture is an essential element of inductive Bible study.

We are dependent on the Holy Spirit when studying the Scripture to reveal truth (John 16:13), to give spiritual discernment (1 Corinthians 12:11) and to soften our hearts. The enemy of our soul is looking to snatch away the Word sown in our hearts (Mark 4:15) and prevent us from bearing fruit. In prayer we welcome the Spirit's work in our souls and fight the spiritual battle that ensues whenever truth goes forth. Since hardheartedness is as much a danger for the believer as the non-believer,[1] we need the Spirit to soften our hearts and expose our blind spots. To cultivate a posture of prayer in inductive study, I suggest prayer before, during and after the study.

BEGINNING

Prayer before studying settles our hearts and minds so that we can become mindful of God's presence. It is often helpful to tell God about the things we are worried about and release those concerns to him so that we can be fully present and alert to his Word and his

Spirit. When our enthusiasm for Bible study is low, we pray that God will increase our passion for his Word. We ask the Spirit to bring us wisdom and insight, and to give us soft hearts. If we are studying in a group, it's helpful to pray for a spirit of love and the ability to listen to each other well.

DURING

Prayer while studying is the most neglected spiritual practice in inductive Bible study. It is as if we start the journey with God but go it alone until we meet up with him at the final destination. A posture of prayerfulness includes staying actively connected to the Spirit in the midst of studying. This usually looks like short "arrow" prayers sent up during the interpretation phase. These prayers can range from praise ("Jesus, this is so cool . . .") to petition ("Help! I don't understand"). I particularly recommend that groups stop and pray when the discussion feels stuck or clarity isn't coming. It is amazing what thirty seconds of silence in the midst of a study can do to the group dynamic and understanding of the text. Likewise, asking God, "What am I missing?" or "Is there anything more you want me to see?" during the study expresses humility and openness to God's work in our lives.

ENDING

As described in chapter eleven, in the application phase of inductive study we are listening for an invitation from the Lord. Rather than rushing into discussion about how the passage connects with our lives, we ask the Spirit to guide us. As Eugene Peterson observes, "God does not put us in charge of forming our personal spiritualities. We grow in accordance with the revealed Word implanted in us by the Spirit."[2] God knows exactly what we need (and what he has prepared for us). Listening to him for how he would have us respond to the Scripture is a way that we seek his will and allow him to shepherd us.

PRACTICUM
Personal Liturgy Before Bible Study

Prewritten prayers (often referred to as liturgical prayer) are a wonderful resource for the spiritual life. Scripture recast as prayer provides consistent and thoughtful content. Regular use of a liturgy enables us to pray with clarity and in alignment with biblical truth regardless of how we are feeling on a particular day.

At a friend's suggestion, I created a personal liturgy to use while writing this book. I enjoyed the process of searching the Scriptures for verses to ground my work and writing prayers to express my need for the Holy Spirit's work in and through me. Using the liturgy each time I sat down at my desk to write helped me to stay centered in Jesus and reliant on him.

A personal liturgy can also be used to prepare your heart for Bible study. A simple framework provides a natural flow to the prayer: (1) entering God's presence, (2) seeking God's help and (3) offering your time of study. To write your own liturgy, pick one verse (or other relevant Scripture) from each section and turn it into a prayer, using your own words.

Entering God's Presence

Psalm 27:8-9: "Come," my heart says, "seek his face!" Your face, LORD, do I seek. Do not hide your face from me.

Psalm 118:19: Open to me the gates of righteousness, that I may enter through them and give thanks to the LORD.

Hebrews 4:16: Let us therefore approach the throne of grace with boldness, so that we may receive mercy and find grace to help in time of need.

Seeking God's Help

Jeremiah 17:9-10 (NIV): The heart is deceitful above all things and beyond cure. Who can understand it? "I the LORD search the heart and examine the mind, to reward each person according to their conduct, according to what their deeds deserve."

Mark 4:8: "Other seed fell into good soil and brought forth grain, growing up and increasing and yielding thirty and sixty and a hundredfold." And he said, "Let anyone with ears to hear listen."

Romans 10:17: So faith comes from what is heard, and what is heard comes through the word of Christ.

Offering Your Time of Study

1 Samuel 3:10: Now the LORD came and stood there, calling as before, "Samuel! Samuel!" And Samuel said, "Speak, for your servant is listening."

Psalm 19:7: The law of the LORD is perfect, reviving the soul; the decrees of the LORD are sure, making wise the simple.

Ephesians 1:17-18: I pray that the God of our Lord Jesus Christ, the Father of all glory, may give you a spirit of wisdom and revelation as you come to know him, so that, with the eyes of your heart enlightened, you may know what is the hope to which he has called you.

Here is an example using the first verse in each section.

Lord Jesus, I'm entering this time in Bible study to seek your face and be near to you. I want to know you; please reveal more of yourself to me through the Scriptures. I ask you to use your Word to search my heart. Holy Spirit, enable me to see things about myself that I'm blind to. Speak to me now through your Word. I am listening.

15

Determining Genre

In chapter ten I identified the second step in interpretation as "define the genre." In that step we are asking ourselves, *What kind of literature am I dealing with?* How we read and interpret text changes depending on the genre. Genres are implicit contracts between authors and their audiences. For example, as soon as you see, "Once upon a time . . ." you know you are reading a fairy tale and adjust your expectations accordingly. Likewise, people in the ancient world would readily recognize the different kinds of writing heard in the synagogue or a house church.

Below is an alphabetized list of the primary genres found in the Bible.[1] A description of the characteristics of each will enable you to identify the genre. This is followed with comments about how to adjust your study and interpretation accordingly.

Apocalyptic
Characteristics. Dramatic descriptions of visions received by a prophet; fantastic images of angels and animals; often written in poetry rather than prose; concerned with final judgment and the end of history.

How to study. Note hope and warning. Ask, "Who is being judged and why?" and "What are the marks of the righteous or faithful?" Read for impact rather than details. Use imagination to fill out images and note their emotional impact.

Architectural/Design Instructions
Characteristics. Descriptions of various materials, measurements and instructions for assembly.[2]

How to study. Convert units of measurement into modern equivalent. Sketch or imagine the object. Ask, "What emotional or cognitive impact would this object have had on those who saw it?"

Census

Characteristics. Lists of names, clans, tribes; use of numbers.

How to study. Summarize numbers in a table. Identify pattern used. Note standouts or places where pattern is broken. Consider the significance of the standouts.

Epistle

Characteristics. Author(s) and recipient identified; often includes greetings, blessing, exhortation and benediction.

How to study. Reconstruct the problem being addressed. Distinguish universal statements from particulars of situation.

Genealogy

Characteristics. Lists of names; description of relational connections.

How to study. Identify pattern or structure of list. Note changes or exceptions. Read about key individuals in surrounding narratives.

Greco-Roman Biography

Characteristics. A narrative that follows a person's public life; extensive description of their death; meant to entertain, honor a hero and teach.

How to study. Imagine yourself as a disciple of the protagonist. Pay attention to what the hero teaches through actions and words. Ask, "What does how they died reveal about their character?"

Greco-Roman Historiography

Characteristics. A narrative that includes genealogical records, speeches, travel narratives and instruction given in the context of meals.

How to study. Discern the significance of the events. Pay attention to teaching and action of key characters. Ask, "What values and practices are promoted?"

Hymn/Creed

Characteristics. Often poetic; focused on God's character and activity.

How to study. Imagine singing the hymn in a first-century house church. Ask, "What does this hymn/creed claim about Jesus?" and "How is the author using it to advance his argument?"

Instruction/Law

Characteristics. Begin with "do" or "do not," etc.; verbs are in command form.

How to study. Note promises and consequences of various behaviors. Consider how obedience would have affected individual and communal life. Ask, "What are the underlying values expressed through this command?"

Myth

Characteristics. Stories set in remote past; traditional stories that represent the worldview, beliefs, principles and fears of a society.

How to study. Read for meaning rather than facts. Identify transcendent truth communicated through the story.

Narrative

Characteristics. Stories with a plot line; major and minor characters.

How to study. Follow key characters. Pay attention to what God says and does. Note tension and resolution in the storyline.

Parable

Characteristics. Short stories about everyday life; often begin with "The kingdom of God is like . . ."

How to study. Identify one main point rather than allegorize every element of the story. Interpret the points of reference for the original audience. Notice the unexpected turn in the story. Highlight the central action and primary characters.

Poetry

Characteristics. Composed in verse, not prose; uses images and metaphors; often uses parallelism.

How to study. Read out loud. Fill out the images. Pay attention to how it affects you emotionally.

Prophecy

Characteristics. Often poetic; spoken on behalf of God.

How to study. Research historical context (see table 7.1). Notice warnings and promises.

Proverbial Wisdom

Characteristics. Collection of short sayings; practical advice about people and their behavior; themes interwoven rather than arranged in logical or sequential order.

How to study. Think of a modern situation where the idea is applicable. Ask, "What is the wisdom communicated here?" Identify the themes in a collection of proverbs rather than focusing on individual sayings.

Speculative Wisdom

Characteristics. Often poetic; reflections on experience.

How to study. Consider the motivations of the speaker. Be aware that the speaker may not speak for God; thus not everything found in speculative wisdom is true. For example, we know from Job 42:7 that God rebuked Job's friends for speaking wrongly about him, thus sections in Job recording speeches by his friends are speculative wisdom.

Speech

Characteristics. Speaker and audience identified; quotation marks around multiple paragraphs.

How to study. Identify context of the speech. Envision being a member of the audience hearing the speech. Ask, "How might the speaker have delivered various parts of the speech?" and "What response was the speaker hoping for from the audience?"

PRACTICUM
What's This?!

Identify the characteristics and genre of the following passages.

Passage	Characteristics	Genre
Ecclesiastes 2:12-17		
Philippians 2:6-11		
Exodus 15:1-18		
Deuteronomy 1:5-8		
Matthew 6:1-3		
Daniel 12:1-4		
Genesis 6:1-4		

16

Research Tools

A pile of battered books lay in the middle of the table where my I had my first experience with manuscript Bible study. Most of them were completely unfamiliar to me. Over the course of the weekend, our leader introduced them as tools that are useful in understanding the world of the author and the original audience. It took me a while to learn how to use the various resources available, but as I did the richness of the Scripture became more and more apparent.

Here is a brief introduction to the research tools that I regularly use when studying the Bible and preparing to teach. (Chapter nineteen addresses the use of commentaries. They aren't included here as I don't consider them to be an essential research tool.) These introductions describe what a particular reference tool has to offer, how it is arranged and how they might be used. Buying these books is an invaluable investment for every Christian.[1] Please be aware that printed books (or their electronic form) are much more reliable than the information found on the Internet. As with anything written about the Bible, the content must be weighed against the Scripture itself.

BIBLE BACKGROUND COMMENTARY

A Bible background commentary covers the cultural background of the Bible verse by verse. Each book of the Bible has its own chapter (listed in the order used in the Bible, not alphabetically). Each chapter begins with an introductory section covering authorship, date, setting, purpose and genre, and then works its way through the entire biblical book, section by section. When using a Bible background commentary, be careful to distinguish between background information and interpretation.[2]

BIBLE DICTIONARY

Formatted like an encyclopedia with short articles arranged in alphabetical order, a Bible dictionary is good for researching historical background and cultural context. Use it to learn about people, places, and what a word or phrase meant at the time of the author. If you aren't able to find a particular word, identify the general category to which it belongs. For example, in the parable Jesus tells in Luke 19:11-27, a nobleman gives each of ten slaves a pound. The word *pound* is not listed in my Bible dictionary, but it can be found in the article on "money."

CONCORDANCE

A concordance is good for finding cross-references, determining where else the author used a particular word, and for looking up the meaning of the original Hebrew or Greek. "Exhaustive" concordances list every occurrence of every word in the Bible and are arranged alphabetically. (The sections on "the" and "he" can be a little overwhelming.) They look somewhat like telephone books, with three columns of tiny print on every page. Each biblical word is in bold type, followed by all the instances where that word was used in the Bible. If you can't find the scriptural reference for the word you are seeking, look up the verse in the version of the English Bible used by the concordance to find the equivalent word.

Next to the reference is a portion of the sentence in which the word is found; you must look up the verse in a Bible to read it fully. The word itself is represented by its first letter in italics. The third element of each entry is a number. The number can be used to look up the word in the Hebrew and Greek dictionaries provided at the back of the concordance. Regular type numbers refer to words in the Hebrew dictionary; italicized numbers represent Greek words.

For example, when studying Luke 19:1-10 I wanted to know more about the word *lost*, since it was a part of Jesus' summary statement. In *Strong's Exhaustive Concordance*, under the heading "lost," the entry looks like this:

Lu 19:10 to seek and to save that which was *l. 622*

In the Greek dictionary at the back of the concordance, the entry for *622* includes a Greek word, a pronunciation guide, two more numbers referring to the root words from which this one is derived, a definition and the words that *622* can be rendered in English. This information deepens my understanding of the severity of being lost.

Back at the entry for "lost," I can see every other instance Luke used the word (which led me to the three parables in Luke 15) and where the word is used by other biblical authors. By surveying the seventeen uses of *lost* in the Old Testament, I discover that the metaphor of lost sheep for God's people is used four times (Psalm 119:176; Jeremiah 50:6; Ezekiel 34:4, 16). Those references provide further fodder for my interpretation of Jesus' interaction with Zacchaeus.

CROSS-REFERENCING BIBLE

Some Bibles include cross-references in the margins or as footnotes. Be aware that most of these will not be exhaustive, nor will they all be relevant. For example, my Bible lists four Old Testament verses next to its note for Luke 19:8, when Zacchaeus vows to pay back four times what he has taken. In reading all four of them, I find that three are very useful, but the fourth isn't. These are the only cross-references given for the entire Zacchaeus story; there are no references to the various passages found in the concordance about the people of God as lost sheep. Consequently, I recommend that you look in multiple research tools when identifying Old Testament quotations and allusions rather than relying solely on a cross-referencing Bible.

When studying the New Testament inductively, avoid cross-references to other parts of the New Testament unless the original audience would have had access to them. For example, Mark's Gospel was written before the other Gospels, so Luke, Matthew and John are not useful in understanding Mark. On the other hand, since Luke was written before Acts and by the same author, cross-references in Luke are invaluable for deepening our understanding of Acts. Remember that the goal in cross-referencing is to shine more light on the author's intended communication to the original audience. If the original audience wouldn't have known your Bible's cross-referenced material (because it wasn't written yet or not widely distributed) it should be off limits during your study.

Words and images can carry a heavy freight of meaning with only a passing reference between those who are familiar with the same stories. Biblical authors are able to evoke strong Old Testament associations with just a word, such as *mountain* or *shepherd*. Such indirect references that infer shared cultural knowledge are called allusions. The writer may not have a specific Scripture in mind, but rather a medley of biblical stories. If you suspect an allusion is being made but don't find a cross-reference in your Bible, try using another resource such as the *Dictionary of Biblical Imagery*.[3]

DICTIONARY OF BIBLICAL IMAGERY

Whereas a Bible dictionary is indispensable for filling out historical and cultural context, the *Dictionary of Biblical Imagery* provides understanding of the connotations of biblical images. The *Dictionary of Biblical Imagery* is used to shed light on biblical images, symbols, metaphors, motifs and figures of speech. For example, the article on "water" describes both the significance of physical water in ancient Israel but also covers the various ways water is used metaphorically in both the Old and New Testaments. The resource is also an excellent tool for identifying cross-references. Arranged like an encyclopedia, it is a good companion to a Bible dictionary.

ENGLISH DICTIONARY

Often, we have a vague notion of what a word means and can understand its general sense when it is used in a sentence, but we aren't able to give a definition of it. Humility pays off when we admit that we aren't sure of a word's meaning. For example, I was recently in a manuscript study of Genesis 2—4. When we reached the section in which the Lord God tells the serpent, "I will put enmity between you and the woman," some brave person raised their hand to ask, "What is enmity?" Immediately, ten other people in the room made motions and noises to indicate that they had the same question but had been too embarrassed to admit it. Taking the time to look up *enmity* and learning that it

means "mutual hostility, animosity, and violence" aided our understanding of the passage. Never hesitate to use a standard dictionary
when you are unsure of the meaning of a word.

INTERLINEAR BIBLE

An interlinear Bible can help you determine which Hebrew or Greek
word is used in a passage. It shows the original Hebrew or Greek text with
the literal English translation typed below each word. I use an interlinear
New Testament that includes the *Strong's Concordance* number (see above).
By comparing the *Strong's* numbers in a passage, I can tell where English
translators have used synonyms in different verses to translate the same
word used by the original author. This information is useful when building
interpretations based on the use of repetition and in making associations
between sections of the text that the original audience would have heard
but have become obscured in translation. When used in conjunction with
the language dictionaries at the back of *Strong's,* an interlinear Bible can
also make it quicker to determine the Hebrew or Greek meaning.

MAPS

Maps are an invaluable resource in helping students of the Bible to locate
the places referenced, understand distances and perceive relationships between them. In many biblical narratives, the weight of the story is missed
because we don't recognize the significance of a place. For example, in
Luke's account of Jesus' rejection at Nazareth, Jesus refers to "the widow
at Zarapheth at Sidon" and "Naaman the Syrian." Both of the places
mentioned are Gentile lands relatively close to Nazareth that had been
fierce enemies of Israel for centuries. Jesus' claim that God favors folks
like the widow and Naaman isn't just uncomfortable, it is incendiary.

For maps I particularly like *Nelson's Complete Book of Bible Maps and
Charts.*[4] This compact resource has a chapter for each book of the Bible
and includes background material, a chart of literary structure, an outline
and maps that show all the places referenced in that particular book.
Remember, however, that the information about structure and outline
are inherently interpretative and shouldn't be viewed as definitive.

STUDY BIBLE

There is a wide variety of types and quality of study Bibles on the market. Many have useful maps and introductory material for each biblical book. However, I discourage the use of study Bibles in inductive study because I have found that when using them the reader is more drawn to the explanatory notes than to the Scripture text itself. Though there may be some helpful cultural background material included, most of the notes are interpretive in nature. The author(s) of the study Bible approach the Scripture with a particular theological lens, sociological perspective or discipleship agenda. Their reading of the Scripture tends to be deductive rather than inductive.

Research tools enhance inductive Bible study by giving us insight into the world of the biblical authors and their audiences. Of course, it is possible to do a basic manuscript study without these tools. However, with their aid new vistas of understanding emerge, subtle beauty is uncovered and the weight of a text is more fully felt.

PRACTICUM
Where Do I Go for Help?

Read Matthew 4:1-25. Which of the following *three* resources would be most helpful when doing research for an inductive study of this passage? Why?

- Bible background commentary
- Bible dictionary
- Concordance
- Cross-referencing Bible
- *Dictionary of Biblical Imagery*
- English dictionary
- Interlinear Bible
- Maps
- Study Bible

17

Identifying Structure

Common practice among Christians (as well as biblical scholars) is to focus on isolated pieces of Scripture. We read a passage without much thought as to what comes before or after; we use reference material to study particular words; we quote individual verses when encouraging friends. However, as Grant Osborne observes, "Parts have no meaning apart from the whole."[1] The only way to accurately interpret the author's intending meaning of a particular word or verse is to understand it in relationship to the rest. With the exception of the Psalms and Proverbs, which are collections of distinct poems or aphorisms, *where* the material comes in the overall schema of the book matters. Thorough inductive study involves observing both content (*what* words are used) and structure (*how* those words are arranged).

In this chapter, I will introduce practices that are useful in identifying both overall structure and structural elements within and between sections. Before proceeding to those practices, however, a word must be said about the significance of structure.

The relationship between various parts of a book can be envisioned as a pyramid (see figure 17.1). The pyramid is the book as a whole, with each layer representing successive units of communication: words, sentences, paragraphs, scenes, sections. "In the pyramidal approach, the mind is able to grasp all the particulars and see them in relationship to the book as a whole."[2] Interpretation that uses a pyramid approach (identifying the relationship of each part to the whole) instead of a chain approach (identifying the relationship of each part to that which comes before or after) pays attention to structural design in addition to narrative progression.[3]

Artists (including writers) communicate through form as well as content, arranging material in such a way as to reinforce their primary message. This can be seen most obviously in the world of architecture.

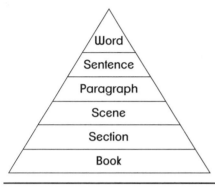

For example, Frank Lloyd Wright designed buildings that mirrored and blended into their natural surroundings to reflect his philosophy of harmony between humanity and the environment. Likewise, the Eiffel Tower, which was built as the entrance arch to the 1889 World's Fair, made a striking statement about France's place among industrializing nations through its massive height and iron latticework. The design choices of the biblical authors are similarly significant and can be seen in a book's overall structure as well as in the structure of various parts.

Figure 17.1.

Determining overall structure is like figuring out the type and purpose of a building—noting the difference, for example, between a three-story colonial-style library and a single-level ranch-style home. It is useful to work on understanding the overall structure of a book before jumping into manuscript study, although this early work should be regarded as preliminary and open to revision after inductively studying the various parts. The overall structure of a book is determined through a three-pronged process: charting, identifying the organizational principle and locating a statement of the book's central message.

Charting enables us to see the basic shape of the book. To create a preliminary chart, begin by quickly reading through the entire book. If the book is more than eight or ten chapters long, read the first and last chapters and thumb through the material in between, noting primary characters and major events.[4] Try dividing the book into three or four sections. Like determining units of thought (see chapter ten), section divisions are marked by significant changes in time, location, characters or topic. It helps to write a short title for each section of the book.

When dividing a book into major sections, we are looking for the author's *organizing principle,* the primary factor used by an author to arrange material. The organizing principle of a book might be determined by looking at its table of contents; the titles of sections sometimes make the organizing principle explicit. This *Bible Study Handbook,* for example, is organized in three sections—"Foundations," "Building Blocks" and "Tools"—which gives you a sense of what the priorities were as the book was written. Using the image of construction, the organizing principle is the convictions and skills needed for studying the Bible inductively.

Biblical narratives are usually organized around key figures (e.g., 1 Samuel), geographic movement (e.g., Exodus) or subject matter (e.g., John). Prophetic books and epistles tend to use thematic organizing principles. Some are arranged as sets of questions and answers (e.g., Habakkuk), warnings and promises (e.g., Isaiah), or a series of topics (e.g., 1 Corinthians).

The third aspect of determining overall structure is identifying the statement of *central message.* Often the core message of the book is stated succinctly in one or two sentences. Sometimes the statement is made by the narrator (e.g., John 20:31), but often it comes from the mouth of the protagonist (e.g., Luke 19:10). Once you've determined the statement of central message, check your chart and organizing principle. The organizing principle should reinforce the central message. If you can't discern how the organizing principle supports the central message, it is likely that you haven't yet understood the author's design of the book.

To illustrate how these three aspects of overall structure work together, let's consider the book of Genesis. The book divides naturally into five sections. It appears that its organizational structure is the patriarchs of Israel (see table 17.1).

Table 17.1

Genesis 1—11	Genesis 12—23	Genesis 24—26	Genesis 27—36	Genesis 37—50
Pre-history	Abraham	Isaac	Jacob	Joseph

While creating the chart, I noticed that each section includes one or more scenes where God makes promises to the main characters. Of these promises, it appears that the statement of the book's central message is encapsulated in the Lord's call to Abraham: "I will make you a great nation. . . . In you all the families of the earth shall be blessed" (Genesis 12:2-3). The core message is supported by the structure: progression from creation and Fall, to the covenant made with Abraham, reaffirmed to Isaac and Jacob, and ending with the account of God's sovereign use of Joseph to bless Egypt and the people of Israel. In light of the central message, it is appropriate to revise the organizing principle from "Israel's patriarchs" to "God's promises to the patriarchs." This overall structure of Genesis provides an interpretative context for understanding individual scenes such as the sacrifice of Isaac (Genesis 22) or Jacob wrestling with the angel (Genesis 32).

Structural elements *within* and *between* sections of text can be determined by assessing where and how the various laws of composition are used.[5] My freshman year of college, I took a New Testament survey class. One day, the professor commented that the Gospel of Mark was an enigma and didn't hold together. He assumed that Mark's stories were placed randomly, in no particular order. A few months later, when I participated in my first Mark manuscript study, I learned that nothing could be further from the truth. Mark's arrangement of material is masterful. The professor either hadn't taken enough time with the text or hadn't been trained in the laws of composition.

Lists of the laws of composition vary in length and nomenclature. It is beyond the scope of this handbook to attempt to describe all of them. However, there are four "laws" that are particularly common in biblical literature: inversion, parallelism, alternation and progression. The following explanations and examples will help students of the Bible appreciate the care taken by biblical authors in designing their work.

Inversion is used "to spotlight that truth which is central and pivotal in a series of truths."[6] A section of material that is inverted is called a *chiasm* (for the Greek letter *x*). In a chiasm, the main point is surrounded by symmetric pairings of material. This technique is seldom seen in contemporary literature, but was very popular among biblical authors. "In

Hebrew it's common to put the punch line in the middle of the story."[7] I find it helpful to think of a chiasm as a carefully made sandwich: bread, lettuce, tomato, cheese, meat, cheese, tomato, lettuce, bread. The crucial idea is in the middle. Luke employs this technique in Luke 4:16-20:

- Jesus stood up
  - He was given the scroll
    - He unrolled the scroll
      - Bring good news to the poor
        - Sent to proclaim release for the captives
          - Recovery of sight for the blind
        - Let the oppressed go free
      - Proclaim the year of the Lord's favor
    - He rolled up the scroll
  - He gave the scroll back to the attendant
- Jesus sat down

Luke uses inversion to highlight that "recovery of sight for the blind" (a metaphor for salvation[8]) was Jesus' primary purpose in ministry. This elaborate chiasm is contained in one paragraph.

Chiasms can be made at any level of the pyramid. Here is one using five consecutive scenes in Mark:

- 2:1-12: Jesus heals paralytic;
  Pharisees question in their hearts
  - 2:13-17: Jesus eats with sinners;
    Pharisees question disciples about Jesus
    - 2:18-22: people question Jesus about disciples;
      Jesus teaches about old and new wineskins
  - 2:23-28: disciples eat while traveling;
    Pharisees question Jesus about disciples
- 3:1-6: Jesus heals man with a withered hand;
  Pharisees plot to kill Jesus

Arranging these five stories using inversion is Mark's way of indicating that Jesus' teaching about the old and new wineskins is the key to understanding why the Pharisees were resistant to Jesus' ministry.

Parallelism uses pairings to highlight the significance of particular content. Luke used it extensively in his Gospel:

- the angel announces a miraculous birth to Zechariah/the angel announces a miraculous birth to Mary (Luke 1)
- Jesus calls Peter/Jesus calls Levi (Luke 5)
- Jesus sends the Twelve/Jesus sends the seventy-two (Luke 9—10)
- Jesus heals the blind man as he enters Jericho/Jesus grants salvation to Zacchaeus as he leaves Jericho (Luke 18—19)

Such pairings invite comparison and contrast. Significant points are made through the process of comparison and contrast rather than through explicit statement. For example, the comparison of Zacchaeus's salvation and the healing of the blind man reveals that Zacchaeus's estrangement from God and the people of Israel was like being blind.

Alternation is switching back and forth between two different subjects to emphasize a series of truths. For example, in Mark 3:7-35 the storyline alternates twice between dangerous crowds and intimate scenes with his followers.[9] In 1-2 Kings, the narrative switches back and forth between the kings of Judah and their counterparts in Israel. Like parallelism, through employing the technique of alternation, the author invites the reader to reflect on comparisons and contrasts.

Progression is the arrangement of material in an order that causes "a particular truth to stand out prominently by its recurrence in each successive literary unit."[10] Progressions can end in a climax or an anticlimax. For example, in Mark 4:35—6:6 there is a repeated element of Jesus' miraculous power. The scenes in this section move from Jesus stilling a storm to exorcising a legion of demons to healing a chronically ill woman and then raising a girl from the dead. The use of progression leads the reader to anticipate something incredible in the final scene. When Jesus came to his hometown, "he could do no deed of power there"; Mark's comment "He was amazed at their unbelief" (Mark 6:6) signals that this progression is intended to teach something about faith.

Biblical authors layer literary techniques, communicating at multiple levels simultaneously. In addition to the progression found in Mark 4:35—6:6, we also find examples of parallelism and inversion. Parallelism is used in the first two scenes (Mark 4:35—5:20) of the "mighty works" section. The stories of the storm and the demoniac are paired: both describe the transformation of chaotic destruction to complete peace as a result of Jesus' rebuke. The next scene (Mark 5:21-43) uses simple inversion. The scene has the healing of the bleeding woman in the middle, "sandwiched" by Jesus' interactions with Jairus. The two healings are tied together further by the repetition of twelve years and the word *daughter*.

Discerning literary structure requires careful observation. Part of the joy and delight of inductive study is discovering various elements of structure. As a friend of mine commented at the end of a manuscript study of John 1—4, "Not only are the stories of Jesus beautiful, but the way John constructs the book is beautiful."

PRACTICUM
Charting Amos

Using the table below, create a chart of the book of Amos. In the process, look for a statement of the primary theme and examples of inversion, parallelism, alternation or progression.

Reference:				
Title:				

Organizing principle:

Statement of core message:

Inversion:

Parallelism:

Alternation:

Progression:

18

Imagination

When I was in high school, I stayed up until almost 2 a.m. on a school night to finish reading *Gone with the Wind*. I had been captivated by the story. I felt as if I had gone to the antebellum South in a time machine. A few months later I watched the movie and was sorely disappointed. Scarlet O'Hara's clothes were beautiful and Clark Gable played a very handsome Rhett Butler, but I didn't like it. The scenes in the movie weren't like the scenes in my head. I had imagined the characters, costumes and settings a certain way, and I preferred my imaginative rendering to that of the movie director.

Using your imagination is a natural part of reading. Through our imagination we are able to "watch" the story in our minds. Some authors provide a lot of detail so that we can imagine something close to what they envisioned when writing their story. Other authors paint general images and leave it to the reader to fill in the details. By and large, readers that use their imagination more fully have greater enjoyment, understanding and retention of what they read.

In his book *Luke: The Gospel of Amazement*, musician Michael Card describes William Lane's exhortation to a group of seminarians: "We must learn to read the Bible at the level of informed imagination."[1] Part of Lane's reasoning is that Jesus' primary method of teaching (parables) required the use of the imagination. Through his seemingly simple stories, Jesus invited his audience to bring their whole selves in contact with his Word, not just their minds. "The imagination is the vital bridge between the heart and the mind."[2] Thus, when Jesus said to the teachers of the law who were criticizing his choice of friends, "Which of you, having a hundred sheep and losing one of them . . ." (Luke 15:3), he was inviting empathetic listening and engaging their imaginations. Jesus wanted these leaders to put themselves in the position of the shepherd, to feel his anxiety when he realized that a sheep was missing and in danger, his elation when he found the sheep, his affection as he hoisted the sheep onto his shoulders, and his joy as he called his friends to celebrate with him. Jesus could have said instead, "I've come for sinners" (and in fact he did). However, knowing his reason for eating with tax collectors wasn't enough; he wanted the Pharisees to share his heart for the lost, and so he engaged their imaginations as a way to access their hearts. Ultimately, he was asking them to put themselves in his shoes as the Good Shepherd, to see the situation from his point of view.

When imagining a biblical scene, you have a choice about which point of view to use. You can imagine it from outside the scene, like watching a play or a movie from the audience. This point of view is valuable and often enables you to grasp the drama of the text at a fuller level. Alternately, you can imagine it from *within* the scene, by picturing yourself as one of the characters. I call this "entering the text." Entering the text enables us to observe from within and accesses a broader range of our senses. For example, imagine yourself as one of Simon's fishing partners in Luke 5:1-11, standing on the shore cleaning your nets after a futile attempt at fishing. You might feel the soreness in your back and shoulders from a night of hard work or the coarseness of the net in your hands as your fingers pluck out slimy lake-weed. You might smell the sweat-soaked clothes of your fellow fishermen, or the stench of decay as the remains of previous days' fishing rot along the shore line. You might hear the sound of seagulls squawking as they vie with each other for food, or the chatter of the crowds who have come to see Jesus.

Entering the text increases the quality of our observation and can lead to greater depth of understanding. Using our imagination can amplify every aspect of inductive study. Use of the imagination is particularly helpful when studying a familiar passage. Try stepping into the shoes of a character you might not normally choose (even the antagonist). Changing point of view can enliven our experience of the text and shine new light.

When leading small groups, I sometimes give the group an assignment before their individual time of study. For example, at a study of Luke 19:1-10 I might say, "Imagine you are a reporter for the *Jerusalem Star*, a tabloid newspaper like the ones found in grocery store checkout lines. If you were writing a feature article about this encounter between Zacchaeus and Jesus, what would your headline be? How about the trailer? What photos would you include?" I find these "Entering the Text" exercises to be effective because they require the use of imagination. Key observations particular to the content are made, and the drama of the text is accessed. Important questions are brought to the surface. Additionally, groups always enjoy hearing what other members have written or drawn.

Here are a variety of "Entering the Text" exercises:

- *Reporter:* Write a brief summary as if you are a reporter writing a story on an event/character.

- *Journal entry:* Write a brief journal entry as though you are one of the characters in the narrative.

- *Eyewitness account:* Write or share in pairs as if speaking from the perspective of an eyewitness to the event (as though you are on trial and asked to give details).

- *Dramatic acting:* Act out the passage as it is being read aloud (works well with traveling scenes).

- *Dramatic reading:* Ask several people in the group to participate and read the passage dramatically. (This works really well with passages in which there's dialogue.)

- *Director:* Imagine you are directing the passage as a scene in a movie; what camera angles or soundtrack might you use?

- *Five senses:* Pick a sense (touch, smell, sight, hearing, taste) and then listen to the passage being read with that sense in mind. Discuss what each "sense" perceived in the passage.

- *Drawing:* On a sheet of paper with a few square blank "cartoon" blocks, draw scenes from the passage.

- *Be the recipient:* Imagine being the original audience hearing this letter or book read in your house church. How does it make you feel? What questions does it make you want to ask the author?[3]

Engaging with the Bible creatively and accessing the resources of our imagination enables us to perceive emphasis, tone, nuance, emotional-motivational force and aesthetic appeal that might be otherwise overlooked or misunderstood. Whether we observe the text from within or from outside of the scene, using imagination, empathy, identification and sensory experiences helps us "tune in" to the author's and original audiences' emotional response to the passage.

At the end of a year-long manuscript study of Mark, my teaching partner and I created an evening simulation in which the group read aloud the entire book of Mark in one sitting. We asked the members of the group to meet us at a particular location dressed as people living in Rome in A.D. 60 (which amounted to a lot of bed sheet togas and sandals). At the appointed time, they were met by a messenger who told them that a scroll written by John Mark had just been received and that they were to come to the secret meeting room at once. The messenger reminded them that the city was filled with Roman soldiers and informants, eager to find followers of Jesus and throw them to the wild animals in the arena. They would need to proceed in groups of no more than three and keep their destination and purpose a secret. After giving directions to the secret meeting room, the messenger vanished. Carefully, a little on edge as they imagined the danger Mark's original audience was in, they made their way across campus and into a hidden garret. By candlelight and in hushed voices, we read through Mark from beginning to end. The text we had studied so closely and been impacted by took on a new level of significance and depth when heard under these conditions. By accessing our imaginations, we entered into the text together and felt the impact of Mark's words at a whole new level.

PRACTICUM
Great Love

Read Luke 7:36-50. Imagine yourself in the scene, first as a servant, then as a Pharisee, and finally as the woman who anointed Jesus. What do you notice about the passage from each perspective?

Servant:

Pharisee:

Woman:

How did this exercise impact you?

19

Commentaries

A quick search for "Bible commentaries" at Amazon.com will produce over 40,000 entries. As the name implies, a commentary is a book written by a biblical scholar or teacher, commenting on a particular book of the Bible. They are organized linearly, with a chapter about background information, followed by an interpretation of each section, moving sequentially through the biblical text. Some commentaries include the author's own translation of the Hebrew or Greek text. Almost all commentaries address the range of meaning of original language words, often arguing for a particular interpretation.

By and large, commentaries use a "chain approach" to interpretation: each verse is examined closely, and relevant scholarship about word usage and theological significance is explained. Verse by verse, the writer takes the reader through a biblical book. Unlike the pyramid approach described in chapter seventeen, the chain approach is less concerned with how the various parts relate to the whole. In fact, most of the commentaries on my bookshelves do not include a final chapter in which themes are reviewed and synthesized. The chain approach pays careful attention to each tree but often misses the shape and beauty of the forest.

There are different kinds of commentaries. On one end of the spectrum are commentaries written by biblical studies professors to share their research with the scholarly community. These can be quite dense and technical, filled with extensive information about textual criticism, analysis of syntax and consideration of linguistic context. Scholarly commentaries rarely make comments about the implications and application of the text.

On the other end are popular commentaries written for the layperson. These often include contemporary illustrations and pastoral suggestions for application.[1] In between the two poles lie commentaries written for pastors and serious students of the Bible. They aren't quite as technical as the scholarly commentaries. There are also unpublished commentaries available online, though these are of such varying quality it is better to avoid them all together.[2]

I find commentaries useful in inductive Bible study if handled thoughtfully. They are particularly helpful for providing background information about the author, date, audience, reason for writing and historical setting of the book you're studying. Some commentaries provide an outline of the book, which can be a useful reference when discerning the overall structure and organizing principle of the book (see chapter seventeen). Remember, however, that the bulk of a commentary is the interpretative work of the author. As noted in chapter one, we tend to abdicate the work of understanding the Bible to experts. It is too easy to encounter something confusing or unclear and seek out the opinion of an expert before we've worked at finding the answer within the text itself. The following guidelines are important to maintain an inductive approach to Bible study, while at the same time benefiting from the members of the body of Christ who serve through biblical scholarship.

Thoroughly study the text on your own first. A blank manuscript is always the best place to begin a study.[3] Robert Traina suggests that "it is best to approach a passage without first looking at previous studies so as to avoid reducing the threshold of perception by prejudicing the mind."[4] Once you have read about a passage in a commentary, your natural instinct will be to tune into the elements described by the commentator to confirm or challenge his opinion. Your mind is already moved along a certain line of reasoning, thus undermining thoroughness in observation or breadth of questioning.

Regard the commentator as a member of the community around the text rather than as the teacher. Publishing makes it possible for us to enter into "conversation" with a broad range of thinkers and leaders. Rigorous discussion with biblical luminaries like F. F. Bruce, John Stott and I. Howard Marshall is stimulating and always leads to deeper understanding of the text, even when we disagree with some of their conclusions. When I pull out a commentary, I envision the author joining me around the table, contributing to the discussion by adding their observations, questions and interpretations. However, the same rule applies to the commentator as to everyone else in the Bible study: all that is said must be substantiated by the text. Often, a commentary brings to light an observation that I had previously missed, but how the commentator uses that observation to build his argument may involve leaps not substantiated by the text.

Know the theological perspective of the commentator. How we understand the Bible is strongly influenced by our theological presuppositions. We can learn from those who don't share our presuppositions, but we must be aware of what those differences are so that we can weigh their arguments. For example, scholars that don't believe in the supernatural (miracles, demons, Jesus' bodily resurrection, prophecy, etc.) will interpret the New Testament differently than those that do. Likewise, a scholar's work is influenced by their hermeneutical assumptions (rules of interpretation), such as belief in authorial intent or a Marxist or feminist approach to the Scripture. To check the perspective of a commentator, read the back cover to see their church affiliation, where they studied theology and where they teach. (You can easily research the statement of faith of a seminary or denomination online.) Can you tell if they believe in miracles? Do they think Jesus is God? Do they believe in his bodily resurrection? (These three factors are often an effective litmus test of orthodoxy.)

Consult two or three commentaries. When using a commentary for a difficult passage, read at least two or three different opinions. Using multiple sources will enable you to see if a particular scholar's perspective is widely held. If you find multiple different interpretations of the same passage, use the various views to help you to dig in further to the text.

PRACTICUM
Identifying Presuppositions

Look at two different commentaries—commentaries you either own or can borrow from a friend or the library. Read the cover, table of contents and introductory material, then flip through the commentary, reading a paragraph here and there. Fill in the following chart to discern each commentator's theological presuppositions.

	Commentary #1	Commentary #2
Title		
Author		
Date written		
Education of author		
Institutional affiliation		
Explicitly stated presuppositions (found in cover material, preface or introduction)		
View of Jesus		
From what you know of this author, how might their approach to faith and the Bible affect their interpretation of this particular book?		

If you selected two commentaries on the same book of the Bible, read entries about the same passage in both. What additional light does this shine on their perspective?

20

Studying Poetry

Roughly one-half of the Old Testament is written in poetic form rather than in prose. This includes the Psalms, the rest of the Wisdom literature and the Prophets. Poetry is used less often in the New Testament, though it stills shows up in hymns (e.g., Philippians 2:5-11), songs (e.g., Revelation 5:9-10), quotations of psalms or prophets (e.g., Galatians 4:27) and when an author wants to emphasize his point (e.g., 1 John 2:12-14). Of the seventeen genres listed in chapter fifteen, five use poetry.

Poetry was popular in the ancient world. "Whole national epics and key historical and religious memories were preserved in poetry. We say 'preserved' because one major advantage of poetry over prose is that is more readily memorized."[1] The rhythm, structure and vivid language make poetry a perfect device for teaching in an oral culture. The people of ancient Israel didn't need to be literate or have a copy of Isaiah's scroll to remember his ringing messages from the Lord. They could participate in communal singing without ever seeing a printed copy of the Psalms. The poetic form enabled them to learn, remember and ruminate on these stirring compositions.

Literature students are taught to do "close readings" of poetry. That process is remarkably similar to manuscript study. The principles of inductive study described in this handbook work well when studying biblical poetry.[2] Paying attention to the following elements will enhance your study of biblical poetry: format, structure, orality, image/ metaphor and clusters of meaning.

Format. When creating a manuscript for a section of text written in poetic form, keep the formatting found in the Bible. In poetry, the length and indentation of various lines is part of the communication. Without poetic formatting it is difficult to recognize a poem's structure and hear its rhythm.

Structure.[3] Common characteristics of Hebrew poetry include the use of parallelism, repetition and alphabetic acrostics. All three of these writing techniques facilitate memorization.

Parallelism uses balance or symmetry to underline key ideas. Most often this involves restatement of an idea in the first and second lines of a sentence with slight alterations of language. For example,

> Let me abide in your tent forever,
>> find refuge under the shelter of your wing. (Psalm 61:4)

Repetition can be found at a variety of levels in a Hebrew poem: a phrase (e.g., "My God, my God," Psalm 22:1), a refrain (e.g., "His steadfast love endures forever," Psalm 118:1, 2, 3, 4, 29) or an entire verse (e.g., "O LORD, our Sovereign, / how majestic is your name in all the earth!" Psalm 8:1, 9). Identifying the most repeated element of a psalm is an effective way of honing in on its core message.

Alphabetic acrostics (in which the first letter of every line spells out the Hebrew alphabet) were used by both psalmists (e.g., Psalm 25) and prophets (e.g., Lamentations 1; 2; 4). Since most of us will not be studying these poems in the original Hebrew, we aren't able to identify which employ alphabetic acrostics without the aid of a Bible background commentary. (See chapter sixteen for more information about research tools.)

Orality. Hebrew poetry was meant to be heard, not read silently. Remember that the Psalms are lyrics to songs used in Israel's corporate worship rather than for personal devotions. To get the full impact of the poetry, read it out loud a few times and pay attention to what effect it has on you emotionally.[4] How would you describe the tone of the poem? (Is it regal? Desperate? Triumphant?) Does the tone shift? If so, why does it shift?

Images and metaphors. Biblical poetry makes extensive use of images (e.g., "cows of Bashan," Amos 4:2), metaphors (e.g., "The Lord is my shepherd," Psalm 23:1) and similes (e.g., "The wicked are . . . like chaff,"

Psalm 1:4). Imagery invites the use of your imagination and appeals to the senses (not just sight and sound but also smell, taste and touch). Consider the various shades of meaning carried by the image. Ask, "How would this image have sounded to the original audience?" Remember that these images are symbolic and should not be taken literally. As Fee and Stuart explain, "You need to appreciate symbolic language (metaphor and simile) for what it is intended to evoke and then to 'translate' it into the reality it is pointing to."[5]

Clusters of meaning. Like prose, poetry can be broken into units of thought.[6] These units are generally called paragraphs when applied to prose, but in poetry I prefer to call them "clusters of meaning." Clusters of meaning in poetry can be seen by a shift in topic, image, direction of the speech (toward God, enemies, other people) or mood. After identifying the clusters, label each succinctly. Then look for patterns in their order. Do you see a progression? Is a comparison or contrast being drawn? How does the construction of the poem reinforce its central message?

I have illustrated each of these elements on one of my favorite biblical poems, Psalm 1 (see figure 20.1). For an ancient Hebrew listener, this psalm vividly communicated the benefits of pursuing righteousness through devotion to the law. By identifying its use of parallelism and repetition, filling out its images and similies, and labeling its clusters of meaning, the contrast between the righteous and wicked jumps off the page.

Almost one third of the Bible is written as poetry, yet most of it is relatively unexplored by Christians. We enjoy familiar psalms and prophetic passages (like Psalm 23 and Isaiah 53), but we run into crosscultural challenges when we stray too far off the beaten path. We can tell that the poetry is meant to be evocative, but we are left flat. This might be because the images don't seem relevant (e.g., "Awake, O harp and lyre!" Psalm 57:8) or we can't easily envision them (e.g., "In exultation I will divide up Shechem / and portion out the Vale of Sukkoth," Psalm 108:7). By studying the Bible's poetry inductively, we are able to bridge the cultural gap and experience the incredible riches of the Bible's poets and prophets. Inductive study will allow you to see even familiar passages with fresh eyes and meet the Lord to whom they point.

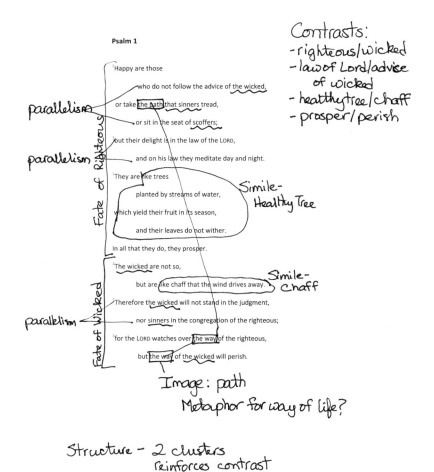

Figure 20.1.

PRACTICUM
Broken Cisterns

- Read Jeremiah 2:9-13 out loud and note what effect it has on you emotionally. How would you describe its tone?

- Mark use of parallelism and repetition.

- Identify any images or metaphors.

- Break the text into clusters of meaning and give each a label.

- Taken together, how might you state the core message of this passage?

Jeremiah 2:9-13

Therefore once more I accuse you,

    says the LORD,

and I accuse your children's children.

Cross to the coasts of Cyprus and look,

5   send to Kedar and examine with care;

    see if there has ever been such a thing.

Has a nation changed its gods,

    even though they are no gods?

But my people have changed their glory

10   for something that does not profit.

Be appalled, O heavens, at this,

    be shocked, be utterly desolate,

        says the LORD,

for my people have committed two evils:

15   they have forsaken me,

the fountain of living water,

    and dug out cisterns for themselves,

cracked cisterns

    that can hold no water.

21

Group Study

Christians are "better together." This is true in inductive Bible study as well as in life. Chapter five described the benefits of small groups studying together: amplifying our experience in the Scripture, developing friendship and creating a launch pad for common mission. This chapter will address some of the practical aspects of group inductive study: the role of the leader, attitudes, ground rules and timing.

ROLE OF THE LEADER

In inductive Bible study, the group leader does not explain the text, answer the group's questions or lecture.[1] Their role is more like a traffic cop, signaling when it is time to cross the street, whose turn it is in the intersection, and when it is time to stop. The traffic cop's goal is not to tell the drivers where to go but to help the cars get through a crowded space quickly and without collisions. In Bible study, the leader directs the flow of the conversation, guiding the group through the inductive process, encouraging healthy interaction and ensuring that the group uses its time well. They do this by explaining the inductive method, helping the group abide by the group rules and deciding which order to discuss the group's questions.[2] More than any other member of the group, the leader pays attention to the process of study and keeps the group continually looking back to the text for understanding. Groups must resist the urge to look to the leader for answers about the meaning of the text, and leaders must resist the urge to be "experts." The quality of the group dynamic and the depth of discussion is greatly improved when the leader responds to a comment or question with, "What do the rest of you think?" and "Do you agree or disagree?" (Additional tips for small group leaders can be found in appendix A.)

ATTITUDES

The attitude or posture of each group member is particularly significant in small group inductive studies. In a lecture hall, someone's cynicism, apathy or hostility doesn't have much impact on the rest of the audience's ability to learn (unless, of course, the person picks a fight with the lecturer). A student that doesn't really want to be in class can be sullen, withdrawn or distracted without affecting those sitting nearby. The opposite is true in communal inductive study. Studying the Bible with a small group is like being part of a basketball team. If one member of the team checks out in the middle of the game, the whole team is affected. The same is true if one member of the team hogs the ball or insists that only he can score. The quality of each person's participation matters.

Since we gather in Jesus' name, our attitude should be shaped by his values. This includes humility, gentleness and being as concerned about another's interests as our own.[3] Too often we don't listen well because we are more concerned about the next point we want to make than with what someone else has seen in the text. Paul calls us to "pursue love" in the community of faith (1 Corinthians 14:1). In small group Bible study, pursuing love looks like drawing one another out, taking each other's contributions seriously and disagreeing respectfully.

Inductive study lends itself to vigorous discussion and even disagreement, but the text is the arbitrator of truth, not the most stubborn person or the one with the loudest voice. Debate in manuscript study should be driven by a mutual commitment to understand the text, not the need to be "right." Cultivating (and praying for) love of the truth and one another can make the process of studying together as transformative as the content of the study itself.

GROUND RULES

I find the following ground rules to be helpful in creating good group dynamic and faithfulness to the inductive method:

1. Only refer to other parts of the Bible that the original audience would have known.
2. Separate observations from interpretation. An observation is a statement of fact. Everyone looking at the text can agree on an observation. If there isn't agreement, the comment is interpretative.
3. All answers must be substantiated by the text itself. Ask each other, "Where do you see that in the text?" Appeals to outside authorities (such as "My pastor says . . .") are off limits.
4. Disagree respectfully and offer counter-evidence from the text.
5. If you find something funny (and you will), share it with the whole group and not just the person next to you.
6. Gently call each other back to the text if someone goes on a tangent.
7. Work hard to listen to one another and build on each other's comments.

TIMING

A common problem in small groups using inductive study is running out of time for application. Remember our third conviction from chapter one? Understanding requires application.

Application may be the last phase, but it certainly is not the least. We are not true to the spirit and purpose of inductive study if our small groups forgo the application discussion.

The key factor in ensuring that a group will complete the entire process and end on time is a leader who is paying attention to pacing. It is helpful to have group members be cognizant of pacing as well. The group is more likely to respond well when a leader says, "Let's move on," even if individuals have more they'd like to discuss in a particular section, if the group has agreed in advance to preserve time for application.

The pacing template in figure 21.1 can be expanded to fit the time allotted for a small group. Many groups that meet for ninety minutes will want to use the sixty-minute template, and allot the other thirty minutes to fellowship, worship or praying together. In an hour-long study, it is difficult to study more than one page of manuscript, but if the group is able to spend one-and-a-half or two hours for manuscript study, a longer section can be tackled. The additional time should be proportionally split between the categories listed above. If time allows, discussion in pairs or triads before the entire group discusses enhances the process. (This is particularly important when there are more than a dozen participants.)

Suggested Pacing for a 1-Hour Inductive Bible Study

5-10 minutes: Introduction and individual study
10 minutes: Group shares observations and questions
25-30 minutes: Group discussion answering questions
2 minutes: Leader summarizes
10 minutes: Application
3 minutes: Prayer

Figure 21.1. Suggested pacing

Like a game of soccer, it is easy to learn the rules and jump into playing together, particularly if the group has a "coach" to provide a little guidance. As much as I love studying the Bible on my own, nothing can compare to group manuscript study that is marked by eagerness to dig into the Scriptures and love for one another. Together we observe more thoroughly, inquire more deeply, think more clearly—and have more fun!

PRACTICUM
Make Your Best Contribution

The contribution of every member of a small group Bible study is necessary for the group to become a true community around the Word. The more individuals grow in their ability to contribute effectively, the better the group experience is for everyone.

The chart below describes ways to contribute to a small group during its various phases: individual study, discussing in pairs and discussing with the group as a whole. These practices are essential to healthy small group Bible studies, but they are also applicable to other types of social or work gatherings.

Think back to the last small gathering you participated in (this might be a Bible study group, a book club, a team meeting, etc.). Put an "S" by the one or two items in which your participation was strongest. Put an "I" by the one or two items which could be improved.

Individual Study	Pairs Discussion	Group Discussion
___ Give your full attention to observing the text	___ Draw each other out	___ Participate fully
___ Articulate your questions	___ Ask follow-up questions	___ Pay attention to the flow of the conversation
	___ Acknowledge new insights	___ Disagree respectfully
		___ Consider alternatives
		___ Share the laughter

Once you have identified a few areas for improvement, look for opportunities in the coming week to put them into practice. Record one insight here from those experiences.

Tips for Small Group Leaders

Studying the Bible together inductively is a lot of fun, but it can get pretty chaotic without someone leading the small group. The role of a Bible study leader is a lot like a traffic cop on a busy street: signaling when to go and when to stop, deciding whose turn it is in the intersection, helping pedestrians cross the street safely. Like a traffic cop, a small group leader pays attention to the entire situation rather than an individual car or a personal destination. Their role includes

- explaining the inductive method (the first handout in appendix B can be used to introduce inductive study; the second handout is a tool to help a group learn how to pay closer attention to the text)

- helping the group abide by the ground rules (see chapter twenty-one)

- deciding which questions and in which order to discuss as a group

- encouraging the group to keep looking to the text

- pacing the group discussion so that there is adequate time for application

- summarizing the core message

- selecting application questions

The annotated outline of a one-hour manuscript study explains how specifically to guide a group through the inductive process. If the group has more than an hour to study together, each category can be expanded proportionally. For tips about how much biblical text to cover in a session, read more about selection in chapter twelve.

ANNOTATED OUTLINE OF A ONE-HOUR
INDUCTIVE BIBLE STUDY

- Introduction—2 minutes (a little longer the first day)
  - » Share cultural background and context information.
  - » Read the passage out loud.
- Individual time—5 minutes
  - » Give group members time to study the passage individually.
  - » Encourage them to
    1. look for the specifics such as who, what, when, where and how
    2. look for connections within the text such as repetitions and contrasts
    3. enter the text experientially by becoming one of the characters in the story
    4. write down the questions that come to their mind
- Share observations/questions together—15 minutes
  - » Ask: "What do you see here, and what questions do you have?" To encourage the sharing ask open-ended questions such as "What else did you see?" and "What else did you notice?" Do *not* ask *content* questions such as "Where were Jesus and the disciples going?" or "Who did Jesus encounter on the road to Samaria?" These kind of questions shut down the sharing process because they are not open-ended.
  - » Note the questions group members raise, but remind the group that you won't be discussing them till later.
  - » This time should be lively.
- Answer questions together—25 minutes
  - » Starting with the beginning of the text, walk through the passage using questions generated by the group.
  - » Use your own questions when necessary to cover the key sections of the text.

> » Encourage the group to base their answers on evidence from the text itself and the context. Do not let the group use cross-references except for Old Testament passages that are alluded to in the text.

> » Keep them in the text, and help them develop good questions and answer them from the passage, its context and the Old Testament background. If you have helped the group observe well, the group itself becomes self-correcting.

- Summarize—3 minutes

> » After walking through the passage and answering the questions as a group, a few main themes should emerge. Summarize those with a few sentences.

> » Try to use the language of the text and the group as much as possible.

- Process/apply—10 minutes

> » Help the group process and apply the passage.

> » Have some possible application questions ready to go.

> » This is where Jesus will solidify what he has been speaking to the group about in the study. He will transform them by his Word as they make specific applications and then do them.

Remember that you are the facilitator of the group's learning, not a lecturer. The biggest mistake that small group leaders make is talking too much. Inductive study is highly participatory and interactive. The goal is for the participants to discover the truth of God's Word themselves, not to have it explained to them by a teacher. Studying the Bible inductively helps a group build a shared understanding of the text (see chapter five). Small group leaders facilitate this process of communal discovery by regularly asking the group, "What do you see in the text?" and "What do the rest of you think?" As you create space for the group in engage with the text and each other, you will have a front row seat to watch the Holy Spirit at work in the community through God's powerful Word.

Introduction to Inductive Bible Study

Goals

1. Discover what a biblical author intended to communicate to his original audience.
2. Encounter Jesus and be transformed by his Word.

Implications

1. God works through human authors who made choices of words, phrases, illustrations, etc.
2. Studying the Bible is a crosscultural experience for us because we don't live in the ancient world that the original audience did.
3. It takes effort and humility to think about the author and audience rather than expect the Bible to be written directly for us.

Three Steps

- *Observation*—What does the text say?

- *Interpretation*—What does the text mean?

- *Application*—How does the text speak to my life?

Observation

Look for 7 FACT-finding questions—questions to determine . . .

- the SETTING or CONTEXT—Who? Where? When?

- the EVENT or IDEA—What? How? Why?

- the RESULT or CONSEQUENCE—So?
- word RELATIONSHIPS—repetitions, similarities, contrasts, cause to effect, general to particular, particular to general, etc.
- LOGICAL CONNECTORS—but, for, therefore, so that, because, if . . . then.
- UNITS of thought—change in location, time, theme, characters, thought or actions
- Old Testament QUOTES or allusions

Interpretation

1. Ask good questions:
   - Use the language of the text.
   - Include in your question the issue that troubles or intrigues you.
   - Refer to the original audience.
2. Answer your questions from the text:
   - Use the immediate context to define meanings.
   - Develop theories that hold multiple observations together.
   - Use cultural and historical background to answer through the lens of the author and original audience.
3. Summarize the core message.

Application

- Pray for the Holy Spirit to lead you.
- Turn the main point(s) into questions for reflection.
- Look for places in your life that are similar to one of the characters or the situation.
- Look for promises, commands and/or an example to follow or avoid.
- Be specific.
- Choose an action that you can take in the next two days.
- Share your insights/plans with another.

Paying Attention to the Bible

Observing a passage closely involves paying attention to three areas:

1. context—the narrative, historical and cultural setting of a passage, which shed light on its significance and meaning
2. content—the facts that make up the story
3. connections—strategies used by authors to make their point

Context

Context Element	How to Determine	Example
Narrative context	Note the stories immediately before and after. Look for major repetitions or contrasts with those stories. Where does this passage happen within the course of the book?	The healing of the blind man as Jesus enters Jericho (Luke 18:35-43) immediately precedes the story of the restoration of Zacchaeus as Jesus is leaving Jericho (Luke 19:1-10).
Historical context	Where does this passage fit within the big story told by the entire Bible? Locate the passage in relationship to key biblical events. If reading a prophetic book, read about the history of Israel at that time in the historical books of the Old Testament.	Jesus' comments about the fall of the Temple in Mark 13 happen forty years before the destruction of the Temple by the Roman army (Acts 3—4). First John is written late in the first century by one of the last remaining eyewitnesses of Jesus' life, death and resurrection (1 John 1:1-3).
Cultural context	Research author, audience, and time and purpose of writing in a Bible dictionary. Continually ask, "What did the author intend to communicate to the original audience?" Look up key or confusing words and concepts in a concordance or Bible dictionary. Put yourself in the shoes of the audience to feel the weight of a passage. Ask the questions the audience might ask, rather than twenty-first-century questions.	*Baptism* (Mark 1:5): "Non-Jews who were converting to Judaism would immerse themselves in water, probably under the supervision of a religious expert. John's baptizing activity fits this model." (Craig S. Keener, *The IVP Bible Background Commentary: New Testament* [Downers Grove, Ill.: InterVarsity Press, 1993], p. 135.) *Knowledge of good and evil* (Genesis 2:9): A Jewish idiom for independent moral choice (e.g., Deuteronomy 1:39; 2 Samuel 19:35). (John Goldingay, *Old Testament Theology: Israel's Gospel* [Downers Grove, Ill.: InterVarsity Press, 2003], p. 132.)

Content

Content Element	Example	Pay Attention
Characters	A blind man, crowds, Simon Peter, the Pharisees	Note both individuals and groups; note which are major and minor
Descriptors of characters	Short, angry, rich, muttering	Note adjectives, verbs, adverbs and emotions for each.
References to any member of Trinity	God, Father, Jesus, Lord, Holy Spirit, Son of Man, Rabbi, etc.	Note the different titles used and who uses them. Particularly notice everything Jesus says and does.
Character interactions and relationships	Peter to Jesus: "Go away from me, Lord" (Luke 5:8); Jesus touches the leper (Mark 1:41)	Note when dialogue or monologue; note speaker for each quotation.
Places and setting	Jericho, sycamore tree, house, wilderness, synagogue, a banquet	Look up each place on a map; note distance between locations.
Time references	Now, in those days, later, in the year of, immediately	Notice the length of time passed between actions and events since the preceding story.
Primary event(s)	Miracle, confrontation, teaching, travel	Note if there is one primary event or a few woven together. If so, ask yourself how these events are related to each other.
Action (verbs)	Mark 1:17: "Follow Me" (command in present tense) "and I will make you become fishers of men" (NASB) (promise in future tense)	Note imperatives; notice shift between past, present and future tense.
Old Testament allusions or quotations	"Clothed with camel's hair, with a leather belt around his waist" (Mark 1:6/2 Kings 1:8); "eat bread in the kingdom of God" (Luke 14:15/ Isaiah 25:6)	Use a Bible with cross-references or a Bible background commentary to find exact references in Old Testament; read the context of the Old Testament reference.
Numbers	"He summoned ten of his slaves and gave them ten pounds" (Luke 19:13); "He was in the wilderness forty days, tempted by Satan" (Mark 1:13)	Calculate size or amount into a modern unit of measurement. Some numbers, such as 6, 7, 12, 40 and 70, have symbolic overtones and indicate an Old Testament allusion.

Connections

Connection Element	Definition	Example
Repetition	Reiteration of same the term	"Holy" (Leviticus); "seed" (Mark 4:1-20)
Continuity	Repeated use of similar terms, phrases, ideas	Three lost and found parables (Luke 15)
Series or progression	The relationship between parts of group with common characteristics; can be indicated by use of *and, moreover, furthermore, likewise* or *then*	"In the beginning was the Word, *and* the Word was with God, *and* the Word was God" (John 1:1)
Contrast or alternative	Association of opposites; often indicated by use of *but, some . . . others, not . . . but, although . . . yet, though . . . yet.*	The righteous and the wicked (Psalm 1); "*Some* were convinced by what he had said, while *others* refused to believe" (Acts 28:24)
Comparison	Association of things that are alike but vary in some way; sometimes indicated by use of *even as, as* or *so*	Four kinds of soil in parable of the sower (Mark 4:1-20); "*As* the Father has sent me, *so* I send you" (John 20:21)
Images, symbols, metaphors	Expression of a secondary idea distinct from the original meaning of the term	"Olive tree" (Romans 11:24); "living water" (John 4:11)
Cause to effect	Progression from the reason for an action or condition to the result; a situation that leads to a response; sometimes indicated by use of *so that, that* or *immediately*	Paralytic obeying Jesus' command to stand up (Luke 5:24-25); "Suddenly there was an earthquake, so violent *that* the foundations of the prison were shaken; and *immediately* all the doors were opened" (Acts 16:26)
General to specific	Movement from a general idea or activity to particulars about that idea	"The LORD is my shepherd, I shall not want" followed by specific ways the author is cared for by the Lord (Psalm 23)
Climax	Progression from lesser to greater to greatest	Tempted by desire, desire conceived, sin birthed, sin fully grown, sin gives birth to death (James 1:14-15)
Reason	Words such as *for, because, since, as* and *whereas* reveal reasoning or explanation	"Blessed are the poor in spirit, *for* theirs is the kingdom of heaven" (Matthew 5:3); "I heard the sound of you in the garden, and I was afraid *because* I was naked" (Genesis 3:10)

Connection Element	Definition	Example
Inference	A conclusion based on an event or statement; often indicated by use of *therefore, wherefore, consequently* or *accordingly*	"Many of the Jews *therefore*, who had come with Mary and had seen what Jesus did, believed in him" (John 11:45); "Be perfect, *therefore*, as your heavenly Father is perfect" (Matthew 5:48)
Condition	A statement that is only true or will happen if something else is true or happens; indicated by *if, if...then* or *provided that*	"*If* you love me, you will keep my commandments" (John 14:15)
Temporal statements	The relationship between an action and the time the action can come to pass; indicated by *when, then* or *whenever*	"Blessed are you *when* people revile you and persecute you" (Matthew 5:11)

Adapted from Robert Traina, *Methodical Bible Study* (Grand Rapids: Zondervan, 1980), pp. 50-52.

Appendix D

Laws of Composition

Extended Version

Category	Definition	Example
Repetition	Reiteration of the same term	"Holy" (Leviticus); "seed" (Mark 4:1-20)
Continuity	Repeated use of similar terms, phrases, ideas	Three lost and found parables (Luke 15)
Series or progression	The relationship between parts of group with common characteristics; can be indicated by use of *and, moreover, furthermore, likewise* or *then*	"In the beginning was the Word, *and* the Word was with God, *and* the Word was God" (John 1:1)
Contrast or alternative	Association of opposites; often indicated by use of *but, some . . . others, not . . . but, although . . . yet, though . . . yet* There are two different Greek words for *but*. One is weaker than the other; it can be translated as *and* or *but*. The weaker word doesn't indicate a sharp contrast. A primary interpretation should not be based on a logical argument using *but* unless you have checked which Greek word is used. This can be done by using an interlinear Bible (described in chapter sixteen).	The righteous and the wicked (Psalm 1); "*Some* were convinced by what he had said, while *others* refused to believe" (Acts 28:24)
Comparison	Association of things that are alike but vary in some way; sometimes indicated by use of *even as, as* or *so*	Four kinds of soil in parable of the sower (Mark 4:1-20); "*As* the Father has sent me, *so* I send you" (John 20:21)
Images, symbols, metaphors	Expression of a secondary idea distinct from the original meaning of the term	"Olive tree" (Romans 11:24); "living water" (John 4:11)

Category	Definition	Example
Cause to effect	Progression from the reason for an action or condition to the result; a situation that leads to a response; sometimes indicated by use of *so that, that* or *immediately*	Paralytic obeying Jesus' command to stand up (Luke 5:24-25); "Suddenly there was an earthquake, so violent *that* the foundations of the prison were shaken; and *immediately* all the doors were opened" (Acts 16:26)
Effect to cause	Progression from the result to what caused it	"Submit to one another out of reverence for Christ" (Ephesians 5:21)
General to specific	Movement from a general idea or activity to particulars about that idea	"The Lᴏʀᴅ is my shepherd, I shall not want" followed by specific ways the author is cared for by the Lord (Psalm 23)
Specific to general	Movement from a particular idea or activity to the general category	The healing of Simon's mother-in-law followed by healing many people (Mark 1:30-34)
Climax	Progression from lesser to greater to greatest	Tempted by desire, desire conceived, sin birthed, sin fully growth, sin gives birth to death (James 1:14-15)
Reason	Words such as *for, because, since, as* and *whereas* reveal reasoning or explanation	"Blessed are the poor in spirit, *for* theirs is the kingdom of heaven" (Matthew 5:3); "I heard the sound of you in the garden, and I was afraid *because* I was naked" (Genesis 3:10)
Means to an end	Explanation of purpose or intent; *so that* or *in order that* is often used	"These are written *so that* you might come to believe" (John 20:31)
Inference	A conclusion based on an event or statement; often indicated by use of *therefore, wherefore, consequently* or *accordingly*	"Many of the Jews *therefore*, who had come with Mary and had seen what Jesus did, believed in him" (John 11:45); "Be perfect, *therefore*, as your heavenly Father is perfect" (Matthew 5:48)
Condition	A statement that is only true or will happen if something else is true or happens; indicated by *if, if . . . then* or *provided that*	"*If* you love me, you will keep my commandments" (John 14:15)
Temporal statements	The relationship between an action and this time the action can come to pass; indicated by *when, then* or *whenever*	"Blessed are you *when* people revile you and persecute you" (Matthew 5:11)

Category	Definition	Example
Explanation or analysis	The presentation of an idea or event followed by its analysis	"Destroy this temple, and in three days I will raise it up," followed by John's explanation that Jesus was referring to his crucifixion and resurrection (John 2:19-22)
Preparation or introduction	Inclusion of background or setting for events or ideas that follow	Luke 3:1-2 describes who was in power at the time of Jesus' birth
Interrogation	A question or problem followed by its answer; if a question is rhetorical and unanswered, it is meant as a declarative statement	Romans 6 begins with four questions
Juxtaposition	The placing of incidents or ideas side by side in order to clarify or interpret each other	Alternation of Jesus' teaching and miracles (Mark 1:21—3:6)
Inclusion	The reporting of one event within the reporting of another event	Jesus' cleansing of the Temple told between the cursing and withering of the fig tree (Mark 11:12-25)

Adapted from Robert Traina, *Methodical Bible Study* (Grand Rapids: Zondervan, 1980), pp. 50-52.

Resources

Books About Bible Study

Charpentier, Etienne. *How to Read the Old Testament.* New York City: Crossroad Publishing Company, 1985.

Dyck, Elmer, ed. *The Act of Bible Reading.* Downers Grove, Ill.: InterVarsity Press, 1996.

Fee, Gordon, and Douglas Stuart. *How to Read the Bible for All Its Worth.* Grand Rapids: Zondervan, 1993.

Grahmann, Robert. *Transforming Bible Study.* Downers Grove, Ill.: Inter-Varsity Press, 2003.

Kuhatschek, Jack. *Applying the Bible.* Grand Rapids: Zondervan, 1990.

Books for Researching Context

Keener, Craig. *The IVP Bible Background Commentary: New Testament.* Downers Grove, Ill.: InterVarsity Press, 1993.

Marshall, I. Howard, A. R. Millard, J. I. Packer and D. J. Wiseman, eds. *New Bible Dictionary,* 3rd ed. Downers Grove, Ill.: InterVarsity Press, 1999.

Nelson's Complete Book of Maps and Charts, 3rd ed. Nashville: Thomas Nelson, 1996.

Ryken, Leland, James C. Wilhoit and Tremper Longman III, eds. *Dictionary of Biblical Imagery.* Downers Grove, Ill.: InterVarsity Press, 1998.

Walton, John H., Victor H. Matthews and Mark W. Chavalas. *The IVP Bible Background Commentary: Old Testament.* Downers Grove, Ill.: InterVarsity Press, 2000.

Videos for Introducing Inductive Bible Study

2100 Productions. *The Discovery Series: Learning How to Engage with Scripture.* Madison, Wis.: InterVarsity Christian Fellowship/USA, 2006. Three- to four-minute videos introducing the central elements of inductive Bible study: Observation, Interpretation, Application. For sale online at https://store.intervarsity.org/dvd-cd/bible-missions.

———. *The Transformation Series*. Madison, Wis.: InterVarsity Christian Fellowship/USA, 2012. Three- to four-minute videos introducing the character traits needed when studying the Bible inductively: Curiosity, Attentiveness, Trustworthiness. For sale online at https://store.intervarsity.org/dvd-cd/bible-missions.

Preprinted Manuscripts

The InterVarsity Store sells all the books of the Bible in manuscript format, in three translations. They have obtained permission from the publishers to print the number of copies ordered, but do not have permission to send the manuscripts electronically or to grant permission to make copies. To order, contact the InterVarsity Store at 1-866-265-4823 or ivstore@intervarsity.org.

Acknowledgments

Christian leaders don't develop in isolation; they are nurtured in community and developed by mentors. I am no exception. I'm deeply grateful to the InterVarsity staff team in Los Angeles in the late 1980s/early 1990s for making manuscript Bible study the center of our life and ministry. Our years together were some of the richest in my life as we built a common understanding of the Gospel of Mark and sought to embody that understanding on campus. Many of the ideas in this book were developed by that team. I've merely sought to gather and articulate our insights about inductive study for a broader audience.

God has blessed me with remarkable mentors who have been loving friends as well as skilled coaches. Lisa Adamovich Engdahl's passion for the Scripture and commitment to make space for the Word was infectious. She was the first to affirm my teaching gifts and gave me many opportunities to learn and grow. Lisa, more than any other leader, has shaped my understanding of the spirituality of study and teaching. Al Anderson walked with me through darker days and provided affirmation of God's call on my life as a teacher and leader. Bob Grahmann made space for me in the broader ministry of InterVarsity by inviting me to teach and train alongside him. He has been my closest partner in thinking through adjustments and new possibilities for manuscript study in a postmodern world. In this book, he will find echoes of our many conversations and experiments.

I am thankful for the staff at InterVarsity Press who share my love for the Scripture and have been so encouraging about this project. Particular thanks goes to Andy Le Peau for initiating the interaction which led to this book and to my editor, Dave Zimmerman, whose feedback and perspective has been invaluable.

Finally, I am grateful for my family and all their love and support. My father provided a model of rigorous thinking and of discipline as a writer in addition to his love and affirmation. My mother has been a true servant, helping me to juggle my many responsibilities and filling in the gaps as needed. My stepmother's life of courageous leadership as a woman in a field previously dominated by men has been a constant source of inspiration as I've developed as a female leader and teacher in the evangelical world. My husband has been my best friend and greatest fan. His insightful questions and constructive input have helped me at every stage of writing.

notes

Introduction

[1]Throughout this handbook, unless otherwise indicated, the New Revised Standard Version of the Bible is used. See chapter thirteen for more information on selecting a translation for your inductive study of the Word.

Chapter 1: Centrality of the Word

[1]See chapter nineteen for instruction on selecting and using commentaries.

[2]The medieval church's assumption of geocentrism had more to do with the biases of ancient Greek philosophers than it did with the Scriptures.

[3]Sir Arthur Conan Doyle, *A Scandal in Bohemia* (n.p., 1891).

[4]Daniel P. Fuller, "An Investigation of the Literary Structure of the Gospel of Mark," Master's thesis, Fuller Seminary, Pasadena, Calif., 1952, p. 57.

[5]Read this testimony and more at <www.bereansafari.org/testimonials/>.

[6]Joel B. Green, *Seized by Truth* (Nashville: Abingdon, 2007), pp. 11-12.

[7]Dietrich Bonhoeffer, *Life Together* (San Francisco: Harper & Row, 1954), p. 82.

[8]Doug Schaupp, "Unleashing a Biblical Revolution: The Life and Ministry of Paul Byer," written for a class at Fuller Seminary, Pasadena, California, 2001, pp. 2-3.

Chapter 2: Power of the Word

[1]St. John's Abbey, *The St. John's Bible,* viewable in context at <www.loc.gov/exhibits/stjohnsbible/images/itw0016as.jpg>.

Chapter 3: Authority of the Word

[1]Don Richardson, *Eternity in Their Hearts,* 3rd ed. (Grand Rapids: Regal, 2005), p. 86.

[2]Ibid., p. 74.

[3]Donald Bloesch, *Holy Scripture* (Downers Grove, Ill.: InterVarsity Press, 2005), p. 200.

[4]Ben Witherington, *Letters and Homilies for Hellenized Christians,* vol. 2 (Downers Grove, Ill.: InterVarsity Press, 2008), p. 333.

[5]Christopher J. H. Wright, *The Mission of God: Unlocking the Bible's Grand Narrative* (Downers Grove, Ill.: InterVarsity Press, 2006), p. 54.

Chapter 4: Water for the Soul

[1]N. T. Wright, *Evil and the Justice of God* (Downers Grove, Ill.: InterVarsity Press, 2006), p. 162.

[2]Eugene H. Peterson, *Eat This Book: A Conversation in the Art of Spiritual Reading* (Grand Rapids: Eerdmans, 2006), p. 17.

[3]James H. Evans Jr., *We Have Been Believers* (Minneapolis: Fortress Press, 1992), p. 102.

[4]Ibid.

[5]I appreciate the time Gary Deddo, senior editor at InterVarsity Press, gave to answer my questions about the theology of the soul.

[6]A full consideration of how to care for the soul is beyond the scope of this book. I recommend Adele Calhoun's *Spiritual Disciplines Handbook* (Downers Grove, Ill.: InterVarsity Press, 2005).

[7]Ajith Fernando, "Laziness About Objective Truth," unpublished, 2009.

[8]For a "balanced diet" I highly recommend all of the spiritual practices mentioned in this section.

[9]Daniel Coleman, *In Bed with the Word* (Edmonton: University of Alberta Press, 2009), p. 8.

[10]The image of living water is used in the Bible concurrently as a representative of God's law (Psalm 1:3), the Lord himself (Jeremiah 2:13; 17:7-8) and the Holy Spirit (John 4:13-14; 7:37-39).

[11]Fernando, "Laziness About Objective Truth."

Chapter 5: Community Around the Word

[1]Dan Siewert, "Building a House," unpublished paper, 1992.

[2]InterVarsity Christian Fellowship/USA seeks to do this regularly, by calling the entire organization to soak in the text chosen for its triennial Urbana Student Missions Conference for the full year prior to the event. For Urbana 06 the text was the book of Ephesians; for Urbana 09, John 1—4; for Urbana 12, selections from Luke.

[3]Eugene H. Peterson, *Eat This Book: A Conversation in the Art of Spiritual Reading* (Grand Rapids: Eerdmans, 2006), p. 18.

[4]"The Basis of a Biblical Organization," World Vision Christian Leadership Letter, January 1983, p. 3.

Chapter 6: Honor the Author

[1]A. J. Jacobs, *The Know-It-All: One Man's Humble Attempt to Become the Smartest Man in the World* (New York: Simon & Schuster, 2004).

[2]Of course, I think it is incredibly important to read the entire Bible, and cover to cover is an easy way to keep track of your progress.

[3]The different genres in the Bible are important to identify, as the form of a piece of writing affects its interpretation. Chapter seventeen will teach you how to identify the various genres found in the Bible and comment on the implications for studying each.

[4]Donald G. Bloesch, *Holy Scripture: Revelation, Inspiration & Interpretation* (Downers Grove, Ill.: InterVarsity Press, 1994), p. 123.

[5]Ibid., p. 129.

[6]I. Howard Marshall, A. R. Millard, J. I. Packer and Donald J. Wiseman, eds., *New Bible Dictionary*, 3rd ed. (Downers Grove, Ill.: InterVarsity Press, 2008), p. 1057.

[7]Bloesch, *Holy Scripture,* p. 119.

[8]Walter Brueggemann, "Books of Kings," in *New Bible Dictionary*, ed. I. Howard Marshall, A. R. Millard, J. I. Packer and D. J. Wiseman, 3rd ed. (Downers Grove, Ill.: InterVarsity Press, 2008), p. 650.

[9]W. S. La Sor, D. A. Hubbard and F. W. Bush, *Old Testament Survey* (Grand Rapids: Eerdmans, 1991), p. 636.

[10]J. E. Goldingay, "Books of Chronicles," in *New Bible Dictionary*, ed. I. Howard Marshall, A. R. Millard, J. I. Packer and D. J. Wiseman, 3rd ed. (Downers Grove, Ill.: InterVarsity Press, 2008), p. 185.

[11]La Sor, Hubbard and Bush, *Old Testament Survey*, p. 636.

[12]Ibid., p. 178.

Chapter 7: Respect for the Story

[1]Donald Bloesch, *Holy Scripture: Revelation, Inspiration & Interpretation* (Downers Grove, Ill.: InterVarsity Press, 1994), p. 200.

[2]Chapter breaks are not an element of the original texts. In fact, they weren't added to the text until the twelfth century. Their placement is at times arbitrary rather than reflective of the overall structure of a book.

[3]I recommend Sean Gladding, *The Story of God, the Story of Us* (Downers Grove, Ill.: InterVarsity Press, 2010) and Vaughan Roberts, *God's Big Picture: Tracing the Storyline of the Bible* (Downers Grove, Ill.: InterVarsity Press, 2002).

Chapter 8: Attentiveness

[1]Daniel P. Fuller, "An Investigation of the Literary Structure of the Gospel of Mark," Master's thesis, Fuller Seminary, Pasadena, Calif., 1952, p. 68.

[2]Agatha Christie, *The Murder of Roger Ackroyd* (New York: HarperCollins, 2011), p. 76.

[3]H. T. Kuist, *These Words Upon Thy Heart* (Westminster, Penn.: John Knox Press, 1947), p. 79.

[4]Robert Traina, *Methodical Bible Study* (Grand Rapids: Zondervan, 1980), p. 31.

[5]J. H. Jowett, *Brooks by the Traveller's Way* (New York: A. C. Armstrong and Son, 1901), p. 78.

[6]Fuller, "An Investigation of the Literary Structure of the Gospel of Mark," p. 69.

[7]Grant R. Osborne, *The Hermeneutical Spiral* (Downers Grove, Ill.: InterVarsity Press, 1991), p. 23. We are usually more readily aware of when a sentence has been broken unnaturally (e.g., Acts 9:19).

[8]Kuist, *These Words Upon Thy Heart*, p. 79.

[9]N. T. Wright, *Jesus and the Victory of God* (Minneapolis: Fortress Press, 1996), p. 198.

[10]J. Scott Duvall and J. Daniel Hays, *Grasping God's Word* (Grand Rapids: Zondervan, 2003), p. 130.

[11]The *New Bible Dictionary* and *The IVP Bible Background Commentary* are both excellent resources.

Chapter 9: Curiosity

[1]Nancy Ortberg, *Unleashing the Power of Rubber Bands* (Carol Stream, Ill.: Tyndale House, 2008), pp. 149-50.

[2]Chip Heath and Dan Heath, *Made to Stick: Why Some Ideas Survive and Others Die* (New York: Random House, 2007), p. 81.

Chapter 10: Understanding

[1]Shawn Young, "Ask Away," *Student Leadership Journal*, fall 2003, p. 34.

[2]"The Student, the Fish, and Agassiz," *Appendix of American Poems* (New York: Houghton, Osgood & Co., 1880).

[3]Clarence Edward Flynn, quoted by Robert Traina, *Methodical Bible Study* (Grand Rapids: Zondervan, 1980), p. 33.

[4]Paul J. Achtemeier, Joel B. Green and Marianne Meye Thompson, *Introducing the New Testament: Its Literature and Theology* (Grand Rapids: Eerdmans, 2001), p. 91.

[5]Gordon D. Fee and Douglas Stuart, *How to Read the Bible for All Its Worth* (Grand Rapids: Zondervan, 2003).

[6]For a Bible dictionary I recommend I. Howard Marshall, A. R. Millard, J. I. Packer and Donald J. Wiseman, *New Bible Dictionary*, 3rd ed. (Downers Grove, Ill.: Inter-Varsity Press, 1996); for Old Testament background, John H. Walton, Victor H. Matthews and Mark W. Chavalas, *The IVP Bible Background Commentary: Old Testament* (Downers Grove, Ill.: InterVarsity Press, 2000); and for New Testament background, Craig Keener, *The IVP Bible Background Commentary: New Testament* (Downers Grove, Ill.: InterVarsity Press, 1993).

[7]For example, there are many possible meanings of the phrase "the kingdom of God is at hand" (Mark 1:15). If we looked at a more remote context like Mark 4:30-32 for our meaning, we might argue that the phrase means "a small thing that will grow large is at hand." Or, if we looked to even more remote context—first-century Jewish understandings of "kingdom or God"—we might argue that the phrase means "a military victory over Rome is at hand." But neither of those meanings is accurate because the immediate context of the passage (Mark chapter 1) makes it clear that the entire section is about Jesus' kingship. Thus the phrase means "the king of God's kingdom is in your midst, literally at arm's length."

[8]Keener, *IVP Bible Background Commentary: New Testament*, p. 241.

[9]Marshall, Millard, Packer and Wiseman, *New Bible Dictionary*, p. 577.

[10]Cross-referencing other Gospels is also out of bounds, since all that is needed to understand Luke's intended meaning can be found in Luke's text.

[11]The same result can be accomplished by doing a word search at sites like www.biblegateway.com.

[12]See table 8.3 for the description of these elements.

Chapter 11: Response

[1]Ben Witherington III, *Letters and Homilies for Jewish Christians* (Downers Grove, Ill.: InterVarsity Press, 2007), p. 443.

[2]Richard Foster with Kathryn Helmers, *Life with God* (San Francisco: HarperOne, 2008), p. 21.

Chapter 12: Selection

[1]This works fine if the leader provides an overview of the book and regularly asks the group to see the selection of the week within the structure of the whole.

[2]These parables of the pearl of great price and the treasure hidden in a field should be studied together; Jesus sets them up in parallel, so comparing and contrasting them illuminates the meaning of both.

[3]An exception to my two-page manuscript rule of thumb is when the text includes a list (such as Nehemiah 3). The process of observing a list is different from observing a narrative or epistle.

Chapter 13: Creating a Manuscript

[1]Paul Byer, "Ross Letter," unpublished, 1986.

[2]Today, there are those reaching out to Muslims in closed access countries whose entire ministry is built around manuscript study of the Gospels. They have shared with me that the method is remarkably transcultural and needs little contextualization.

[3]Gordon D. Fee and Douglas Stuart, *How to Read the Bible for All Its Worth* (Grand Rapids: Zondervan, 2003), p. 33.

[4]Ibid, p. 41.

[5]Byer, "Ross Letter."

Chapter 14: Prayer

[1]In the Gospel of Mark, both the Pharisees *and* Jesus' disciples are described as having hard hearts (Mark 3:5; 5:52).

[2]Eugene H. Peterson, *Eat This Book: A Conversation in the Art of Spiritual Reading* (Grand Rapids: Eerdmans, 2006), p. 15.

Chapter 15: Determining Genre

[1]Most of this material has been adapted from Gordon D. Fee and Douglas Stuart, *How to Read the Bible for All Its Worth* (Grand Rapids: Zondervan, 1993).

[2]The ancient manuscripts didn't include diagrams or drawings, only written instructions. Today plans for buildings and objects are usually communicated through blueprints or sketches.

Chapter 16: Research Tools

[1]You can also buy Bible software that combines Bible study with electronic collections of dictionaries, concordances and commentaries.

[2]InterVarsity Press publishes a Bible background commentary for each of the New and Old Testaments: John H. Walton, Victor H. Matthews and Mark W. Chavalas, *The IVP Bible Background Commentary: Old Testament* (Downers Grove, Ill.: InterVarsity Press, 2000) and Craig S. Keener, *The IVP Bible Background Commentary: New Testament* (Downers Grove, Ill.: InterVarsity Press, 1993).

[3]Leland Ryken, James C. Wilhoit and Tremper Longman III, *Dictionary of Biblical Imagery* (Downers Grove, Ill.: InterVarsity Press, 1998).

[4]*Nelson's Complete Book of Bible Maps and Charts* (Nashville: Thomas Nelson, 1993).

Chapter 17: Identifying Structure

[1]Grant R. Osborne, *The Hermeneutical Spiral* (Downers Grove, Ill.: InterVarsity Press, 1991), p. 22.

[2]Daniel P. Fuller, "An Investigation of the Literary Structure of the Gospel of Mark," Master's thesis, Fuller Seminary, Pasadena, Calif., 1952, p. 61.

[3]See chapter nineteen for a fuller explanation of the chain approach.

[4]When creating a chart, a Bible with section headings is useful.

[5]Table 8.3 covers many of the laws of composition. The laws of composition work at any layer of the pyramid. I call them "Connections" so as to sound less clinical.

[6]Daniel P. Fuller, "An Investigation of the Literary Structure of the Gospel of Mark," p. 78.

[7]Nigel Beynon and Andrew Sach, *Dig Deeper: Tools for Understanding God's Word* (Wheaton: Crossway, 2010), p. 44.

[8]Dennis Hamm, "Sight to the Blind: Vision as Metaphor in Luke," *Biblica* 67 (1986).

[9]Fuller, "An Investigation of the Literary Structure of the Gospel of Mark," p. 97.

[10]Ibid., p. 78.

Chapter 18: Imagination

[1]Michael Card, *Luke: The Gospel of Amazement* (Downers Grove, Ill.: InterVarsity Press, 2010), p. 11.

[2]Ibid., p. 13.

[3]Adapted from Bob Grahmann, Sharon Conley and Lindsay Olesberg, "Entering the Text," unpublished, May 2002.

Chapter 19: Commentaries

[1]For example, N. T. Wright's New Testament for Everyone series translates insights from years of rigorous scholarship into guides that are readable and well illustrated.

[2]For electronic versions of reliable commentaries, consider *The Essential IVP Reference Collection* (Downers Grove, Ill.: InterVarsity Press, 2008).

[3]When preparing to teach, I don't open a commentary until I have studied a passage several times on my own or in community.

[4]Robert Traina, *Methodical Bible Study* (Grand Rapids: Zondervan, 1980), p. 25.

Chapter 20: Studying Poetry

[1]Gordon D. Fee and Douglas Stuart, *How to Read the Bible for All Its Worth* (Grand Rapids: Zondervan, 2003), p. 197.

[2]My understanding of how to study poetry has been greatly enhanced by coteaching with Ali Borger-Germann.

[3]See chapter seventeen for more on how structure interacts with message.

[4]When reading poetry, breathe at the appropriate punctuation marks rather than the end of the line.

[5]Fee and Stuart, *How to Read the Bible,* p. 208.

[6]Chapter ten described identifying units of thought as the first step of interpretation. However, studying poetry is fluid, thus the phases of observation, interpretation and application are interwoven.

Chapter 21: Group Study

[1]Stan Slade, an American Baptist missionary in El Salvador, witnessed an unexpected benefit of inductive study. In his unpublished article, "Inductive Bible Study and Mission in El Salvador," he describes how revolutionary manuscript study is among the poor who have no experience of "functional democracy." Due to their experiences with the government, the landowners and the church, most Salvadorians had no expectation that their voices would be taken seriously in any significant decision-making process. The leadership style used in manuscript study uses its influence to call out their participation and let *them* determine the questions, answers and conclusions made regarding the passages of the Bible studied.

[2]Some people prefer to call this type of leadership "facilitation"; I maintain the use of the word *leadership* because Bible study leaders exercise influence, a key aspect of leadership.

[3]See Matthew 11:29; 1 Timothy 3:3; Philippians 2:3-4.